"Joseph Harrod draws from the riches (... help us to think deeply about prayer. He.... .. . . prayer that will not only answer many of your questions but also enhance both theological discernment and practical devotion."

—Joel R. Beeke
president, Puritan Reformed Theological Seminary

"Joe Harrod has written a wonderful guide to improve our communication with God. The 40 questions span the spectrum from biblical and theological issues to historical models and practical guidance for praying. These chapters which are deeply researched and documented are written in a form that would appeal to new believers as well as more experienced Christians looking to refresh their prayer life. Dr. Harrod isn't afraid to examine some of the thorny questions about prayer, including: Does God answer the prayers of unbelievers? Does prayer change God's mind? And, is it acceptable to argue with God in prayer? This book would be a valuable resource for college courses in Christian spirituality as well as study groups for the local church. I highly recommend it and trust it will be eagerly received by all readers."

—Tom Schwanda
associate professor, emeritus of Christian formation and ministry,
Wheaton College

"Dr. Joe Harrod writes an amazing book on prayer! It is both practical and rich in depth. It answers so many of the questions that we are all asking to understand our call to pray. Dr. Harrod will warm your heart and challenge your mind, leading you to adore the Savior who invites you to call upon his great name!"

—Aaron Harvie
senior pastor, Highview Baptist Church

"What air is to this terrestrial globe, so is prayer to the kingdom of God. It is vital for life in the kingdom, though if the truth be told, far too many of us wrestle with the discipline of prayer. When we should be wrestling in prayer, to use a Pauline image, we are wrestling just to be diligent and disciplined in praying. Joe Harrod's study of prayer through the medium of 40 questions—surely this must be the first time that prayer has been discussed via such means—is an excellent reminder of prayer's necessity. May close study of it also make us, its readers, men and women who pray— and that with passion and assiduity!"

—Michael A.G. Haykin
chair and professor of church history,
The Southern Baptist Theological Seminary

"Joe Harrod's *40 Questions About Prayer* is faithful to Scripture, clearly written, and extremely helpful for Christians seeking to grow in their understanding and practice of prayer. I think many churches and ministry groups will find this book perfectly formatted for group discussions. Highly recommended!"

—Robert L. Plummer, PhD
Collin and Evelyn Aikman Professor of Biblical Studies
The Southern Baptist Theological Seminary

"In *40 Questions About Prayer*, Joe Harrod provides a sound and accessible resource for Christians who have questions about prayer. This fine book is anchored in Scripture and will be proven helpful for any Christian who wants to grow a prayerful life. As a pastor, I am excited about this excellent work and will recommend it for use in our church."

—Jamaal Williams
lead pastor of Sojourn Church, Midtown, Louisville, KY;
president, Harbor Network

40 QUESTIONS ABOUT
Prayer

Joseph C. Harrod

Benjamin L. Merkle, Series Editor

40 Questions About Prayer
© 2022 Joseph C. Harrod

Published by Kregel Academic, an imprint of Kregel Publications, 2450 Oak Industrial Dr. NE, Grand Rapids, MI 49505-6020.

This book is a title in the 40 Questions Series edited by Benjamin L. Merkle.

The Greek font, GraecaU, is available from www.linguistsoftware.com/lgku.htm, +1-425-775-1130.

ISBN 978-0-8254-4692-4

Printed in the United States of America

22 23 24 25 26 / 5 4 3 2 1

To Tracy
All my love, always.

Contents

Part 4: Prayer in Practice

Part 5: Prayer in Historical Context

Foreword

Perhaps it is one of the primary indications of our fallenness that when we pray, we seldom feel the gravity and reality of what we are actually doing: talking to God himself. Knowing God through his Son Jesus is the supreme privilege of any human. And it is a glorious blessing to worship God, to serve him, and to learn about him. Beyond these we also experience the inestimable gift of him speaking to us by means of his written self-revelation, the Bible. But think of it: in prayer we actually get to talk with God.

Maybe it is because of the ease and frequency in which we enter into prayer that we often fail to appreciate the reality and profundity of talking with the king and creator of the universe on his holy throne in heaven. Or possibly it's because we are accustomed to seeing those with whom we converse, whereas in prayer we are speaking with one who is invisible to us. In any case, isn't it strange that talking with God can sometimes seem mundane and, shall we admit it, even boring?

Another matter influencing our attitude toward prayer may be the fact that we often see so little come of our prayers. We can't help but wonder, *Why is this? Is there something wrong with me? Is there something wrong with my prayers?* And it is here that my friend and colleague, Joe Harrod, meets us with *40 Questions About Prayer*.

What Christian doesn't have many questions about prayer?

For example, what Christian hasn't asked, "What does it mean to pray 'in Jesus's name'"? It's more than just special words to add at the end of our prayers. And to hear many say the phrase (often so quickly as to be almost indecipherable), it borders on the "meaningless repetition" that Jesus warned against in Matthew 6:7. So what does it really mean, and how do we pray "in Jesus's name"?

And there are so many other questions we all have about prayer, such as:

- May we pray to the Holy Spirit?
- If God is sovereign, why pray at all?
- Does God hear the prayers of unbelievers, since they cannot really come "in Jesus's name"? And if not, should we teach our young, unconverted children to pray?

- What does it mean to "pray without ceasing," as we're commanded in 1 Thessalonians 5:17?
- Is it acceptable to use written prayers in church?
- What should we do if our mind often wanders in prayer?
- And perhaps most of all, why don't we receive more answers to our prayers?

The need for such an encyclopedic resource like *40 Questions About Prayer* is obvious.

When I was in college, the first Christian book I ever bought was on prayer. And I did so because I had so many questions about prayer, and both wanted and needed help with my prayer life. Would that this book had been available fifty years ago!

I read *40 Questions About Prayer* with as much eagerness as I did that first book on prayer, and I'm so glad I read it. I've done a lot of reading, writing, and teaching on prayer in the past half-century, but I still learned a great deal about prayer from this book. One of my favorite chapters is, "How Might Christians Pray Scripture?" I've seen this one concept of turning the words of Scripture into the words of your prayers instantly and permanently transform the prayer lives of countless believers. I'm excited to know you'll be learning about that in the pages to come.

This book is saturated with Scripture—exactly what you want in a book about prayer. Ultimately, we want the Word of God to teach us how to talk with God. Second, it is clear. Joe Harrod is a scholar, but he is also a faithful churchman, and he has written this book primarily in service to ordinary believers and the local church. Third, it is useful. Beside the great benefits of an individual reading of *40 Questions About Prayer*, this book would also serve well as a classroom text or a small group study on prayer. Each of the brief chapters closes with questions to consider privately or to discuss with others. Fourth, as I've already noted, its breadth—forty specific questions answered—makes it spectacularly helpful.

I've had the privilege of knowing Joe Harrod for well over a decade. He has earned three degrees in theology and was one of the first graduates from our PhD program in Biblical Spirituality here at The Southern Baptist Theological Seminary in Louisville, Kentucky. Initially I met Joe in one of my doctoral colloquia. I was immediately impressed with his research abilities. He always did more than the minimum requirements in any writing project, displaying an unusual depth of research, even beyond the recommended resources. He has an inquisitive and analytical mind, which makes him just the kind of person for writing answers to forty separate questions as this project required.

But being a good scholar does not by itself make a good writer on prayer. I've come to know Joe Harrod much deeper as a friend and colleague in our Biblical Spirituality department in the last several years. He is first and foremost a man of God. He is a deeply devoted follower of Christ, and this manifests itself in his home, his church, and in his relationships with students and fellow faculty. I know this man and this book, and I highly commend both to you.

—Donald S. Whitney
Louisville, Kentucky

Introduction

It is hard to limit oneself to only forty questions about the topic of prayer, for there are many things we long to know. The questions in this book are ones that I have asked and that others have asked me. The first time I remember praying was the day my father died. On that day, my prayers seemed to go unanswered and God felt very far away. I am thankful I did not give up on prayer after that experience. I have thought about prayer much since then, now more than thirty years removed, and I hope some of the reflections in this book will be helpful to you as you wrestle with the mystery of prayer.

Throughout the book I have tried to engage a variety of Christian traditions of prayer while anchoring fast to Scripture. My hope is that the reflections in this book lead readers back to Scripture often, even while recognizing that there are aspects of the practice of prayer where considerable freedom exists. That said, some readers will notice that I have prioritized Protestant authors even as I have included Roman Catholic and Eastern Orthodox writers. Spirituality is inseparable from theology. Adopting particular practices without considering their underlying doctrinal commitments is unwise. Scholarly readers will notice I have not mentioned topics like the Orthodox practice of stillness (*hesychasm*), the Jesus prayer, centering prayer, or mystical prayer. I have questions about these kinds of prayers, to be sure, but I have concentrated on discursive prayers here.

The flow of this book is as follows: After four general questions about prayer, we examine a series of theological questions related to prayer before turning to a number of questions about prayer in the Bible. Then we consider some practical questions about prayer and end with three questions about prayer and history. During the writing of this book, other questions about prayer arose, including those about contemplative prayer, prayer in the global church, prayer among women, and praying for and with those who are disabled. There is simply not enough time or space to answer these questions here.

The list of people I need to thank is very long. At the risk of omitting or offending many whose help has been welcomed and timely, I will not try to mention every name, but I do want to thank Dustin, Eric, Junior, and Michael: acquaintances who became friends and friends who became brothers. I offer my gratitude to Pastors Aaron Harvie and Jeff (and Jana) Goodyear for providing feedback on specific chapters. I am thankful for their pastoral insights in this process. Many of my colleagues at The Southern Baptist Theological Seminary have contributed to this book in various ways, some taking time to read drafts of chapters and offer encouragement or suggestions of a refocus of my efforts, some by their own writings and teaching on prayer, others by the way that they have prayed over the years. I am especially grateful to my colleagues in the Biblical Spirituality department, including Michael Haykin, Matthew Haste, Stephen Yuille, and to Dustin Bruce, the Dean of Southern's undergraduate school, Boyce College. I am particularly grateful to Don Whitney for writing the foreword to this book and for many years as a mentor and a friend. I appreciate Dustin Brown's help in finding key sources at a pivotal time. Several graduate students at The Southern Baptist Theological Seminary read portions of this manuscript and offered helpful suggestions: Timothy Bitz, Ben Khazraee, Robbie Piel, Scott Reeder, Zachary Thoenen, and Kenneth Trax. Robert Hand, Deborah Helmers, and Shawn Vander Lugt at Kregel have been very helpful editors and I appreciate their insightful comments and questions. For our sons, thank you for asking to pray and for praying for me. Finally, for my wife Tracy, without whom this book would not be, I am sorry that I have not led you in prayer the way I should have and am so thankful for your prayers which are powerful in their working. All my love, always.

PART 1

General Questions About Prayer

What Is Prayer?

Students of Western thought know well the Latin of philosopher René Descartes's famous maxim *cogito ergo sum* ("I think, therefore I am"). It may be fitting to adapt this saying for the beginning of our discussion: *oro ergo sum* ("I pray, therefore I am"). We begin our series of questions on prayer by acknowledging the basic human impulse to pray and the fact that prayer, in almost all cultures, is something that faithful people can grow in. We conclude with a survey of definitions of prayer before identifying a fitting one for this book.

Prayer Is a Common Part of Religion

Prayer, or something like it, exists in many religions. Prayer is a central experience in the three Abrahamic religions of Judaism, Christianity, and Islam.[1] The experience of prayer in Islam and Judaism varies from the ritualized daily fivefold ṣalāt (Islam) or the threefold ʿamidah/tefillah (Judaism) to free prayers of devotion to the mystical contemplations of Kabballah and Sufism. Prayers of petition thrive in some branches of Hinduism and Buddhism while it is virtually absent from others. Among various nature religions, prayer takes the forms of communication with or devotion to deity.[2] Some atheists even pray.[3] Even though there is wide disagreement between

---

1. For a detailed survey of similarities and differences between prayer in these faiths, see Clemens Leonhard and Martin Lüstraeten, "Prayer," in *The Oxford Handbook of the Abrahamic Religions*, eds. Adam J. Silverstein and Guy G. Stroumsa (New York: Oxford University Press, 2015).
2. "Nature religions" includes various forms of pagan and neo-pagan practice such as Wicca, Druidism, or goddess spiritualties. See Janet Goodall, Emyr Williams, and Catherine Goodall, "Pagan Prayer and Worship: A Qualitative Study of Perceptions," in *The Pomegranate* 15, no. 1–2 (2013): 178–201.
3. A Pew Research Center study showed an increase in the number of atheists who prayed "seldom/never," from 87 percent in 2007 to 97 percent in 2014. See https://www.pewforum.org/religious-landscape-study/religious-family/atheist/#frequency-of-prayer.

such groups about what "prayer" means, its widespread practice is telling. Tim Keller summarizes this situation well when he writes, "Prayer is one of the most common phenomena of human life."[4]

Prayer Is Learnable

By describing prayer as part of religion and so common a part of human experience, we might err in assuming it is fixed or immutable, not admitting to change or growth. We can all learn to pray or learn to pray differently. Yet if prayer is so basic to human experience, in what ways is it learned? Why might speech so basic require change or even growth? One analogy comes from normal human development. Newborns and infants possess the ability to communicate basic needs, but as any parent can attest, such communication is often inarticulate. Normally, as children mature, so do their ability and capacity for increasingly nuanced and meaningful relational conversation. So it is with prayer.

When asked by his disciples for instruction on prayer (cf. Luke 11:1), Jesus offered guidance willingly. The prayers of a recent convert may reflect the simplicity of the tax collector's prayer: "God, be merciful to me, a sinner" (Luke 18:13). Such a prayer is true and beautiful. Over time, however, he will likely learn to see other needs—especially the needs of others—and find other ways of expressing his heart to a listening heavenly Father. In an earlier century, Pastor Andrew Murray (1828–1917) emphasized this dynamic: "Though in its beginnings prayer is so simple that the feeblest child can pray, yet it is at the same time the highest and holiest work to which man can rise."[5] Learning to rise in prayer is a theme addressed throughout this book.

A Working Definition

Definitions of prayer abound. Donald Bloesch cataloged around a dozen different definitions from secular, philosophical, and varying Christian traditions.[6] One recent definition is that prayer is "the primary speech of the true self to the true God."[7] In the early medieval period, John of Damascus (c. 660–c. 750) said, "Prayer is an uprising of the mind to God or a petitioning of God for what is fitting."[8] Question 178 of the Westminster Larger Catechism

---

4.   Timothy Keller, *Prayer: Experiencing Awe and Intimacy with God* (New York: Dutton, 2014), 36.

5.   Andrew Murray, *With Christ in the School of Prayer* (Urichsville, OH: Barbour, 1992), 2.

6.   Donald G. Bloesch, *The Struggle of Prayer* (Colorado Springs: Helmers and Howard, 1988), 14–18.

7.   Ann and Barry Ulanov, "Prayer and Personality: Prayer as Primary Speech," in *The Study of Spirituality*, eds. Cheslyn Jones, Geoffrey Wainwright, and Edward Yarnold, SJ (New York: Oxford University Press, 1986), 24.

8.   John of Damascus, "An Exact Exposition of the Orthodox Faith," in *St. Hilary of Poitiers, John of Damascus*, eds. Philip Schaff and Henry Wace, trans. S. D. F. Salmond, vol. 9b, A

asks, "What is prayer?" and answers, "Prayer is an offering up of our desires unto God, in the name of Christ, by the help of his Spirit; with confession of our sins, and thankful acknowledgment of his mercies."[9] More recently, Tim Keller has called prayer "a *personal, communicative response to the knowledge of God*."[10] There is no shortage of definitions, yet we must adopt a definition for asking and answering the questions that compose the balance of this book. The definition we choose will be shaped inherently by our worldview. The following summary is an adaptation of James Herrick's helpful synthesis of the main elements of the Christian worldview: God exists as "a personal, creating, and wholly other God"; the Bible, as the revealed Word of this God, has supernatural authority; everything else that exists owes its existence to God and thus owes God worship and obedience. We bear the consequences of our first parents' fall into sin, which consequences include "spiritual confusion, a state of spiritual separation from God and the inevitability of physical death." Jesus is God incarnate, and through his life and death accomplishes reconciliation between God and humans. History is moving toward a decisive judgment with people held accountable for their sins. The God who made all things orders and sustains his world, and prayer is part of his sustaining and ordering of all things. God intervenes in human affairs, at times, through prayer.[11]

For this book, I have chosen to prioritize the definition of seventeenth-century British Baptist John Bunyan (1628–1688). Bunyan developed this definition in his tract *I Will Pray with the Spirit* (1663) while imprisoned as a religious dissenter. According to Bunyan,

> Prayer is a sincere, sensible, affectionate pouring out of the heart or soul to God, through Christ, in the strength and assistance of the Holy Spirit, for such things as God hath promised, or, according to the Word, for the good of the Church, with submission, in Faith, to the will of God.[12]

Bunyan's definition includes (1) a rich description of the practice of prayer ("sincere, sensible, affectionate pouring out of the heart or soul"), (2) a

---

Select Library of the Nicene and Post-Nicene Fathers of the Christian Church, Second Series (New York: Christian Literature Company, 1899), 70.

9. Westminster Assembly, *The Westminster Confession of Faith: Edinburgh Edition* (Philadelphia: William S. Young, 1851), 363.

10. Keller, *Prayer*, 45 (italics original).

11. See James A. Herrick, *The Making of the New Spirituality: The Eclipse of the Western Religious Tradition* (Downers Grove, IL: InterVarsity Press, 2003), 32–33.

12. John Bunyan, *I Will Pray with the Spirit, and I Will Pray with the Understanding Also, or, A Discourse Touching Prayer, from I Cor. 14.15*, 2nd ed. (London: 1663), 4–5. I was happy to find that Fred Sanders, a gifted theologian in the Methodist tradition, has also featured Bunyan's definition of prayer in his *The Deep Things of God: How the Trinity Changes Everything* (Wheaton, IL: Crossway, 2010), 214.

Trinitarian emphasis ("to God, through Christ, in the strength and assistance of the Holy Spirit"), (3) fitting delimitations ("for such things as God has promised, or according to his Word"), (4) the ecclesiological context ("for the good of the church"), and (5) an appropriate attitude ("with submission in faith to the will of God"). Throughout this book, we will consider each of these elements more fully as we consider questions about the biblical foundations, theology, and practice of prayer.

Bunyan's definition, as an observant student noted recently, describes *petitionary* prayer, or prayer that asks things of God. This is not the only kind of prayer, as we will see in our second chapter, but for many reasons that will become clear throughout this book, it is the most common sort of prayer. That Bunyan mentions prayer in the name of the triune God and in the context of the church sets his definition apart from competing definitions. If we ignore these two elements, our understanding of prayer can easily veer away from the richness of a fully biblical practice.

Summary

Prayer is part of the basic human experience and appears in nearly every religion and culture. Prayer, in its most basic expression, is talking to God. This speech may be little more than an urgent, unplanned cry for help or it might be an intentional part of a daily life focused on seeking fellowship with God. Prayer is communication that we can learn and grow in as we mature in our spiritual lives. This fact does not mean that "mature" prayer must be inherently complicated, long, or nuanced, even though it might be all of these things. The fact that prayer is learnable and that we may grow in it is part of the impetus for this book and its various questions. Those who "call upon the name of the Lord" (Gen. 4:26), to use the earliest biblical expression for prayer, might have many motives for doing so. One of those motives, hopefully, is wanting a closer relationship, or "communion," to use a richer word from a bygone era, with God. Growing in prayer is one important way that believers come to know God.

REFLECTION QUESTIONS

1. How would you define prayer?

2. What do differing definitions of prayer have in common?

3. Why do you think definitions of prayer vary so much?

4. How have you experienced growth in prayer?

5. Why do you think prayer is so prevalent in world religions?

What Are Various Types of Prayer?

In the first chapter we called prayer a "pouring out of the heart or soul to God." This language is that of communication and communion. Following a classic definition by John Bunyan, we also said that this communication is "for such things as God has promised, or according to his Word," which involves asking, supplication, or petition. Petitionary prayer is our default mode of speaking to God, for we recognize quite easily how insufficient are our resources for life and how inexhaustible his provision is. Without undermining the place of petitionary prayer, which is addressed in many of the questions in this book, this chapter considers other types of prayer such as intercession, confession, thanksgiving, and adoration. The earliest Christians practiced these sorts of prayer as faithful Jews had done before them and thus these prayers deserve our attention.

Paul's words in 1 Timothy 2:1–2 begin our discussion of the variety of prayers. Here, Paul implores Timothy to make "supplications" (*deēseis*), "prayers" (*proseuchas*), "intercessions" (*enteuxeis*), and "thanksgivings" (*eucharistias*) on behalf of all people, especially those having political power, in order that Christians might "lead a peaceful and quiet life." Presumably, Paul believed these four ways of speaking to and with God could bring about this condition of stability for the church. Similarly, in Philippians 4:6, Paul uses various expressions for prayer when he exhorts the church to avoid anxiousness and instead to make their requests known to God by "prayer" (*proseuchē*) and "supplication" (*deēsei*) with "thanksgiving" (*eucharistias*). Paul indicates that these ways of speaking to God could calm worried hearts. Neither passage presents a comprehensive view of prayer and both passages place "prayer" alongside other ways of speaking to God, thus we should not make too much of these distinctions even as we appreciate the differences.[1] In what follows,

---

1. On this point, see Martin Dibelius and Hans Conzelmann, *The Pastoral Epistles: A Commentary on the Pastoral Epistles*, trans. Philip Buttolph and Adela Yarbo, Hermeneia

we will consider intercession, confession, thanksgiving, and adoration, four common kinds of prayer, more closely.

Intercession: Others-Focused Prayer

If "supplication," or petitionary prayer, generally focuses on *our* own needs and situation, intercessory prayer focuses on the situation and needs of others. In the Old Testament, intercession is one of the responsibilities of those who would lead the people of God: the patriarch Abraham; priests like Aaron or Joshua; prophets like Moses, Samuel, Elijah, Daniel, and Amos; lay leaders such as the elders of the community; and kings like David or Hezekiah all interceded on behalf of others. It may be that the patriarch Job's regular sacrifices on behalf of his children (Job 1:5) served an intercessory function. The prophet Isaiah foretold that the Lord's servant "makes intercession for the transgressors" (Isa. 53:12), and New Testament texts like Romans 8 and Hebrews 7 and 9 connect this type of prayer with Jesus. Although intercession is not restricted to leaders alone, those responsible for shepherding God's people ought to see intercession as a particular burden and responsibility of their ministry. God calls every Christian, though, to the ministry of intercession by virtue of naming us "a holy priesthood, to offer spiritual sacrifices acceptable to God through Jesus Christ" (1 Peter 2:5).

Patrick Miller, in his study of prayer in the Bible, notes that intercessory prayer might take a number of forms.[2] That is, there is no particular phrasing that we must follow when interceding for others, although Scripture gives us many examples of intercession (see Questions 18 and 35). From 1 Timothy 2:1, we understand that it is right that Christians intercede for "all people." We ought to intercede for other Christians within our congregations and larger circle of relationships, asking God particularly to meet specific needs as we become aware of them. It is also right for us to make intercession on behalf of Christians we do not know. As we hear of Christians suffering deprivation or persecution around the world, we may intercede on their behalf, seeking comfort for them from God (2 Cor. 1:3–4) and asking his will to be done on earth in their circumstances (Matt. 6:10). When we hear of the gospel expanding in the midst of totalitarian opposition, we can pray for a continued spread of the word. Even when we are unaware of particular needs, we might intercede generally on behalf of other Christians in light of God's revealed will for all believers that they might grow in holiness, forsaking sexual immorality (1 Thess. 4:3); that they might experience spiritual wisdom and understanding

---

(Philadelphia: Fortress Press, 1972), 36. As early as the 230s, Christians noted this passage and the varieties of prayer. See Origen, *Origen: An Exhortation to Martyrdom, Prayer, and Selected Works*, ed. Richard J. Payne, trans. Rowan A. Greer, The Classics of Western Spirituality (Mahwah, NJ: Paulist Press, 1979), 83.

2. Patrick D. Miller, *They Cried to the Lord: The Form and Theology of Biblical Prayer* (Minneapolis: Fortress Press, 1994), 267.

(Col. 1:9); that they might walk in a manner worthy of their calling (Eph. 4:1); and so forth. Every ethical imperative to which believers are called provides occasion to pray for other Christians, whether their faces and stories are familiar to us or remain unknown. It is also fitting for Christians to intercede on behalf of strangers, that their faith might be stirred to trust Christ or to trust Christ more, whatever the situation may be. Furthermore, Christians should intercede on behalf of those who by their open declaration are sinners, opponents of the gospel, enemies of God, and even our own enemies (Matt. 5:44), asking that "God may perhaps grant them repentance leading to a knowledge of the truth" (2 Tim. 2:25). Though from our perspective such a person may be far from hope, we cannot see God's hidden and eternal plans, for only God knows the extent to which the prayers of other Christians have led to our own saving faith. As the great medieval theologian Thomas Aquinas wrote regarding praying for sinners, "No man should be denied the help of prayer."[3]

Confession: Grace-Focused Prayer

As he lay dying, the aged North African bishop Augustine (354–430) asked friends to copy several of David's psalms onto large sheets that could adorn his walls so he could read them from his bed in order to prepare himself to meet God. In later generations, Christians came to call these particular Scriptures "penitential psalms," or psalms that help believers confess sin.[4] Though a Christian's sins—past, present, and future—are forgiven in Christ, we continue to sin. When we sin, our experience of relational nearness to God is disrupted; yet God is so kind as to allow us to continue to draw near to him in prayer, even when we feel far away. Confession is often the start of restoring our sense of nearness to God.[5]

Considered as a group, these penitential psalms describe the inward experience of unconfessed sin as a heaviness (Pss. 32:4; 38:4) or weakness (Pss. 6:2; 32:3; 102:3) or weariness (Pss. 38:5–8; 143:4). They help us recognize the physical and emotional effects of harboring sin. Then, these psalms also speak of confession as freedom. Though God knows our sin, confession is necessary (Pss. 32:5; 51:4). We have confidence that God hears our confession (Pss. 6:8–9; 38:9; 102:1–2; 130:4, 7) particularly because of his prior faithfulness toward us (Pss. 102:18–22; 143:5–6). These psalms also motivate us by picturing the joy of restoration that confession brings (Pss. 32:1–2, 11; 51:8, 12, 15; 130:4).

---

3. Thomas Aquinas, *Summa Theologiae*, 2.83.7, https://aquinas.cc/la/en/~ST.II-II.Q83.A7.Rep3.
4. The seven penitential psalms are Psalms 6, 32, 38, 51, 102, 130, and 143. See Question 16 below.
5. Although this book does not permit space to explore nuances of sin, one classic treatment is that of John Owen, *Indwelling Sin*, in *Overcoming Sin and Temptation*, eds. Kelly M. Kapic and Justin Taylor (Wheaton, IL: Crossway, 2006), 229–407. This work also appears in vol. 6 of Owen's *Works*.

The Old Testament provides other rich examples of confession, from David's acknowledgment before the prophet Nathan, "I have sinned against the LORD" (2 Sam. 12:13), to Daniel's prayer on behalf of his exiled people, "O Lord . . . we have sinned and done wrong and acted wickedly and rebelled" (Dan. 9:4–5). Surprisingly, the idea of confessing sin comes up less frequently in the New Testament. When it does appear, confession involves *public* acknowledgment of one's sin.[6] The verb "confess" (*homologeō*) carries a lot of theological significance, but here we will focus on the simple definition of "agreement."[7] With regard to prayer, confession is our agreeing with God about our sin and its effects, and then seeking mercy, forgiveness, and renewed fellowship. Scripture offers us great hope of forgiveness and purification at this point: "If we confess (*homologōmen*) our sins, he is faithful and just to forgive (*aphē*) us our sins and to cleanse (*katharisē*) us from all unrighteousness" (1 John 1:9).

What exactly are we to confess *about* our sin? First, we are to agree with God that specific actions we have committed, thoughts we have considered, or attitudes we have harbored are sinful when they transgress God's moral boundaries. This is the kind of confession we see most often in the Bible.[8] Second, we confess specific things we have left undone, known as sins of omission. These sins might include words of forgiveness or restoration that we have withheld, occasions where we should have given testimony of God's goodness yet remained silent, acts of charity that we ignored, and the like. The question of whether we ought to confess *past* sins that we have previously mentioned to God is a disputed matter, for if God has forgiven and cleansed us through the blood of Christ in light of previous confession, it seems that continuing to bring them up again and again expresses uncertainty as to whether God has really "remove[d] our transgressions from us" as far as east is from the west (Ps. 103:12). Similarly, the question of whether we ought to confess our sinful *nature* is disputed also, "For [God] knows our frame; he remembers that we are dust" (Ps. 103:14).

Reformer John Calvin suggests that confession ought to take priority in our prayers.

> To sum up: the beginning, and even the preparation, of proper prayer is the plea for pardon with a humble and sincere confession of guilt. Nor should anyone, however holy he may be, hope that he will obtain anything from God until he

---

6. So Matthew 3:6; Mark 1:5; Acts 19:18; and James 5:16. The context of 1 John 1:9 is ambiguous regarding public or private confession.
7. In different contexts, this verb might mean to declare something publicly, to swear allegiance, to admit a fact, to make a public commitment, and so forth.
8. See Miller, *They Cried to the Lord*, 246.

> is freely reconciled to him; nor can God chance to be propi-
> tious to any but those whom he has pardoned. Accordingly,
> it is no wonder if believers open for themselves the door to
> prayer with this key.[9]

Prayers of confession might begin by inviting God's penetrating gaze into
our soul: "Search me, O God, and know my heart! Try me and know my
thoughts!" (Ps. 139:23). David does not ask God to undertake this investiga-
tion in order that God might learn something; God already knows everything
about David's life (139:1–5) and is completely present (139:7–16). Rather, like
David we ask God to search us in order to help *us* see and "discern [our] errors" and expose our "hidden faults" (Ps. 19:12).

Confessing our sin before God—that is, agreeing with him about the
sinfulness of our sins—must be matched by repentance toward God. Baptist
theologian John Gill (1697–1771) identified six kinds of repentance: natural,
national, external, hypocritical, legal, and evangelical. The first five kinds are
common enough in the world, and observable in Scripture, but only the final
sort ("evangelical" or gospel-focused repentance) brings true restoration. Its
hallmarks, according to Gill, are "a true sight and sense of sin," "a hearty and
unfeigned sorrow for it," a genuine shame and detestation of the sin we confess, and "a resolution, through the grace of God, to forsake sin."[10] Prayer is
the proper place for repentance to occur.

Thanksgiving and Adoration: God-Focused Prayer

One mark of spiritual growth is coming to love God for who he is and expressing this love in prayers of thanksgiving and adoration. The biblical foundation for our love of God is "because he first loved us" (1 John 4:19). Christians
"bless God" and remember "all his benefits," including forgiveness, redemption,
and the way he satisfies our soul (Ps. 103:2–5). As we grow in our walk with
God, so grow our motives for loving him. Bernard of Clairvaux (1090–1153),
the charismatic leader of a monastic community in what is now France, wrote
of four degrees of love for God, moving from self-motivated love of God for his
benefits to a purer love of God for who He is.[11] Much later, the early evangelical
theologian Jonathan Edwards (1703–1758) also noted growth and change in

---

9. John Calvin, *Institutes of the Christian Religion*, ed. John T. McNeill, trans. Ford Lewis
Battles, vol. 1, The Library of Christian Classics (Louisville, KY: Westminster John Knox
Press, 2011), 1:3.20.9.

10. John Gill, *A Complete Body of Doctrinal and Practical Divinity: Or a System of Evangelical
Truths, Deduced from the Sacred Scriptures*, new ed., vol. 2 (London: Tegg & Company,
1839), 366–69.

11. For a modern translation, see Bernard of Clairvaux, "On Loving God," in *Bernard of
Clairvaux: Selected Works*, trans. and ed. G. R. Evans, The Classics of Western Spirituality
(Mahweh, NJ: Paulist Press, 1987), 173–205.

our love for God that overflows in speech: "The true saint, when under great spiritual affections, from the fullness of his heart, is ready to be speaking much of God, and his glorious perfections and works, and of the beauty and amiableness of Christ, and the glorious things of the gospel."[12] What Edwards wrote regarding our speech surely applies to our prayers.

Presbyterian minister and Bible commentator Matthew Henry (1662–1714) gives timeless perspective on thanksgiving: "Our errand at the throne of grace is not only to seek the favour of God, but to give unto him the glory due unto his name . . . by a grateful acknowledgment of his goodness to us."[13] Following Paul's lead, we are also to offer thanksgivings for "all people" (1 Tim. 2:1), which Paul regularly did in his letters. We can never separate our love for God from the blessings of gospel transformation, but through the inward ministry of the Holy Spirit, gospel transformation allows us to see God with new eyes and consequently to praise him with purified mouths (cf. Isa. 6). Prayers of adoration and thanksgiving focus on God, not on us or our needs. Without drawing a hard and fast distinction, prayers of thanksgiving often come from reflection on what God has done and prayers of adoration from consideration of who God is in himself.

Prayers of adoration focus on who God is, as he has revealed himself in Scripture and as he makes himself known in experiential communion and fellowship. As mentioned earlier, prayer is one important way we express a growing, deepening love for God. Put simply, humans talk about those whom they love. What happens, however, if we struggle to adore God in prayer? As we grow in the path of discipleship, Christians sometimes encounter an awkward phase where our adoration of God might seem forced. It is important for us to acknowledge this awkwardness in order to grow in our prayer lives.

Adoring God for who he is sometimes seems awkward because we are so accustomed to self-love. The apostle Paul understood that every human can see God's glory in the work of creation, but described our common problem: we do not naturally honor or thank God (Rom. 1:18–21). Turning our attention away from ourselves is unnatural because our nature is distorted by sin, which is why we depend on the ministry and mercy of God's Spirit, working within us, to help us worship God aright. Paradoxically, confessing our difficulty of adoring God is often an important first step in learning to adore him.

Another reason that prayers of adoration can seem difficult, especially to new believers, is that we have vague or distorted ideas about who God reveals himself to be because coming to know God takes time and effort. We come to know God the Father experientially through our union with Jesus Christ,

---

12. Jonathan Edwards, *Religious Affections*, in *The Works of Jonathan Edwards*, vol. 2, ed. John E. Smith (New Haven, CT: Yale University Press, 1959), 252.
13. Matthew Henry, *A Method for Prayer: Freedom in the Face of God*, ed. J. Ligon Duncan III (Fearn, Scotland: Christian Heritage, 1994), 79.

who himself is the perfect image of God (2 Cor. 4:4; Col. 1:15), and through the transforming presence of the Holy Spirit (2 Cor. 3:18). We come to know God and to clarify vague ideas about him by giving our attention to hearing, reading, and meditating upon Scripture, for it is here that he makes himself known. As we read the Bible, we ought to pray as Moses, "Please show me your glory" (Exod. 33:18), and to look expectantly for God to do just that. As we grow more familiar with the Bible, we can also grow deeper with God through deepening our theology.

At its best, theology is the study of God that leads us to prize him and praise him. Over time, theology moved from a pastoral task in the ancient church, to the monastic scriptoriums of the medieval period, to the classrooms of academies in the high Middle Ages, before coming full circle in Reformation pulpits. Although "theology" is a legitimate discipline of academic study, it is also the calling of all who would follow God.

Anytime we speak about God and go beyond quoting Scripture, we are engaging in the task of theology, and theology can help us cultivate adoration for God. How so? Consider that the field known as *biblical* theology can help us adore God as we step back to see the grand story of Scripture: creation, fall, redemption, and new creation. *Historical* theology moves us to adore God for his faithfulness in each generation of preserving and defending the faith. What most readers likely hear in the word "theology," though, is *systematic* theology. Systematic theology helps define the parameters of true faith by deep reflection on specific areas of doctrine, such as the attributes of God, the person and work of Christ, the promises of the gospel, the hope of Christ's return, and similar areas. Within each area of systematic theology, Protestants have long identified specific *loci* (Latin for "places")—including the doctrines of God (theology proper), the doctrine of the person of Christ (Christology), the doctrine of the Holy Spirit (pneumatology), and the doctrine of the Trinity—as particular areas that concern the person of God. How might reflection on these *loci* prompt adoration? The following reasons barely scratch the surface.

Theology proper reminds us that Yahweh alone is to be completely adored (Deut. 6:4–5), for he alone is the living and true God (Jer. 10:10), uniquely holy (Exod. 15:11), alone able to redeem (Isa. 43:11–13), whose will is never thwarted (Dan. 4:35), whose glory fills the heavens (Ps. 8:1) but who dwells with the lowly (Isa. 57:15), whose attributes include incomparable love, knowledge, wisdom, righteousness, justice, truth, patience, compassion, self-existence, and so many more. As we consider Jesus Christ, with Paul we proclaim him "God over all, blessed forever" (Rom. 9:5), whose incarnation makes communion between humans and God possible, who is the unique mediator between God and man (1 Tim. 2:5), who "in every respect has been tempted as we are, yet without sin" (Heb. 4:15), who humbled himself and is to be exalted and worshiped (Phil. 2:5–11), who is our wrath-bearing substitute

(2 Cor. 5:21), who exercised direct control over nature, disease, demons, and death. Jesus is Lord! The Spirit who hovered over creation (Gen. 1:2) now washes and renews us inwardly (Titus 3:5–6) and works to transform those who behold Christ into the very image of Christ (2 Cor. 3:17–18), even as he brings to fruition various virtues (Gal. 5:22–23) and acts to guarantee the deposit of salvation in the gospel (Eph. 1:13). These are but some of the reasons for which we adore the triune God in prayer.

Does Sequencing Matter?

Should Christians sequence various kinds of prayer in a particular way? One popular acronym for helping Christians remember these different prayers is Adoration, Confession, Thanksgiving, and Supplications (A.C.T.S.). This approach is simple, memorable, and has probably been the way that hundreds of thousands of Western Christians have learned to pray for decades. Some suggest that the sequencing of this acronym follows the pattern of the Lord's Prayer and follows a theological priority of beginning by adoring God, which leads to confession of sin, prompts thanksgiving for mercy received, and ends with supplications for our needs.[14] Another popular approach, though less memorable, suggests a sequence of confession, followed by adoration and thanksgiving, intercession, and finally supplication for one's own needs.[15] Apart from placing petitionary prayer last, these two influential models differ on what kind of prayer ought to come first, each source offering thoughtful, biblical reasons for their sequencing. How might we sort out this difference?

It may be helpful for us to recognize that while models like these are "biblical" inasmuch as they seek to make sense of the Bible's teaching on prayer, the Bible gives us great freedom in how we pray. Faithfulness to Scripture would not require us to include all of these types of prayer every time we pray. When we are moved to awe at the work of God, we might respond appropriately with an extended time of adoration, asking nothing, focusing all attention on him. Similarly, when God's Spirit convicts us concerning sin, we might respond with an extended prayer of confession. We might vary our pattern, sometimes beginning with confession, other times beginning with adoration, still other times petitioning God for urgent needs. Freedom would allow us to follow either model, or no model, with near infinite variation. The helpfulness of such models comes in their reminder of the diversity of prayer.

---

14. See, for example, R. C. Sproul, "A Simple Acrostic for Prayer: A.C.T.S.," https://www.ligonier.org/blog/simple-acrostic-prayer.

15. Frank Houghton, et al., *Quiet Time: An InterVarsity Guidebook for Daily Devotions* (Downers Grove, IL: InterVarsity Press, 1977), 15–16. The introduction of "intercession," thankfully, prevents the acronym C.A.T.S.

Summary

In this chapter, we've considered several of the diverse kinds of prayer found in the Bible. Our human "default mode" is supplication, or petitionary prayer, focused on our own needs. But the Bible also calls us to give attention to prayers of confession, thanksgiving, adoration, and intercession. In confession, we agree with God about our sin and seek restoration of fellowship. Adoration focuses on worshiping God for who he is while thanksgiving emphasizes what God has done in our lives and the lives of others who have responded to the gospel. Intercession allows us to fulfill our calling as priests to God as we beseech God on behalf of others. Each kind of prayer is biblical and fitting for those who would walk closely with God.

REFLECTION QUESTIONS

1. How is intercession different from supplication?

2. What are some challenges you have faced in adoring God through prayer?

3. What is the benefit of beginning times of prayer with confession or adoration?

4. Which kind of prayer is the most difficult for you? Why so?

5. Why is confession of sin so important for the Christian life?

Why Must the Bible Inform and Guide Prayer?

Prayer is part of what it means to be human. In this chapter, we want to consider what role Christian Scripture has, or should have, in shaping prayer. This question may seem odd at first: If prayer is such a normal part of the human experience, wouldn't bringing the Bible into the discussion restrict or constrain prayer? Yes, focusing on biblical parameters for prayer is indeed restrictive—and as I argue in this chapter, such restriction is desirable, for it seeks to conform our practice of prayer to the revealed will of God. After exploring the nature of the Bible, we will consider three ways that it might inform and guide our praying.

The Bible's Attributes Encourage Our Prayers

All Christian traditions value the Bible, yet various traditions hold differing conclusions about what the Bible is and why it is valuable. Protestants overwhelmingly consider Scripture as the final and best authority for theology and practice. Throughout this book, we will consider important reflections on prayer offered by women and men during the church's long history, but Scripture takes precedence over their suggestions. The priority of Scripture is bound up in its nature and attributes, particularly in its sufficiency, authority, and inspiration.

The Bible does not answer every question we might ask about prayer. For example, should Christians keep a journal in which they record their prayers and God's answers? Are prayers shared through text messages different from prayers spoken in person? Is it better to pray in the morning or in the evening? The fact that the Bible does not address these particular questions does not diminish its teaching on prayer or somehow render it outdated, for Scripture tells us everything we *need* to know in order to pray: God exists, he created everything (including us), he invites us to pray, he delights in our prayers, he moves in response to the prayers of his people, and so on. Another way of saying that the Bible tells us everything we need to know about prayer is what theologians call the Bible's *sufficiency*.

The doctrine of Scripture's sufficiency has a twofold focus. First, it emphasizes the fact that the Bible gives everything that sinners need in order to be saved. Second, the Bible tells believers how to live faithfully. On this second point, theologian Gregg Allison offers a helpful reflection: "Scripture provides everything that Christians need to please God fully. For every task that God calls believers to do, he completely equips them to accomplish his will through his Word (and, certainly, empowered by his Spirit)."[1] We will consider the ministry of the Holy Spirit in prayer in several of this book's questions, but here we affirm that Scripture is a sufficient guide to our prayer. God tells us everything we need to know in order to pray.

We trust in Scripture's sufficiency because of the related doctrine of its *authority*. God created all things and governs them by his authoritative speech (Heb. 1:1–3). As creator, God has the prerogative to rule his creation and express his boundaries for faith and obedience. God is the ultimate author of Scripture and thus the Bible has God's authority. God chooses to reveal himself in creation and through Scripture. Both forms of revelation show us true things about God, and we are obliged to learn and follow these truths rather than to follow our own hunches or formulations about what we think God is like or what we suspect he might require. God reveals what he requires for people to live faithfully, including information about prayer. So as we seek to better understand prayer, we must understand prayer as it appears in the Bible, both positively (by way of affirmation) and negatively (by way of opprobrium). Because God is the author of Scripture (by way of human authors, to be sure), we can trust what the Bible says about prayer to be true.

The Bible has authority and sufficiency because it is *inspired*. In popular culture, to say a book, movie, or song is "inspired" might recognize some exceptional quality: a poignant turn of a phrase, a memorable plot, an enjoyable scene. Though Protestants will differ on some details, in general what we mean by inspiration is that although human authors are responsible for giving us the physical text of the Bible and their unique authorial stamp is evident, God is the Bible's ultimate author.[2] The apostle Paul put it this way: "All Scripture is inspired by God and profitable for teaching, for reproof, for correction, for training in righteousness; so that the man of God may be adequate, equipped for every good work" (2 Tim. 3:16–17 NASB 1995). The English word "inspired" is the Greek *theopneustos*, the "out-breathing of God." Since God is its

---

1. Gregg Allison, *50 Core Truths of the Christian Faith: A Guide to Understanding and Teaching Theology* (Grand Rapids: Baker, 2018), 32.
2. Here I affirm what theologians have long called "verbal plenary inspiration."

ultimate source, Scripture is profitable in many ways. Here we focus on the ways that Scripture is profitable with regard to its teaching on prayer.

First, Scripture teaches us what prayer is and what it is not. Positively, Scripture shows us so many godly people praying that we have a lifetime of worthy examples. Negatively, it shows us people whose prayers God rejects or refuses to hear. Scripture offers reproof when we stray into practices of prayer that mimic pagan practices or self-righteous religion. It offers correction for wrong theologies of prayer. Then, because all those who are saved have an external righteousness given them by Jesus, not a native righteousness, Paul suggests Scripture trains us in this new just standing before God; that is, because we are rebellious children, we need to relearn how to enjoy fellowship that was broken in the garden of Eden when our first parents gave in to sin. Finally, because Scripture is inspired, it can prepare us for every good work, including prayer.[3] What are some specific ways, then, that the Bible should inform and guide our prayer?

The Bible Shows People at Prayer

Scripture provides numerous and important examples of people praying, and we can learn much about prayer by paying attention to these accounts. With Paul, we believe that "whatever was written in earlier times was written for our instruction, so that through perseverance and the encouragement of the Scriptures we might have hope" (Rom. 15:4 NASB). Readers may notice that I have emphasized a descriptive role of Scripture here rather than a prescriptive one. This emphasis reflects the freedom found in Scripture. Other scholars have recognized the interesting fact that while prayer was so central to worship in the old covenant, the law prescribes no technique, no form, nor any ritual regarding prayer in Israel.[4] In a similar way, prayer was vital to Jesus's experience and to that of his disciples and the earliest Christians, yet the New Testament is virtually silent with regard to prescriptive forms or ritual observance. Where Scripture is prescriptive, however, we want to understand its requirements and order our practice faithfully.

The Bible Reveals Our Weaknesses in Prayer

Another reason that we ought to listen to the Bible's teaching on prayer is that Scripture can reveal blind spots, weaknesses, and areas for growth in our prayers. We read of the early church "devoting themselves to prayer" (Acts 1:14) and ask if we are similarly devoted. We hear Paul encourage the

---

3. Although the constraints of this series dictate chapter word counts, I mention here the importance of even greater confidence in Scripture by noting its infallibility and inerrancy. Since God cannot lie, his Word is utterly trustworthy and will never lead us astray.

4. See Christopher R. Seitz, "Prayer in the Old Testament or Hebrew Bible," in *Into God's Presence: Prayer in the New Testament*, ed. Richard N. Longenecker (Grand Rapids: Eerdmans, 2001), 16.

Philippians not to let anxiety overwhelm them but instead to pray (Phil. 4:6) and consider how debilitating our own worries can be. We hear the longing prayers of the psalmist for God to show him wonderful things and bend his heart toward obedience (Ps. 119:18, 36) and struggle to remember when we sought such spiritual growth rather than physical gain. Scripture serves as a guide for us to evaluate our own practices of prayer against an authoritative standard. Such reflection is often challenging, for we come to see how weak our faith is and how shallow our requests often are; yet we can be comforted in the fact that, our Lord excepted, all of the positive examples of people who prayed well were people like us: created in God's image but liable to weakness and dependent upon God's grace. Here we find hope: though they were weak as we are, they were able to pray. God heard their prayers despite their frailties; he will also hear ours.

The Bible Reshapes Our Priorities in Prayer

Were it not for the Bible's examples and teaching on the full spectrum of prayer, my own prayers would be largely self-focused. Even with awareness and reflection on the richness of biblical teaching on prayer, I must fight this tendency to only pray primarily *about* me and *for* me. Returning to John Bunyan's definition of prayer from the first chapter, we recall that prayer involves talking with God "for such things as God has promised, or according to his Word."[5] When we grow in praying "according to his Word," we will come to see how God would have us pray for others and come to pray with a godward focus. We will still pray about ourselves, but the things we learn to ask will be expanded and formed through God's priorities. Throughout their lives, Christians should come to Scripture over and over again to grow in their understanding of God's promises and requests consistent with his Word. In subsequent questions we will consider how specifically to approach the Bible in this way.

Summary

The various questions that form the balance of this book reiterate the central theme of this chapter: Scripture is our best and authoritative guide for prayer. That we give priority to Scripture does not mean we need not or should not listen to other Christians when they seek to teach us about prayer. In humility, we realize that others may have better understood what the Bible teaches about prayer or more faithfully appropriated this teaching than we have! Though we all have the privilege of reading and interpreting Scripture, we are not all equally skilled in this task and thus we value the place of community, where God has appointed teachers and peers to help us read faithfully. As we listen to the teaching of others about prayer (or about any other

---

5.   See Question 1. Bunyan, *I Will Pray*, 4–5.

aspect of faith), we always return to the Bible to evaluate their answers in light of God's standard. The Bible reveals truths about prayer that God, in his kindness, has chosen to make known to us in order that we might pray faithfully. These truths form a theology of prayer, and in Section 2 of this book, we will consider several important questions about this theology.

REFLECTION QUESTIONS

1. Why should the Bible inform and shape our prayers?

2. How do the concepts of sufficiency, authority, and inspiration relate to prayer?

3. What are some ways that you have been "reproved and corrected" (2 Tim. 3:16) by Scripture in your own prayer life?

4. How does the Bible's role of equipping believers for "every good work" (2 Tim. 3:17) affect prayer?

5. Why do you think some people resist the Bible's teachings about prayer?

How Does the Gospel Shape Christian Prayer?

While we might not always have the gospel in the front of our minds when praying, the message of Jesus incarnate, buried, raised, ascended, reigning, and returning is distinctively important for Christian prayer. Prayer flows from the gospel, and disconnected from the work of Christ, prayer, and our very faith upon which prayer rests, is vanity. Some Christians separate prayer from the gospel. They may think of the gospel as a message exclusively for nonbelievers that has little to do with prayer. In answering this chapter's question, I hope to show how prayer depends upon the gospel and how the gospel leads us to deeper prayer. We begin with a definition of "gospel" before exploring, briefly, various aspects of its multifaceted message and how each aspect deepens and directs our prayers.

The Gospel Is About Jesus

Because the term "gospel" has been used often and differently among Christian traditions, it seems important at the outset of this chapter to describe how it is being used here.[1] The gospel is the good news that God has acted decisively through Jesus to reconcile sin-alienated people to himself: "Christ also suffered once for sins, the righteous for the unrighteous, that he might bring us to God" (1 Peter 3:18). Though created to be God's image-bearers, the pinnacle of his creative work, Eve and Adam disobeyed God and incurred his wrath over their transgression. Thus every human thus born as a son or daughter of these first parents is born a sinner and stands condemned before God's just standard (Rom. 3:23). Sin brings death and judgment, both temporal and eternal, upon all. In his abundant mercy and grace, God sent forth his unique Son Jesus,

---

1. One recent book that presents the gospel clearly is Greg Gilbert, *What Is the Gospel?* (Wheaton, IL: Crossway, 2010).

the only truly righteous man, to live and die on behalf of sinners. Through his death, Jesus has borne the sins of the world. Those who trust Christ as the sin-bearing Lamb of God (cf. John 1:29) are united to Christ; are declared "not guilty" (justified) before God; are adopted as his sons and declared to be heirs of his kingdom; have the very Spirit of Christ living within (Rom. 5:5); and are declared to be holy, even as we grow into the very image of Christ, who himself is the very image of God. In Christ, God has brought us into relationship with himself, and prayer is language of this union.

Jesus's Obedience and Our Prayer

When considering Jesus's work in salvation, it's common to describe his accomplishment in terms of his *active* and *passive* obedience. Christ's *active* obedience refers to his living a morally blameless life, perfectly fulfilling God's standards in every letter of the law, accomplishing as the last Adam what the first Adam did not: perfect obedience. As we will see at various places in this book, Jesus's active obedience involved prayer through which he resisted the devil and yielded himself to "drink the cup of God's wrath" for sinners (cf. Matt. 26). God imparts Jesus's righteousness to those whom he saves, and this righteousness is nourished in the soil of prayer.

The idea of Jesus's *passive* obedience encompasses all that he suffered for sinners in order to endure God's judgment that was rightly ours. Elsewhere we will notice Jesus's practices of prayer, but one easy-to-overlook part of Christ's passive obedience is his *restraint* in prayer. Citing the Old Testament prophet Isaiah, and a forward-looking description that anticipated the work of God's chosen servant, the early church affirmed that Jesus was "like a sheep he was led to the slaughter and like a lamb before its shearer is silent, so he open[s] not his mouth" (Acts 8:32; cf. Isa. 53:7). It is hard for us to fathom that at his arrest, Jesus could have appealed to his Father who would have immediately sent him "more than twelve legions of angels" to secure his freedom (Matt. 26:53), yet Jesus chose to restrain his lips. Herein is a great irony of the gospel: Jesus chose *not* to pray that we might enjoy the freedom *to* pray. What a marvelous truth this is!

Jesus Is a High Priest Who Hears Prayer

One connection between prayer and the gospel is Hebrews 4:14–16. Here, Christians are reminded of the confidence by which we may "draw near" to God in prayer with an expectation of finding mercy and help when needed *because* of Christ's person and work. Here, Jesus's real incarnation ("for we do not have a high priest who is unable to sympathize with our weaknesses") renders him a truly sympathetic high priest while his resurrection and ascension ("who has passed through the heavens") afford all believers everywhere unlimited access to his listening and receptive ear. This text provides believers a gospel-centered motivation to pray. Because the nature of Jesus's priestly ministry is considered more fully elsewhere in this book (Question 7), we will only mention this particular gospel connection in passing here.

God Is an Adopting, Listening Father

The doctrine of adoption provides a second link between prayer and the gospel. While many Christians often focus on gospel truths such as Christ's atonement or the Father's justification of sinners (and for good purpose), we must remember that God has "predestined us for adoption . . . through Jesus Christ" (Eph. 1:5). God now treats us as sons (Heb. 12:5, 7), giving us "discipline" (*paideian*, formative instruction or correction). We have "received the Spirit of adoption as sons, by whom we cry, 'Abba! Father!'" (Rom. 8:15). Adoption (*huiothesia*) is a fundamental change in our relationship with God:

> But when the fullness of time had come, God sent forth his Son, born of woman, born under the law, to redeem those who were under the law, so that we might receive adoption as sons. And because you are sons, God has sent the Spirit of his Son into our hearts, crying, "Abba! Father!" So you are no longer a slave, but a son, and if a son, then an heir through God. (Gal. 4:4–7)

Our relationship changed, we join with Jesus in praying "our Father" (Matt. 6:9) with sincerity. We are not merely mimicking his language, it has become our language. His Father is indeed our Father. We are part of the Trinitarian "family": sons of the Father, brothers of Christ, bound together by the Spirit. We are no longer outsiders. We have God's ear, and he hears our prayer (Ps. 65:2).[2] The theological truth of adoption, God brings us into his family, encourages us to pray.

Pardoned, Righteous, and Free to Speak

As already mentioned, when many Christians think about the "gospel," they focus on the doctrine theologians call *justification*, God graciously declaring sinners "not guilty" and giving them ("imputing" is the normal term) Christ's righteousness. Like adoption, justification is a legal declaration that God makes on behalf of sinners (Rom. 3:20–28). When we think of Christ's righteousness in relation to prayer, we might consider Jesus's prayer at the raising of Lazarus: "Father, I thank you that you have heard me. I knew that you always hear me, but I said this on account of the people standing around,

---

2. Historian Richard Lovelace makes this point well when he writes, "Christians need to know they have a secure status as adopted sons and daughters of God in order to behave naturally in his presence." See his *Renewal as a Way of Life: A Guidebook for Spiritual Growth* (Eugene, OR: Wipf and Stock, 1985), 143.

that they may believe that you sent me" (John 11:41–42). Jesus's confidence undoubtedly came from many reasons, but one was that sin created no barrier between him and the Father (cf. Ps. 66:18). Paul can quote the psalmist:

> Blessed are those whose lawless deeds are forgiven, and whose sins are covered; blessed is the man against whom the Lord will not count his sin. (Rom. 4:7–8)[3]

Those who have been justified are blessed indeed, for we have confidence that God hears us when we pray! Our confidence is not in our own righteousness, but the righteousness of Christ that God has given us.

Made Holy Through and for Prayer

Because sinners have been declared not guilty on the merits of Christ's life and death, we pursue holiness (moral cleanness and separation from the world) not to earn God's favor but in response to it. Paul says it this way: "For the grace of God has appeared, bringing salvation for all people, training us to renounce ungodliness and worldly passions and to live self-controlled, upright, and godly lives in the present age" (Titus 2:11–12). Christians say no to themselves and to the world and say yes to God *because* his grace has appeared, bringing salvation. This pursuit of separation from the world and devotion to God is known as *sanctification* and prayer is essential to this new path.

Sanctification is God's will for everyone who trusts in Jesus as Lord (1 Thess. 4:3). In John 17, Jesus prayed for his disciples and, by extension, those who would become his disciples through their ministry (17:20), including us. Jesus asked the Father to "sanctify them in the truth," adding "your word is truth" (John 17:17). Though we ought not to overstate its significance, the verb "sanctify" (*hagiason*) occurs in the Greek aorist tense, indicating completed action. It would be reasonable to translate Jesus's statement as "sanctify them and keep them set apart in the truth," or as New Testament scholar David Peterson says, "consecrate them to yourself and keep them in that relationship."[4] Believers are those set apart *through* Jesus's prayer and set apart *for* prayer, for themselves and others.

Prayer is one of God's given means of growing and persevering in holiness for the duration of our lives. Holiness involves growing to love righteousness, to which we are naturally averse.[5] Holiness involves putting off comfortable

---

3. Paul quotes Psalm 32:1–2.
4. David Peterson, *Possessed by God: A New Testament Theology of Sanctification and Holiness*, ed. D. A. Carson, New Studies in Biblical Theology, vol. 1 (Downers Grove, IL: InterVarsity Press, 1995), 30.
5. John Calvin, *Institutes of the Christian Religion*, ed. John T. McNeill, trans. Ford Lewis Battles, vol. 1, The Library of Christian Classics (Louisville, KY: Westminster John Knox Press, 2011), 685.

old patterns of living for self in sin and putting on new patterns of living in righteousness (cf. Col. 3:5–17). Without this holiness, "no one will see the Lord" (Heb. 12:14), yet God has chosen to sanctify his people slowly over time rather than immediately upon conversion. There is no faster way; there is no easier path to holiness. In prayer, we cry out to God to help us press onward in sanctification despite our weakness.

Jesus Rules Over His Kingdom Now

At the outset of his public ministry, Jesus was "proclaiming the gospel of God, and saying, 'The time is fulfilled, and the kingdom of God is at hand; repent and believe in the gospel'" (Mark 1:14–15). His sermon announced that God's reign was now manifest in his presence, even in a rural fishing town in a land occupied by the mightiest empire on earth. All who heard his announcement would have to change their minds and trust this message that God, not Caesar, was really in control. By all outward appearances, Caesar was king, but outward appearances can be deceptive.

When Paul wrote to encourage Christians he had not met, he reiterated Jesus's message that the kingdom of God, God's rule over the world, was at hand *through* Jesus: "If then you have been raised with Christ, seek the things that are above, where Christ is, seated at the right hand of God" (Col. 3:1). Paul's message surely requires faith: (1) Jesus is alive, and not only is he alive, (2) but he is king ("seated at the right hand of God" is kingly language); moreover, (3) Christians are those who have been raised with Jesus. Though we do not see his reign and our nearness, he is king, and we are united to his resurrection *now*. The message of Jesus's rule really ought to encourage our prayer.

Jesus's kingdom and reign will be manifest visibly in time; yet if Jesus is king *now*, and we are raised with him *now*, then Jesus is in a unique position to hear and answer our prayers without hindrance. In prayer, we have an audience with the one who rules all creation, and we are united to him.

The Indwelling Holy Spirit Overflows with Prayer

In an earlier generation, Christian pastors turned to a passage in Zechariah to encourage prayer:

> And I will pour out on the house of David and the inhabitants of Jerusalem a spirit of grace and pleas for mercy, so that, when they look on me, on him whom they have pierced, they shall mourn for him, as one mourns for an only child, and weep bitterly over him, as one weeps over a firstborn. (Zech. 12:10)

Though today we might rarely turn to the minor prophets for instruction on prayer, older interpreters agreed that this passage anticipates what happened at Pentecost—the gift of the Holy Spirit—and they connected this prophecy to the Spirit's ministry of helping believers to pray. In subsequent questions we will consider several of the ministries of the Spirit in relation to our prayer in greater detail and will thus only enumerate these ministries briefly here:

- The Spirit enables us to pray to God as "Abba! Father!" (Gal. 4:6).
- The Spirit helps us in our weakness when we do not know how to pray (Rom. 8:26).
- Believers are to pray "in" the Spirit (Eph. 6:18; Jude 20).

We bring up the ministry of the Holy Spirit in connection with the gospel here because believers sometimes forget that the abiding presence of the Holy Spirit is one of the blessings *of* the gospel. In John 14–16, Jesus makes many promises concerning the presence of the Holy Spirit and the Spirit's ministry: God will give the Spirit to believers forever (John 14:16); the Spirit will teach believers "all things" and help them remember all of Jesus's teachings (14:26); the Spirit will bear witness to Jesus (15:26); the Spirit will guide believers in truth (16:13) and will glorify Jesus (16:14). Those who trust Christ enjoy the abiding presence of the Spirit now, and these forward-looking promises Jesus made are Christians' present experiences through the gospel.

United in Prayer in Christ

As mentioned earlier in this chapter, Christians have been united to Christ in salvation. The passive voice statement "have been united" is intentional, for we do not unite ourselves to Christ. Theologian John Murray describes this union as spiritual and mystical. Union with Christ is "spiritual" because the Spirit of God is the one who unites believers and Christ together by applying the work of Christ that took place outside of ourselves. The union also is spiritual because the union between Christ and believers is a spiritual union. This union is "mystical" because it is mysterious, previously hidden but now brought to light (Rom. 16:25; Eph. 5:32; Col. 1:26).[6] Being united to Christ should encourage us to pray in several ways.

First, we pray in confidence as those who have been brought near to Christ. As with our adoption, we are no longer outsiders to the family of God but *are* God's family. When we pray, we do so from a position of nearness, not distance. Second, we are united to Jesus who was himself a man marked by prayer. We will consider prayer in Jesus's life in greater detail in later chapters, but to read the Gospels (the New Testament books of Matthew, Mark, Luke, and John) is to see Jesus regularly praying. He teaches his disciples to pray, he invites them to join him in prayer, and so we have been united to a great man of prayer who loves prayer and whose ministry remains that of prayer as a

---

6. John Murray, *Redemption: Accomplished and Applied* (Grand Rapids: Eerdmans, 1955), 165–73.

great high priest. Our identity as those who may have been formerly weak in prayer has been changed; we are now united to one who is mighty in prayer and who calls us to pray in faith with him.

Summary

The gospel is about Jesus, and Jesus was, and remains, a man of prayer. His prayers strengthened his obedience to the Father in his life and in his death. The gospel promises that Jesus's obedience is credited to us and that his death is our death, his righteousness is our righteousness, and his access to the Father is now our access. As a great high priest, Jesus prayed for us during his ministry on earth and continues to intercede on our behalf in heaven. The gospel tells us that we have been adopted into God's family and thus have God's attentive ear. Prayer is part of our ongoing growth in conformity to the image of Christ (Rom. 8:29) and thus a vital part of our sanctification. We have been united to Christ, who rules his kingdom now, and have been raised and reign with him. The gospel makes prayer possible and effective.

REFLECTION QUESTIONS

1. What are some aspects of the gospel presented in this chapter that you think about most often? How do these aspects affect your view of prayer?

2. What are some aspects of the gospel you do not think about as often? What are some ways these aspects might enrich your thinking on prayer?

3. How does adoption inform our prayers?

4. How do justification and sanctification relate to our prayers?

5. What is one danger of separating prayer from the gospel?

PART 2

Prayer and Theology

To Whom Do Christians Pray?

We said in Question 1 that prayer is offered "to God, through Christ, in the strength and assistance of the Holy Spirit."[1] Christians pray to God and the God to whom we pray reveals himself as eternal Trinity. How does this revelation affect our prayers? Should it affect our prayers at all? In answering this chapter's question, I want to show how pausing to think deeper about who God reveals himself to be can help us pray with a deeper awareness of his presence. In other questions, we will see how the apostle Paul was particularly attentive to this revelation. In fact, one phrase from Paul's writings offers a helpful starting point. As Paul reflects on the great truth that through the cross both Jew and Gentile could be reconciled and united into "one new man," he locates this reconciliation in relationship with God: "For through [Jesus] we both have access in one Spirit to the Father" (Eph. 2:18). This notion of "access" and its Trinitarian framework are important for our prayers, and we want to consider this importance more fully.

A Summary of Trinitarian Prayer

In Ephesians 2:11–22, Paul shows how God has brought these Greek-speaking Gentiles who were once aliens and strangers into fellowship with God's people Israel through Jesus Christ. His language is that of ethnic and civil identity: "So then you are no longer strangers and aliens, but you are fellow citizens with the saints and members of the household of God" (Eph. 2:19). Wherever you are reading this book, struggles over a sense of cultural alienation are part of your story, but through Christ, God is making one new man to be his holy people and through Christ, "we both have access . . . to the Father" (Eph. 2:18). Jesus has reconciled us (see Question 4) with one another and opened the way for us to come into the presence of the Father (John 14:6).

---

1. John Bunyan, *I Will Pray with the Spirit, and I Will Pray with the Understanding Also, or, A Discourse Touching Prayer, from I Cor. 14.15*, 2nd ed. (London: 1663), 4–5.

What does it mean for us to pray "through him" (*di' autou*)? It means that Jesus is the unique mediator between God and people (1 Tim. 2:5). No one comes before God in prayer but through Jesus. We consider Jesus's experience of prayer and the Lord's Prayer more fully in several questions below, but here we simply mention that when Jesus prayed, he addressed his prayers to the Father (Matt. 11:25; Mark 14:36; John 17:1). When he taught his disciples to pray, he told them to address their prayers to "our Father" (Matt. 6:9; Luke 11:2). In prayer, our access is "toward the Father" (*pros ton patera*).[2] According to Paul, our access to the Father is "in one Spirit" (*en heni pneumati*). Later, we will consider this idea of praying "in" the Spirit in more detail, but here we can simply conclude that none of our prayers reach the Father apart from the ministry of the Spirit.

We Pray to One God

Focusing on prayer and the distinct role of each person of the Trinity is important because we are thinking about God as he reveals himself in his Word, but it is equally important that we retain a biblical mindset and recognize that we pray to one God. There is one God, who exists eternally as Father, Son, and Holy Spirit. God is one in *essence* and three in *person*. There are not three gods, but one God. There is not one god who takes three different expressions, but one God who is three subsistences, each "co-equal and co-eternal."[3] Father, Son, and Spirit share one essence or nature, and when we pray, we pray to the one true God who is eternally triune. The seventeenth-century theologian John Owen (1616–1683) noted this situation well:

> Here is a distinction of the persons, as to their operations; but not at all as to their being the object of our worship. For the Son and the Holy Ghost are no less worshipped in our access to God than the Father himself; only the grace of the Father, which we obtain by the mediation of the Son, and the assistance of the Spirit, is that which we draw nigh to God for.[4]

Owen's quote is very helpful as it helps us avoid the ancient heresy of Modalism. This teaching ignores the biblical distinction between persons and suggests there is one God who manifests himself differently at various points in history, sometimes as Father, sometimes as Son, and other times as Spirit. Thankfully, the ancient church recognized the error in this teaching, yet it

---

2. The preposition *pros* with the accusative indicates an orientation toward its object.
3. See J. I. Packer, *Concise Theology: A Guide to Historic Christian Beliefs* (Wheaton, IL: Tyndale, 1993), 40–42.
4. John Owen, *Communion with the Triune God*, eds. Kelly M. Kapic and Justin Taylor (Wheaton, IL: Crossway, 2007), 420.

is not uncommon to hear public prayers addressed to the Father that thank him for dying on the cross! Of course the Father did not die on the cross, the Son did, and such a prayer probably reveals unreflective theology rather than intentional heterodoxy. Careful Trinitarian reflection, though, can help us uphold truth, even in our prayers.

We Pray to and Through No One Else

Christians pray *through* Christ, *in* the Spirit, *to* the Father and pray to or through no one else. This vision for prayer is decidedly Protestant, for other traditions ascribe a special role to Mary, the mother of Jesus, or to other "saints" with regard to prayer. In the Middle Ages, Thomas Aquinas suggested that Christians ought to offer prayer to other saints that those saints might in turn pray for living Christians: "We pray to the saints, whether angels or men, not that God may through them know our petitions, but that our prayers may be effective through their prayers and merits."[5] Aquinas's perspective was shaped by a theology of merit and grace in which some believers accumulated credit before God and possessed a better standing with God and thus their prayers were considered more effective, a view rejected in the Protestant Reformation. Similarly, *The Catechism of the Catholic Church* envisions Mary as a trustworthy guardian of "the supplications and praises of the children of God" because "she has become the mother of all the living," and thus "we can pray with and to her." Stating this doctrine forthrightly, the *Catechism* says, "The prayer of the church is sustained by the prayer of Mary and united with it in hope."[6] Within Roman Catholicism, Mary's role in prayer is connected to her larger role in the economy of redemption in which she stands as a mediator between the church and Jesus, receiving the prayers of those on earth and communicating them to Jesus.[7] Though long-practiced and popular, these devotional habits are foreign to Scripture. Article 23 of the Italian Reformed *Confession of the Waldenses* states: "That those who are already in the possession of eternal life in consequence of their faith and good works ought to be considered as saints and glorified persons, and to be praised for their virtue and imitated in all good actions of their life, but neither worshiped nor invoked, for God only is to be prayed unto, and that through Jesus Christ."[8] The answer to Question 179 of the Westminster Larger Catechism is likewise helpful on this matter: "God only being able to search the hearts, hear the requests, pardon the sins, and fulfil the desires of all; and only to be believed in,

---

5. Thomas Aquinas, *Summa Theologiae*, 2.83.A.4, https://aquinas.cc/la/en/~ST.II-II.Q83.A4.Obj2.
6. *The Catechism of the Catholic Church*, Part 4, Article 2, Paragraph 2, 673–79.
7. *Lumen Gentium* 69.
8. *The Confession of the Waldenses*, Article 23, *The Creeds of Christendom, with a History and Critical Notes: The Evangelical Protestant Creeds, with Translations*, vol. 3, ed. Phillip Schaff (New York: Harper & Brothers, 1882), 764.

and worshiped with religious worship; prayer, which is a special part thereof, is to be made by all to him alone, and to none other."[9]

Summary

Christian prayer is intentionally Trinitarian: *to* the Father, *through* the Son, *in* the Spirit, yet all prayer is directed to the one true God. The ologian Fred Sanders calls this kind of Trinity-aware prayer "praying with the grain," or prayer that recognizes the structure that really exists in the way God is and in the ways that he relates to us.[10] Praying to God with intentional awareness of each person of the Trinity ought to provoke adoration, for we are meditating on God in his own being. This sort of Trinitarian awareness shaped Paul's prayer of blessing (*berkah*) in Ephesians 1:3–14, where he praises the Father, Son, and Holy Spirit for their unique works in salvation. This text also reminds us that cultivating a Trinitarian awareness helps shape our petitions and intercession as we ask each person of the Trinity to bring his undivided-but-distinct work to bear in our lives and the lives of others.

REFLECTION QUESTIONS

1. When you pray, how do you most often visualize God hearing you?

2. What differences can being aware of God's existing as three persons in one nature make in your prayers?

3. How might being aware of the special works of each person of the Trinity affect your prayers?

4. How might praying to God with an awareness of his nature and work deepen your prayers?

5. How does the idea that we pray to and through no one but God affect your devotion?

---

9. Westminster Assembly, *The Westminster Confession of Faith: Edinburgh Edition* (Philadelphia: William S. Young, 1851), 363–64.
10. Fred Sanders, *The Deep Things of God* (Wheaton, IL: Crossway, 2010), 212–14.

Should Christians Pray to the Son and the Holy Spirit?

In the last chapter, we saw that prayer involves each person of the Trinity. The present question extends that discussion by considering the rightness of praying to the second and third persons of the Trinity. The question is not whether Christians *may* pray to the Son and Spirit, but whether we *should* do so. Answering this question is important for our daily practice of prayer. Perhaps you have never considered praying to the Son or Spirit, or perhaps your prayers regularly invoke them. Experientially, what might we miss by praying only to the Father? Are there errors or imbalances into which we may stray by praying to the Spirit or the Son? We will consider each of these questions in turn.

Praying to the Son and Spirit

On occasion, Christians in the early church prayed to Jesus. In a passage with clear Trinitarian overtones, Stephen "full of the Holy Spirit," beholds the glory of God and sees "Jesus standing at the right hand of God" (Acts 7:55). Stephen's dying prayers are directed to the Son: "Lord Jesus, receive my spirit" and "Lord, do not hold this sin against them" (Acts 7:59, 60). Paul also prayed to Jesus: "Three times I pleaded to the Lord about this [thorn]" (2 Cor. 12:8).

While there are clear biblical examples of prayers directed to Jesus, there are no clear examples of prayers directed to the Spirit. The closest thing to a Spirit-addressed prayer occurs in the doxology of 2 Corinthians 13:14 and in the greeting of Revelation 1:4–5.

> Grace to you and peace from him who is and who was and who is to come, and from the seven spirits who are before his throne, and from Jesus Christ, the faithful witness, the first-born of the dead, and the ruler of kings on earth. (Rev. 1:4–5)

The greeting is certainly Trinitarian, with the reference to the "seven spirits" generally recognized as an Old Testament allusion to the Spirit drawing on imagery from the Old Testament prophet Zechariah.[1] The doxology of 2 Corinthians is likewise Trinitarian: "The grace of the Lord Jesus Christ and the love of God and the fellowship of the Holy Spirit be with you all" (2 Cor. 13:14). While epistolary greetings and doxologies are standard parts of ancient letters, they express a wish or desire on behalf of their writers, namely that the recipients experience the various situations ("grace and peace" or "grace . . . love . . . fellowship") connected to the divine giver of these blessings. In sum, these introductory and closing sections are prayers, but admittedly brief ones.[2] We do not find narratives of Old or New Testament saints praying to the Holy Spirit in the same way that we have examples of prayers to the Father and even to the Son.

Puritan theologian John Owen offers a helpful perspective regarding prayer and the Holy Spirit. This theme was an important one to Owen, who wrote important works on the Spirit, on the Spirit and prayer, and on the communion between believers and God.[3] On the one hand, Owen appeals to Revelation 1:4 to show that believers *may* pray to the Spirit, indicating the Spirit's divine nature and personhood. On the other, Owen suggests that believers might pray to the Father, asking him to send the promised Spirit for comfort and aid, but also that Christians "may pray to him [the Spirit] to come unto us to sanctify and comfort us, according to the work and the office that he hath undertaken."[4] Owen's approach is helpful because it balances the biblical truth that the Spirit is God and therefore worthy of prayer with the principle that the Spirit accomplishes specific ministries among the faithful and that our prayers to him might focus on these ministries. His approach helps us avoid error and imbalance in our prayers.

Potential Theological Imbalances and Errors

The doctrine of the Trinity is a distinctive and essential Christian doctrine, and it matters for our prayer. At various times in the church's history, pastors and theologians have had to confront various errors and heresies related to the Trinity. One error is unitarianism, the idea that God is essentially and personally

---

1.   G. K. Beale, *The Book of Revelation*, New International Greek Testament Commentary (Grand Rapids: Eerdmans, 1999), 189.
2.   To be fair, not everyone is convinced that these passages are prayers. See Fred Sanders, *The Deep Things of God* (Wheaton, IL: Crossway, 2010), 225.
3.   See John Owen, *Of the Work of the Holy Spirit in Prayer*, in *The Works of John Owen*, vol. 4, ed. William H. Goold (Carlisle, PA: The Banner of Truth Trust, 1965); Owen, *Discourse on the Holy Spirit, Works*, vol. 3; and Owen, *On Communion with God*, in *Works*, vol. 2.
4.   Owen, *Holy Spirit*, in *Works* 3:118.

"one."[5] While Scripture is clear that "God is one" (Deut. 6:4), and Christianity is monotheistic, Christians confess that God is three persons in one divine nature. Unitarians in each generation have denied that the Son and Spirit are God in the same essential way that the Father is God, and the church has consistently condemned this approach as error. Unitarians are not praying to the one true living God of the Bible, yet it is possible that orthodox Christians who actually do hold to the divinity of the Spirit and Son might fall into a kind of functional unitarianism by only praying generally to "God," without considering that God means Father, Son, and Spirit, and that each person has special work to do in our lives. At the other end of the spectrum are those who have overemphasized the role of the Son or the Spirit so as to undercut the role of the Father and thus fall into different kinds of theological errors.

It is also possible that by praying to the Spirit or the Son we will encounter imbalanced theology, theology that is tilted differently from the weight revealed in Scripture. Graham Cole calls this situation "disproportion."[6] Such theology is not in error per se, but it simply ignores the proportionality found within God's self-revelation and is an unwise path to follow. When we realize that the Son and Spirit are indeed God and may be prayed to, we might feel disenchanted with praying to the Father, something we have done for a long time, as we explore this newfound freedom. To ignore praying to the Father, though, is to veer away from clear biblical teaching, no matter how right it may be to pray to the other persons in the Trinity.

A final reminder regarding the scope of prayer seems fitting. As we have argued above, "prayer" is most often petitionary, but it is also an expression of worship as believers adore God for who he is or thank him for what he has done in their own lives or in the lives of others. Offering thanksgiving or adoration to the Holy Spirit or the Son is simply a specific way of acknowledging their unique ministries in the work of salvation or in their work within the world. Just as it is fitting for believers to ask the Father to send the Spirit (Luke 11:13), and to do so with the expectation that the Father delights to do this, it is also right for us to ask the Spirit to bring various virtues (e.g., faith, hope, love, patience, kindness, self-control, etc.; cf. Gal. 5:22–23) to fruition in our lives or to help us "understand the things freely given to us by God" or to "teach us" these things (1 Cor. 2:12–13). Likewise, it is fitting for us to thank the Father for putting forth his Son to be a propitiation for us (Rom. 3:25), but it is equally appropriate for us to thank the Son for making propitiation "for the sins of the people" (Heb. 2:17) or for being the "mediator of a new

---

5. The lowercase "u" distinguishes this teaching, which occurred from at least the fourth century on, from the religious Unitarian sect that has the same name (and teaches the same aberrant doctrine).
6. Graham A. Cole, *He Who Gives Life: The Doctrine of the Holy Spirit* (Wheaton, IL: Crossway, 2007), 86.

covenant" (Heb. 12:24) or for not counting "equality with God a thing to be grasped" and humbling himself to the point of death on a cross (Phil. 2:6, 8), and so forth.

Summary

Some readers might be asking, "With all of these caveats, wouldn't it be easier to simply pray to 'God' or the 'Father' all the time? Is praying to the Son or Spirit worth the hassle?" It is never wrong to pray to the Father. Not ever. Praying to the Father is our normal direction for prayer. Praying to the Son or Spirit, though, can help us grow in deeper in our worship because it reaffirms their uniqueness and worthiness. The Son and the Spirit are not just important beings, but in the words of an early church creed,

> And [I believe] in the Holy Ghost, the Lord and Giver of Life;
> who proceedeth from the Father [and the Son]; who with the
> Father and the Son together is worshiped and glorified.[7]

Prayer is one of the important ways that Christians worship and glorify the Father and the Son and the Holy Spirit. Following Owen's advice, praying to the Son and Spirit, "according to the work and the office" that is biblically ascribed to each person, helps us maintain balance and avoid error.

REFLECTION QUESTIONS

1. What theological reasons allow us to pray to the Son and Spirit?

2. What are some potential imbalances of praying only to the Father?

3. What are some potential errors we might commit when praying to the Son or Spirit?

4. What are some specific requests we might make of the Son or Spirit?

5. What are some specific thanksgivings or adorations we might offer to the Spirit or Son?

---

7. Philip Schaff, *The Creeds of Christendom, with a History and Critical Notes: The Greek and Latin Creeds, with Translations*, vol. 2 (New York: Harper & Brothers, 1890), 59.

How Does Jesus's Intercession Strengthen Our Prayers?

Building on our discussion of prayer being offered *to* the Father, *in* the Spirit, *through* the Son in earlier chapters, we focus our attention here on the special ministry of Jesus as our advocate and mediator. Christian theologians have long noted that the New Testament describes Jesus as a prophet, king, and priest.[1] These three roles may seem formal and foreign for many Christians, who know Jesus primarily as a friend of sinners, but each role communicates a different aspect of his saving work. Here we want to ask how Jesus's role as a priest who prays for us might bring us comfort and strengthen our own praying. Maybe this chapter's question is not one that you ask often, but its answer is vital for our spirituality.

Priests Represent Sinful People Before God

As with many biblical terms, "priest" may evoke images drawn from our own experience or from popular media that have little to do with the Bible, thus a short reminder of who priests were seems appropriate. In Scripture, priests represent sinful people before God. Sin separates people from God and thus they cannot approach him directly. In the Old Testament, men like Abel (Gen. 4:4), Jethro (Exod. 18:1), and the mysterious Melchizedek (Gen. 14:18) had priestly roles. After Israel's release from Egypt, God designated Aaron (Exod. 28:1) and his family line (the Levites, Exod. 32:28–29) as hereditary priests for the nation. Priests stand between sinners and God as mediators, representing God to the people and the people to God. As mediators, they offer sacrifices and intercession on behalf of the people they represent.

---

1. Charles Hodge, *Systematic Theology*, vol. 2 (Oak Harbor, WA: Logos, 1997), 459.

Jesus Is the Greatest Priest

The epistle of Hebrews identifies Jesus as a priest. Offering one reason for Jesus's incarnation, the writer explains that Jesus "had to be made like his brothers in every respect, so that he might become a merciful and faithful high priest in the service of God, to make propitiation for the sins of the people" (Heb. 2:17). Jesus is both priest and sacrifice. As the Belgic Confession states, "We believe that Jesus Christ is ordained with an oath to be an everlasting High Priest . . . [who] hath presented himself in our behalf before the Father, to appease his wrath by his full satisfaction, by offering himself on the tree of the cross, and pouring out his precious blood to purge away our sins."[2]

Elsewhere, the author of Hebrews emphasizes Jesus's sympathy for sinners: "For we do not have a high priest who is unable to sympathize with our weaknesses, but one who in every respect has been tempted as we are, yet without sin" (Heb. 4:15). Yet Jesus was unlike other priests in Israel: "The former priests were many in number, because they were prevented by death from continuing in office, but he holds his priesthood permanently, because he continues forever. Consequently, he is able to save to the uttermost those who draw near to God through him, since he always lives to make intercession for them. For it was indeed fitting that we should have such a high priest, holy, innocent, unstained, separated from sinners, and exalted above the heavens" (Heb. 7:23–26). Unlike earthly priests, who ministered in earthly structures "made by hands, which are copies of the true things," Jesus prays for us in the very presence of God (Heb. 9:24). All of the priests in Israel were anticipations of Jesus's priesthood. Jesus's priesthood has important consequences for our salvation and for our new life of faith, including our prayers. As mentioned above, Jesus's ministry gives us *confidence* to draw near to God in prayer and *comfort* that Jesus continually prays for us.

Paul reflected on Jesus's ministry of heavenly intercession in Romans 8:34–35:

> Who is to condemn? Christ Jesus is the one who died—more than that, who was raised—who is at the right hand of God, who indeed is interceding for us. Who shall separate us from the love of Christ? Shall tribulation, or distress, or persecution, or famine, or nakedness, or danger, or sword?

The present tense verb "interceding" (*entynchanei*) underscores both the ongoing interpersonal contact and earnestness of the request.[3] Paul mentioned

---

2. *The Belgic Confession*, Article 21, *The Creeds of Christendom, with a History and Critical Notes: The Evangelical Protestant Creeds, with Translations*, vol. 3 (New York: Harper & Brothers, 1882), 407.
3. BDAG, "ἐντυγχάνω."

Jesus's intercession in connection with the believer's confidence: "What then shall we say to these things? If God is for us, who can be against us?" (Rom. 8:31). The "things" Paul mentions include some of the greatest truths of the faith: that those who are united to Jesus are no longer condemned (8:1); that the abiding Holy Spirit ensures our resurrection from the dead (8:11), allows us to experience victories over sin (8:13), leads us (8:14), reminds us inwardly of the truth that the Father has adopted us (8:16), and prays for us in our weakness (8:26); that believers are being conformed to the image of Christ (8:29); and that God's work of salvation is from eternity to eternity (8:30). Because we belong to Jesus, and this Jesus is in the Father's presence interceding for us, nothing "will be able to separate us from the love of God in Christ Jesus our Lord" (8:39).

The Content of Jesus's Intercession

Paul and the author of Hebrews are confident *that* Jesus is presently interceding in heaven on our behalf, but *what* is Jesus praying? First, Jesus hears the prayers of his people and mediates them to the Father. Peter describes Christians as a "holy priesthood," ordained to offer "spiritual sacrifices acceptable to God *through* Jesus Christ" (1 Peter 2:5, emphasis mine). Our prayers are the sacrifices offered, and they come to God through Jesus. Second, Jesus's intercession fulfills the promises offered to believers. Theologian John Gill provides a helpful summary:

> Once more, Christ executes this office by seeing to it, that all the blessings of grace promised in covenant, and ratified by his blood, are applied by his Spirit to the covenant-ones: and so he sits as a priest on his throne, and sees the travail of his soul with satisfaction; when, as those he engaged for, are reconciled by his death, so they are saved by his interceding life; are effectually called by grace, and put into the possession of what was stipulated and procured for them.[4]

Paul praises the Triune God, "who has blessed us in Christ with every spiritual blessing in the heavenly places" (Eph. 1:3). Jesus prays for the application of these blessings to his brothers and sisters. Finally, Jesus prays for our spiritual flourishing and protection in the midst of suffering. Taking our cues from his earthly prayer in John 17, Jesus prays that God would work in believers in the following ways: "keep them in your name" (17:11) "that they may be one" (17:11); "keep them from the evil one" (17:15); "sanctify them in the truth"

---

4.   John Gill, *A Complete Body of Doctrinal and Practical Divinity: Or A System of Evangelical Truths, Deduced from the Sacred Scriptures*, new ed., vol. 1 (London: Tegg & Company, 1839), 616.

(17:17) "that they may also be in us [the Father and the Son] so that the world may believe that you have sent me" (17:21) and "that they may be with me [Jesus] where I am, to see my glory that you have given me" (17:24).

Comfort and Confidence in Our Intercessor

Jesus always intercedes for us from perfect knowledge of our situations and needs. One of the great blessings of life in the church is having other Christians pray for us. Yet every prayer offered by a fellow believer has one inherent weakness: no other person can know *exactly* what to ask on our behalf, because others cannot *fully* understand our needs nor can they comprehend exactly our situations, nor are they always able to pray when we stand in need of intercession. Not so with Jesus. A letter from a young Baptist student in an earlier century illustrates just how important Jesus's intercession can be for our spiritual comfort:

> Paul speaks of blessings received through the prayers of his fellow Christians; no wonder; therefore, he so often solicits their continuance. But if it be well to be interested in the prayers of fellow Christians, how much more to believe the great High Priest of our profession, Jesus the Son of God, is gone into the holy of holies, with our names on his breastplate, ever to plead in the presence of God for us—for us; oh, transporting thought! Who can doubt the success of such an intercessor. . . . Through his intercession alone I expect my sins to be pardoned, my services accepted, and my soul preserved, guided, and comforted; and, with confidence in his intercession, I cannot doubt but I shall enjoy all [these things].[5]

Summary

During his earthly ministry, Jesus was a man of prayer. The gospel of Luke recounts that Jesus's last act as he ascended into heaven was prayer: "lifting up his hands he blessed them. While he blessed them, he parted from them and was carried up into heaven" (Luke 24:50–51). Now, in the very presence of God, he remains a man of prayer who intercedes on behalf of his adopted siblings. In John 6, Jesus promised that he would receive sinners: "All that the Father gives me will come to me, and whoever comes to me I will never cast out" (6:37). Jesus's intercession gives us confidence and comfort that we are his forever.[6]

---

5. Samuel Pearce to William Summers, in Andrew Fuller, *The Complete Works of Andrew Fuller*, vol. 4, Memoirs of the Rev. Samuel Pearce, ed. Michael A. G. Haykin (Berlin: De Gruyter, 2017), 45.
6. Readers wishing to explore the comfort that Jesus's intercession offers might consult Thomas Goodwin, *The Heart of Christ in Heaven, to Sinners on Earth*, in *The Works of Thomas Goodwin*, vol. 4 (Edinburgh: James Nichol, 1862), 95–150.

REFLECTION QUESTIONS

1. How would you describe Jesus's ministry as priest?

2. Is Jesus's ministry as intercessor something you consider often?

3. In what ways might Jesus's ministry give you confidence in prayer?

4. In what ways might Jesus's ministry give you comfort in prayer?

5. What are some of the things that Jesus prays for you?

How Does the Holy Spirit Help Christians Pray?

One of our most common struggles in prayer is due to uncertainty. Christians may know *that* we need to pray and have a solid method *to* pray, yet lack clarity in *what* to pray in various circumstances, both for ourselves and for others. The complexity of our circumstances, variety of our trials, limiting effects of sin, limited knowledge, distractedness, laziness, or other common-to-life weakness can make certitude in prayer elusive. Confronted with these realities, we long for God's help, but *what* might such help be? In Romans 8:26–27, Paul encourages the Christians in Rome by explaining that one of the hidden ministries of the Holy Spirit addresses this particular experience of weakness as the Spirit prays for believers according to the will of God. Precisely what shape this ministry takes in actual experience requires careful attention, but first the idea of weakness in prayer needs some elaboration.

Uncertainty Is Natural, but Amplified by Sin

In Eden, Adam and Eve enjoyed relational wholeness with one another, with the world, and with their Creator, such that uncertainty in following God's will was present yet minimal; God expressed his will immediately and directly (cf. Gen. 2:16–17). Though theologians debate the extent of Adam's knowledge before the fall, few would hold that humanity's first parents possessed omniscience, because they were, after all, creatures dependent on a Creator. As vice-regents entrusted with working, protecting, and governing the Creator's handiwork, humans enjoyed authority (e.g., ruling over creation exhibited in naming the animals), and this authority was exercised through trust in their Creator-King. Even in Eden, obedience was a matter of faith, for Adam and Eve had to believe that (1) God's commands were true and (2) that God's commands were best. Such trust emphasized the distinction between

Creator and creature, which seems to be the very emphasis targeted by the serpent (cf. Gen. 3:4–5). This trust was a critical component of Adam and Eve's experience of nearness to God, and once broken requires an act of new creation (e.g., regeneration) to be restored.

After the fall, the noetic effects (weakness in knowing) of sin amplify natural uncertainty and affect every aspect of human existence, including prayer. Beginning with the generation of Enosh, Adam, Eve, and their children "began to call upon the name of the Lord " (Gen. 4:26). This calling is the beginning of prayer. Gone was the normative, immediate experience of God's nearness; present is the now-normal experience of God's distance and a longing for him to fulfill his promise to crush the serpent's head (cf. Gen. 3:15). Thus, humans pray. Though prayer is a gracious condescension on God's part in giving willful rebels access to him, for humans it is frequently tainted by self-focused motives (cf. James 4:3), doubt, or simply not knowing what we ought to pray for in a given situation. Uncertainty in prayer is a continual reminder that prayer, as gracious a gift as it is, will always be imperfect, for one party in the relationship (us) will continually struggle to communicate well. Though imperfect, prayer is vital, for it is how people commune with God. This fact of prayer's weakness makes Paul's promise of the Spirit's help in prayer found in Romans 8:26–27 so precious.

How the Spirit Overcomes Uncertainty

What precisely does Paul say the Holy Spirit does to address the common human experience of weakness in prayer? Commentators offer various interpretations of the Spirit's help in Romans 8:26–27. Though longstanding differences exist, all approaches share this: they understand that the Spirit *really is* involved in ministering to Christians' weakness in prayer. One approach understands the Spirit's ministry to be teaching believers that for which they should pray.[1] Another approach understands the Spirit's aid as a charismatic manifestation through the lips of believers.[2] Still another school finds in this passage an elaboration of the Spirit's ministry as the believer's advocate and helper (cf. John 14:16).[3]

The Spirit Prays for Believers

The third approach given above, and the one followed in this chapter, understands Romans 8:26–27 as a hidden ministry of the Holy Spirit meant

1. Older theologians such as John Calvin and John Owen as well as contemporary commentators like Richard Longenecker take this approach.
2. The most detailed modern proponent of this view is Pentecostal scholar Gordon Fee (b. 1934).
3. Many contemporary New Testament scholars take this approach, such as Thomas Schreiner, Douglas Moo, and Colin Kruse.

to encourage Christians in their present experience of weakness and un-certainty in prayer. This ministry is "hidden" in that it takes place imper-ceptibly within believers; the Spirit's "groanings" are just that—the *Spirit's* divine speech and not *our* vocalizations. If it were not for Romans 8:26–27, this ministry would be opaque to believers; yet God is so kind to make the Spirit's ministry known here and thus it is also "revealed" in such a way as to encourage Christians that their imperfect prayers fall on the listening ears of a perfect God.

The ESV's "likewise" (*hōsautōs*) at the beginning of 8:26 connects what Paul is going to say about the ministry of the Spirit with what he has said earlier in the chapter, but what is the best connection point? While the near referent of "groaning" in 8:22–23 might offer a possible link, the main verb in 8:26 is "helps," a verb describing a specific work of the Spirit, and thus "likewise" seems to align more naturally with the Spirit's specific work of bearing witness to believers' adoption (8:16–17).[4] As noted in the discus-sion of the relationship between the gospel and prayer (Question 4), the Spirit offers inward testimony to believers that God has truly adopted them and that they really are accepted into his presence as genuine heirs. "Likewise," the Spirit helps believers in their weakness of praying with lin-gering uncertainty.

The primary verb *synantilambanetai* occurs in only one other New Testament passage and in both instances means something like "comes to the aid of," "assists," or the ESV's "helps" (cf. Luke 10:40). The specific focus of the Spirit's help is with "our weakness." Here, "weakness" (*astheneia*) is very generic: the experience of limitation or incapacity. Attentive readers will note that by his use of the first-person plural Paul has included him-self within the sphere of Christians who experience weakness and need the Spirit's help. The conjunction "for" that begins the next phrase specifies the particular weakness Paul intends: "For we do not know what to pray for as we ought." Although some English translations render this weakness a matter of method by translating the phrase as "for we do not know how to pray as we ought" (NRSV), the pronoun *ti* ("what") is rarely a synonym for *pōs* ("how") and more likely addresses content rather than the form of prayer.[5] The weakness here is one of certainty in praying for the things we ought, yet the final clause of Romans 8:26 promises hope for uncertain be-lievers: the Spirit's intercession.

4.   Geoffrey Smith, "The Function of 'Likewise' (ΩΣΑΥΤΩΣ) in Romans 8:26," *Tyndale Bulletin* 49.1 (1998): 29–38.

5.   See Douglas J. Moo, *The Letter to the Romans*, 2nd ed., New International Commentary on the New Testament (Grand Rapids: Eerdmans, 2018), 546; and Thomas R. Schreiner, *Romans*, 2nd ed., Baker Exegetical Commentary on the New Testament (Grand Rapids: Baker, 2018), 425.

According to Paul, "The Spirit himself intercedes for us with groanings too deep for words." Several noteworthy aspects of this phrase demand attention and elaboration. First, Paul explains the Spirit's ministry with an intensive construction ("the Spirit *himself* intercedes"). Among other things, this phrasing supports the idea of the Spirit's personhood rather than existence as a thing or force. Then, the particular verbs Paul uses for "intercedes" (*hyperentynchanō*, 8:26) and (*entynchanō*, 8:27) are rare in the New Testament, yet both carry the idea of making an appeal on behalf of someone else. Further, the clause begins with the strong adversative "but" (*alla*), indicating that the Spirit's intercession in 8:26–27 is in sharp contrast to human prayer, and 8:27 elaborates this contrast and further clarifies that the issue is one of knowledge and not form. In the clause that ends 8:26, "the Spirit" is the grammatical subject of the verb "intercedes," that is, the Spirit is the one offering confident intercessions, whereas earlier in the verse Paul and other believers are the ones praying with uncertainty.

The Spirit Prays Imperceptibly

As indicated in the synopsis of approaches earlier, some interpreters take Paul's phrase "groanings too deep for words" (*stenagmois alalētois*) as a reference to Spirit-prompted glossolalia (prayer in tongues) within believers. Before merely rejecting this approach because it might be different from our background or simply seems odd, we must ask what leads some interpreters to this conclusion. Those who defend this approach offer various arguments, only some of which are reproduced here.[6] They note correctly that wordless prayer was uncommon in the ancient world in which Paul wrote. They also identify similarities between Romans 8:26 and other passages in Paul's letters where the Spirit is involved in believers' prayers (cf. 1 Cor. 14:14–15 and Eph. 6:18) and insist these passages help clarify the Romans passage. Then, they note that the term *alalētois* might mean "without words" *or* "inexpressible" in different contexts. The challenge with this last argument is that the word in question occurs only here in the Greek New Testament (though appears in other Greek literature outside the Bible) and a near equivalent word (*aneklalētō*, 1 Peter 1:8, more clearly translated "inexpressible") is also used only once. The related word *alalon* (used in Mark 9:17, for example) clearly means "mute," or one unable to speak. In 1 Corinthians 14:14–15, Paul envisions speaking/praying in a tongue (*glōssē*), which is clearly verbal-yet-unintelligible speech. In Ephesians 6:18, Paul implores Christians to pray at all

---

6. For a more detailed presentation of this view, see Gordon D. Fee, *God's Empowering Presence: The Holy Spirit in the Letters of Paul* (Grand Rapids: Baker Academic, 1994), 580–85. See also Schreiner, *Romans*, 426–27 for a helpful survey of other arguments from this perspective, even though Schreiner himself does not believe this passage presents glossolalia.

times "in the Spirit," with no clear reference to either verbal or nonverbal expression. While the 1 Corinthians and Ephesians passages indeed mention the Spirit's work within believers, they both involve *believers* praying, whereas in the Romans passage it is the *Spirit* who is praying. This last point also addresses the first argument: examples of nonverbal prayer were indeed scarce in the ancient world, but those are examples of *humans* praying, whereas in the Romans passage the *Spirit* prays. In Romans 8:26–27, then, the Spirit prays on behalf of believers with silent, yet sure, intercession.

The Spirit Prays According to God's Will

One aspect of our uncertainty in prayer is knowing if our prayers are in keeping with God's will. As redeemed sinners, adopted children, and obedient servants, we really want to order our lives in ways that honor God, whether in big decisions or small. In his model prayer (Matt. 6:9–13; Luke 11:2–4), Jesus taught disciples to pray, "Your will be done," and himself prayed this way in Gethsemane (Matt. 26:42). In Romans 8:27, Paul offers us great hope in regard to ordering our lives around God's will: the Spirit's intercession is always consistent with God's will.

The passage is very humbling as it opens a window into inter-Trinitarian communication. Paul uses an Old Testament circumlocution to describe the Father when he writes, "He who searches hearts knows what is the mind of the Spirit" (Rom. 8:27). In various Old Testament passages, God searches human hearts without effort and thus truly knows those into whose hearts he gazes.[7] No matter what external appearances a person may have, God knows that person accurately and inwardly. Here the one searched is the Spirit, the presence of the definite article and context indicating that it is the Holy Spirit and not a human's own spirit being examined. Though the phrase may seem odd, Paul's logic may be to introduce a comparison to God's certainty of hearing the Spirit's prayers by means of the Old Testament allusion. That is, if the Father who searches *human* hearts knows people as they truly are, how much more truly and perfectly does he know what is in the Spirit's heart?

The syntax of 8:27 emphasizes the Spirit's unity with the Father and thus the saints' hope in prayer. A wooden translation of the phrase might read, "Because according to God the Spirit intercedes on behalf of the saints." The phrase "because according to God" (*hoti kata theon*) occurs prior to the verb "intercedes" (*entynchanei*), and this atypical structure may signal emphasis. While our experience of prayer is one of weakness due to uncertainty, our confidence in prayer comes from the fact that the Spirit intercedes for us completely in line with the Father's plans, for the Spirit and Father are united in purpose, namely our conformity to the image of Christ (cf. Rom. 8:29).

---

7. Such as 1 Samuel 16:7; 1 Chronicles 28:9; Proverbs 15:11; 17:3; 20:27; and Jeremiah 17:10.

One question arises that is not as easily answered from the text: *When does the Spirit pray in this way for believers?* Richard Longenecker suggests that whenever believers pray, the Spirit translates their imperfect prayers into his own groans.[8] J. I. Packer and Carolyn Nystrom seem to follow a similar approach when they write that God "fixes our prayers on the way up."[9] Without placing too much strain on the Greek language, the fact that all the verbs related to the Spirit's ministry in Romans 8:26–27 are present tense may suggest that this ministry is an ongoing work throughout the believer's life as a new creation.

Summary

Though in so many circumstances we struggle to know what to pray, Christians can surely take comfort in this truth: whenever we experience uncertainty with regard to our prayers, in that moment of weakness, we can be assured that the Spirit is interceding on our behalf perfectly.

REFLECTION QUESTIONS

1. What is your most common experience of weakness in prayer?

2. What are some specific times when you have been unsure of what to pray for?

3. What leads some Christians to read Romans 8:26–27 as prayer in tongues? How might you help a friend think through this viewpoint?

4. How does the Spirit's prayer on your behalf free you to pray more confidently?

5. What are some steps you can take to remember the Spirit's ministry in prayer?

---

8. Richard N. Longenecker, *The Epistle to the Romans*, New International Greek Testament Commentary (Grand Rapids: Eerdmans, 2016), 734–35.
9. J. I. Packer and Carolyn Nystrom, *Praying: Finding Our Way through Duty to Delight* (Downers Grove, IL: InterVarsity Press, 2006), 175.

What Does It Mean to Pray "in Jesus's Name" and "in the Spirit"?

In earlier questions we have considered the fact that believers pray to the Father, through the Son, in the Spirit's power, and have seen how Jesus and the Spirit both pray in and for us. This chapter's question considers what it means for Christians to pray in Jesus's name. Among Protestants, it is quite common to hear the phrase "in Jesus's name, amen" at the conclusion of prayers. For many, praying in this way is a sincere act of devotion and a reminder that prayer is a fruit of the gospel, purchased in the new covenant at the price of their Savior's blood. For others, such phrasing is nearly superstition, akin to a magical spell, that ensures the content of the prayer will be heard. Still others pray this way because they have heard others do so, without much reflection on the significance of these words or what they signify. Whether we use certain wording in our prayers or not, every Christian needs to reflect on the fact that Jesus taught us to pray in this way. This chapter considers the biblical and theological significance of doing so and concludes with practical reflection on how we might pray in Jesus's name.

Prayer "in My Name"

The three Synoptic Gospels recount Jesus's speaking of the faithful performing various actions "in my name." Disciples might receive children "in my name" (Matt. 18:5), gather "in my name" (18:20), do "a mighty work" in his name (Mark 9:39), cast out demons (Mark 16:17), and so forth. John's gospel also includes Jesus speaking of actions done "in my name," sometimes by the Father and other times by believers. In this gospel, these instances occur in chapters 14–16, the upper room discourse, and are part of the way that Jesus comforted his shell-shocked disciples after telling them of his soon-coming departure.

John 14 begins with comfort: "Let not your hearts be troubled. Believe in God; believe also in me" (v. 1). Many readers will know John 14 from its common use in evangelistic training or presentations, and it is a powerful passage for these settings because of Jesus's clear assertion that he alone is "the way, and the truth, and the life" and the only way to the Father (14:6). Focusing on the true gospel significance of Jesus's words is not wrong, but we might inadvertently read them in this way and miss their significance for prayer. Jesus is indeed the only way to the Father, for "there is no other name under heaven given among men by which we must be saved" (Acts 4:12), and he is also the only way to the Father in prayer—a fact mentioned three times in John 14.

> Truly, truly, I say to you, whoever believes in me will also do the works that I do; and greater works than these will he do, because I am going to the Father. Whatever you ask in my name, this I will do, that the Father may be glorified in the Son. If you ask me anything in my name, I will do it. (John 14:12–14)

John's gospel is rich in Trinitarian reflection. In chapter 1, John declares that Jesus was "with God" in the beginning, and here Jesus promises that his return to the Father will change the dynamic of prayer for his followers. Fellowship is a key theme in John 16. Having lived in fellowship with Jesus, the disciples, notably Thomas, could not envision being physically separated from him, yet Jesus assures them that his "going to the Father" will be to their advantage as he will be in a position to hear and act upon their prayers in a way different from his then-incarnate experience (16:7). Father and Son are united in purpose.[1] Later in John 14, Jesus promised that the Father would send the Holy Spirit "in my name" (14:26) and that the Spirit would work within his disciples to confirm Jesus's teaching. Jesus reiterated this promise of prayer in John 15:16; 16:23–24, and 26. According to the testimony of Acts 4:29–30, the apostles and disciples prayed in this way:

> And now, Lord, look upon their threats and grant to your servants to continue to speak your word with all boldness, while you stretch out your hand to heal, and signs and wonders are performed through the name of your holy servant Jesus.

---

1. Andreas J. Köstenberger and Scott R. Swain, *Father, Son and Spirit: The Trinity and John's Gospel*, New Studies in Biblical Theology, vol. 24, ed. D. A. Carson (Downers Grove, IL: InterVarsity Press, 2008), 71: "Clearly, this indicates a very close personal family relationship. What is in view here is not an identity of persons, but a unity of purpose. The 'in' language should not be taken as suggesting a 'mystical' relationship between Jesus and the Father."

In that prayer occurring after Peter and John had been released from prison, one rich in Old Testament allusions, the church affirms that God was indeed working "signs and wonders" in their midst "through the name of your holy servant Jesus." Their prayer seeks God's continuing intervention for the sake of the gospel. Just like the earthly rulers who oppose the Son and Father in Psalm 2 (cf. Acts 4:25–26), the Jewish authorities of the day were hostile to the Jerusalem church; in this passage, believers are asking God to "consider" these threats and to allow them continued opportunity to proclaim the gospel. It is noteworthy that these Christians do not include a formulaic mention of Jesus's name, but rather pray with the conviction that their petitions would be heard and that God's continued blessing in response to the proclamation of the good news has been, and would continue to be, "through the name" of Jesus.

To ask "in Jesus's name," then, implies several things. First, it implies our recognition that prayer is inseparable from Jesus's ministry as mediator and redeemer; he is the one who makes our prayers possible. This ministry has consequences for our later discussion of God hearing the prayers of unbelievers. To pray in Jesus's name is to acknowledge that he is the only way to the Father. Second, it implies that our requests are consonant with Jesus's own goal of glorifying the Father. Colin Kruse notes the relationship between our desire and Jesus's desire: "However, a more straightforward interpretation is that 'in Jesus' name' means for Jesus' sake, i.e. in line with his desire and purpose to bring glory to his Father. Thus 14:13–14 would read, 'And I will do whatever you ask for my sake, so that the Son may bring glory to the Father. You may ask me for anything for my sake, and I will do it.'"[2]

Kruse's suggestion is helpful, as it clarifies that praying "in Jesus's name" is not about using particular phrases to unlock prayer but about aligning our requests with Jesus's will and purpose, namely the Father's glory. With this focus in mind, then, we recognize the boundaries of asking in the name of Jesus. Jesus's own words, "whatever you ask of the Father in my name, he will give it to you," ought to encourage believers to pursue the same goal that Jesus did: the glory of the Father in all things. There might be a great many things that we might ask of Jesus that have little to do with magnifying the Father's name through the Son, and John 14–16 gives us no confidence to seek temporal benefits that are here today but vanish like the morning mist. Rather, we have great confidence to pray "in Jesus's name" for those things that he himself sought, the Father's glory being chief among them.

We have seen, thus far, that we pray to the one true God, who exists forever as Father, Son, and Holy Spirit. Though we might pray to the Son or Spirit, our normal direction for prayer is *to* the Father. The Son and the Spirit are at work in the background of our prayers. The gospel declares that we are

---

2. Colin G. Kruse, *John: An Introduction and Commentary*, Tyndale New Testament Commentaries, vol. 4 (Downers Grove, IL: InterVarsity Press, 2003), 299.

united to the Son and that he is our mediator who prays for us and brings our requests before the Father. The Spirit is our advocate and prays for us, helping us in our weakness. In this chapter we consider another way that the Spirit's ministry and our prayers intersect as we ask what it means to pray "in the Spirit" (Eph. 6:18 and Jude 20). As we will see, praying "in the Spirit" is important for our ongoing experience of fellowship or communion with God and also for our fight against unseen spiritual enemies.

Prayer "in the Spirit"

As Paul's emphasis on praying "in the Spirit" in Ephesians 6:18 occurs in the context of spiritual conflict, we will examine some of his teaching here and some in a later chapter below. First, we concentrate on praying "in the Spirit" within the short epistle to Jude. Apart from the beautiful doxology that ends this letter (vv. 24–25) and the author's intention to defend the faith "once for all delivered to the saints" (v. 3), Jude's message is probably less familiar to Bible readers than other parts of the New Testament. Part of Jude's concern is to contrast those who are harming and dividing the church (vv. 17–19) with those who are persevering in genuine faith (vv. 20–23). One hallmark of those dividing the church was that they were "worldly people, devoid of the Spirit" (v. 19). By contrast, genuine Christians "keep yourselves in the love of God" (v. 21), and one of the ways the faithful stay so is by "praying in the Holy Spirit" (v. 20). The significance of such prayer for the health of the church is hard to miss: those who lack the Spirit's presence follow their own "ungodly passions" and "cause divisions" within the church, but those who have the Spirit and maintain fellowship with the Spirit by means of prayer are ministers of mercy to church members struggling with doubt and sin.

Jude's call for faithful believers to pray in the Spirit is part of a threefold approach to experiencing the love of God and such prayer is instrumental for this goal. Jude expresses his main idea in verses 20–21 by means of the imperative verb "keep" (*tērēsate*). Believers are to "keep" themselves "in the love of God" (*en agapē theou*). Jude seems to be describing both God's love for believers and the believers' love for God.[3]

Jude brackets his epistle with confidence in God's loving protection. Believers are those who are "beloved in God the Father and kept for Jesus Christ" (v. 1).[4] In his doxology, Jude ascribes "glory, majesty, dominion, and authority" to the one "who is able to keep you from stumbling and to present you blameless before the

---

3. Thomas R. Schreiner, *1, 2 Peter, Jude*, vol. 37, Christian Standard Commentary (Nashville: Holman References, 2020), 484. "Is Jude exhorting believers to maintain their love *for* God, an objective genitive? Or is he saying that they should keep themselves in the place where they experience God's love for them, a subjective genitive? A decision is difficult."
4. The perfect passive participles of verse 1 clarify that God's work is foundational to the believer's security and experience of God's love: "By God the Father being loved [*ēgapēmenois*] and for Jesus Christ being protected [*tetērēmenois*]."

presence of his glory" (v. 24). Thus, tempting as it might be to read this verse as suggesting that believers must bear the weight of sustaining our good standing with God, which would not be good news at all, we remember that the broader message of the New Testament is that God's love is foundational to our faith: "God shows his love for us in that while we were still sinners, Christ died for us" (Rom. 5:8). God loves us apart from performance (and thankfully so!). So in what sense are we to "keep" ourselves in the love of God?

It might be helpful to consider the situation by describing the love of God in two senses. First, there is the objective reality of God's love, demonstrated in the Father giving his only begotten Son for sinners (John 3:16). In Jude as in Romans, we see that this love God has toward us is based on his gracious disposition and kindness, not our performance; thus is it stable, not variable, and a genuine source of confidence. That is, if God chose to demonstrate his love toward us "while we were yet sinners," separated from him and under the curse of death, then his objective love for us is not based on us reciprocating that love. Second, though, is our experience of God's objective love toward us, viewed from our perspective, which ebbs and flows with our variable expression of faithfulness or unfaithfulness. This seems to be the sense in which we are to "keep" ourselves in the love of God, a point Jude expresses by means of three instrumental participles: "building [*epoikodomountes*] yourselves up in your most holy faith and praying [*proseuchomenoi*] in the Holy Spirit . . . waiting [*prosdechomenoi*] for the mercy of our Lord Jesus Christ that leads to eternal life" (vv. 20–21). For Jude, these three actions are what "keep" us in God's love toward us, that is, our experience of his love, and thus "praying in the Spirit," along with a growing faith and a patient anticipating of Christ's return are vital to our experience of relational nearness to God. While we focus on prayer here, all three actions are important.

So what, then, does it mean for believers to be "praying in the Spirit"? First, the participle translated "praying" in both Jude 20 and Ephesians 6:18 (*proseuchomenoi*) is simply a common Greek word for prayer; it does not denote a special kind of prayer. Second, we recognize that the preposition "in" (*en*) might also be translated "by," "with," or in several other ways, depending upon context. Broadly, doing any action "in the Spirit" (*en pneumati*) involves genuine believers following the Spirit's leadership and acting in the Spirit's power. Sinclair Ferguson summarizes the situation in this way: "Praying in the Spirit is prayer which conforms to the will and purpose of the Spirit."[5] Praying in the Spirit is one action that all Christians are to undertake, for both Jude and Paul address their respective epistles to all believers, not to a select few, nor are their instructions to pray in the Spirit targeted at Christians who possess a special gift of prayer or a distinct manifestation of the Spirit's presence. Considering

---

5.   Sinclair B. Ferguson, *The Holy Spirit*, ed. Gerald Bray, Contours of Christian Theology (Downers Grove, IL: InterVarsity Press, 1996), 188.

Paul's instructions in Ephesians 6:18, Christians are to be "praying at all times in the Spirit" (*proseuchomenoi en panti kairō en pneumati*). "All times" speaks of a consistent need for us to depend upon the Spirit. Though Jude does not give a similar temporal indicator, his threefold actions of building oneself up in the faith, praying, and waiting on the Lord are part of the believer's ongoing life before God, a life in which the Spirit of God takes a central role. One way in which the Spirit can take a central role in our prayers is to allow Scripture to shape our prayers and our requests. We address the practice of this kind of prayer in several places and will not repeat those details here, but if the Spirit is the person of the Godhead most intimately associated with the very inspiration of the Bible, praying "in the Spirit" must surely involve attention to the patterns of prayer that the Spirit has inspired. The Spirit will always lead Christians into greater conformity to Christ's image (2 Cor. 3:18) and this image is shaped by consistent obedience to the revealed Word of God. Praying "in the Spirit" may mean more than merely praying the Bible, but it does not mean less than this.

If believers are to pray "in the Spirit," is it possible that we might sometimes pray "apart from" or "out of" the Spirit? Neither Paul nor Jude speaks of prayer in such a way, so any answer we give will be conjecture, but it seems that the Christians James addressed were praying in a way that did not follow the Spirit's leadership: "You do not have because you do not ask. You ask and do not receive because you ask wrongly, to spend it on your passions" (James 4:2–3). Self-focused prayer would seem to be the best description of praying "apart from" or "outside of" the Spirit. Self-focused prayer cannot merely mean praying about our needs, for if we could not petition God for help in our weakness, we would have no hope. No, the sort of prayer James rebukes is prayer motivated by selfish desires rather than by the Spirit.

Summary

Praying "in Jesus's name" is more than speaking those same words at the conclusion of our prayers. There is certainly no harm in such a phrase, so long as it does not become "vain repetition" or move us to some form of magical thinking. Praying in the name of Jesus means prayer that recognizes the unique role of Jesus as our mediator before God and that pursues Jesus's own goal of bringing glory to the Father. Question 180 of the Westminster Larger Catechism asks, "What is it to pray in the name of Christ?" The answer given is, "To pray in the name of Christ is, in obedience to his command, and in confidence on his promises, to ask mercy for his sake; not by bare mentioning of his name, but by drawing our encouragement to pray, and our boldness, strength, and hope of acceptance in prayer, from Christ and his mediation."[6] Praying in Jesus's name is prayer that magnifies the Father and the Son.

---

6. Westminster Assembly, *The Westminster Confession of Faith: Edinburgh Edition* (Philadelphia: William S. Young, 1851), 364.

Praying "in the Spirit" is so very important for Christians because this sort of prayer is one of the ways that we experience God's love for us. The facts of Jesus's atoning death and continual intercession are proofs of God's love toward us, yet the presence of the Spirit, who is himself the "guarantee of our inheritance" of every spiritual blessing in Christ (Eph. 1:14) and who prays for us (Rom. 8:26), is part of our experience of this inheritance now, the presence of God in our midst. All believers are to pray in the Spirit, at all times, and thus to keep ourselves in the love of God.

REFLECTION QUESTIONS

1. How did you learn to pray in the name of Jesus as a younger Christian?

2. How does praying in Jesus's name change your perspective on prayer?

3. What confidence does Jesus teach us to have in praying in his name?

4. How does praying "in the Spirit" affect our experience of God's love?

5. Does praying "in the Spirit" imply special techniques or special gifts?

Does God Hear the Prayers of Unbelievers?

The questions we have considered thus far have focused on prayer as speech that God invites, hears, and answers within the context of a relationship between himself and the one(s) praying. In this chapter, we want to consider whether God hears the prayers of those who live apart from a relationship with him. More specifically, we want to consider whether God hears the prayers of unbelievers with an intention to act upon their requests. First, we consider briefly what it means to live apart from relationship to God, and then we take up the chapter's question proper.

Life as an Unbeliever

God created everything that exists, including humans, and all things exist through and for him (Col. 1:16). God created men and women "in his image" with a unique capacity for relationship with him and with one another (Gen. 1:27). Our first parents lived in fellowship with God until they chose to transgress his commands, bringing ruin to themselves and God's good world. Though affected by sin, all people retain the knowledge that God exists, because God has shown them his "eternal power and divine nature" through creation (Rom. 1:19–20). People reject this truth, suppress it, and create idols in place of the true God (Rom. 1:23). Idols vary in culture and through time, and may be physical creations or mental images that are falsely ascribed the honor due to the true God alone. In rejecting the true and living God who reveals himself, men and women persist in their sin, which invites God's wrath against their unrighteousness (Rom. 1:18). Unrighteousness makes people enemies of God (Rom. 5:10). This baseline status is true of all unbelievers. Though they be cruel or kind, influential or obscure, old or young, those who reject God are not morally neutral toward him; they are his enemies. This summary sets the stage for answering the question of whether God hears and acts upon the prayers of unbelievers.

Paul identifies "idolatry" as the fallen human response to people's rejection of the true God. Because those living in opposition to the true God are made in his image, they have an innate craving for worship that they will satisfy by making gods in their own image (Rom. 1:23). One idol that people create is that of a god who exists to answer their needs, to fulfill their desires, who allows them to persist in their own distorted and disordered view of reality and gives them the psychological strength to face the world on their own terms. This idol is not a god who answers prayer. The Bible does, however, present some occasions where the true and living God responds to prayers of individuals who appear to be outside typical relationships with Yahweh.

Prayers of Outsiders

Prayer plays a limited role in the universal history of Genesis 1–11.[1] Genesis 6 introduces readers to Noah, "a righteous man, blameless in his generation," who "walked with God" (Gen. 6:9). The prophet Ezekiel grouped Noah with Daniel and Job (Ezek. 14:14), but it is not clear that Noah's prayers are what drew the comparison.[2] We have no biblical testimony of Noah's prayers in the same way that we have a record of the prayers of Job and, as Christopher Seitz has observed, even this evidence is limited.[3] Job was not an Israelite and may have been a contemporary of Abraham. Job's prayer in 42:1–6 is a brief expression of repentance in light of God's awesome self-disclosure in the preceding chapters. At God's request (42:8), Job intercedes on behalf of his three friends who have spoken wrongly of God "and the LORD accepted Job's prayer" (42:9). In this instance, God both prompted and answered the prayers of someone living prior to the covenant with Israel at Sinai. God's covenant with Abram (later Abraham) includes the Lord's willingness to hear Abraham's intercession for the wicked city of Sodom (Gen. 18:22–33).

The prophetic book of Jonah shows the possibility of God hearing and responding to the prayers of pagans. As the prophet runs from God's call to preach repentance to the Assyrian city of Nineveh, he boards a ship in Joppa manned by pagan sailors. The Lord sends a great storm and the sailors "cried out to his god," the captain entreats Jonah to "call out to your god," and Jonah identifies his "God" by the covenant name Yahweh, distinct from the pagan sailors' "god." As Jonah continues his self-focused behavior, the pagan sailors

---

1. J. Gary Millar, *Calling on the Name of the Lord: A Biblical Theology of Prayer*, New Studies in Biblical Theology, vol. 38, ed. D. A. Carson (Downers Grove, IL: InterVarsity Press, 2016), 31. "It is interesting that prayer does not play a hugely significant role in Genesis—many of the key incidents unfold without any reference to anything resembling prayer."
2. Though Daniel in the biblical book of the same name is indeed a man of intercession (Dan. 9), as is Job (Job 42), Ezekiel may have an earlier "Daniel" in mind, a non-Israelite.
3. Christopher R. Seitz, "Prayer in the Old Testament or Hebrew Bible," in *Into God's Presence: Prayer in the New Testament*, ed. Richard N. Longenecker (Grand Rapids: Eerdmans, 2002), 13–14.

shift their prayers to Jonah's God, to Yahweh, crying out, "O LORD, let us not perish for this man's life, and lay not on us innocent blood, for you, O LORD, have done as it pleased you" (Jonah 1:14). Without assuming the pagan sailors experienced a full conversion to Jonah's faith, it is clear that the Lord answered their prayers, which in turn prompts their worship (1:16).

Theological Assessment

Scholastic theologian Thomas Aquinas considered the question of whether or not God answers sinners' prayers. Thomas evaluated John 9:31 and Proverbs 28:9 as key texts. We examine each in turn. John 9 contains a pericope in which Jesus heals a blind man and the event becomes the occasion to expose theological errors on the part of Jesus's disciples and the Pharisees. The Pharisees summon the man whom Jesus has healed, challenging Jesus's righteousness and identity. The healed man lectures the Pharisees on righteousness and prayer: "We know that God does not listen to sinners, but if anyone is a worshiper of God and does his will, God listens to him. Never since the world began has it been heard that anyone opened the eyes of a man born blind. If this man were not from God, he could do nothing" (John 9:31–33). In defending Jesus's identity as the Son of God, an intentional goal of John's gospel, the healed man presents a theological defense related to prayer that might be summarized in this way: "This man prayed that I would receive sight and I received sight. God hears and responds to the prayers of those who worship and obey him. Since God responded to this man's prayers, he is not a sinner but one who worships and obeys God." Lecturing the religious leaders, who were themselves blind to Jesus's true identity, this former blind man proves to be quite the able theologian! Although the point about prayer is not the main thrust of the text, the Pharisees do not rebuke the man on this point, indicating a shared assumption that God would not hear and answer the prayers of those persisting in sin.

Proverbs 28:9 uses a clever play on "hearing" to link obedience to God's law with prayer: "If one turns away his ear from hearing the law, even his prayer is an abomination." The proverb envisions one who refuses to "hear" the *Torah*, God's life-giving instruction, and suggests that God will likewise refuse to "hear" that person's prayers. Similar to John 9, one's willingness to honor God properly affects God's willingness to hear and respond to prayer.

Aquinas suggested that when sinners pray in keeping with their sinful desires, God does not hear and answer their prayers, and their prayers may lead them deeper into sin. Yet if a sinner prays contrary to his wicked desires, "from a good natural desire," God may hear and respond out of mercy.[4] Perhaps an illustration of Aquinas's point will be helpful. A sinner, moved at the sight of a child stricken with cancer, might pray for God to heal the child. In Aquinas's

---

4. Thomas Aquinas, *Summa Theologiae* 2.83.16. https://aquinas.cc/la/en/~ST.II-II.Q83.A16.SC.

view, the prayer would not be offered because it would be to the advantage of the sinner but because that person recognizes the suffering of the situation and is moved from a human sense of pity or compassion to see that suffering alleviated. God might respond to this prayer not because of the goodness of the one offering it nor because he has obligated himself to respond to this person's prayer, but because the request is consonant with God's mercy.

This approach seems to integrate the biblical data well: God has not obligated himself to hear and answer the prayers of those who are dead in their sins (Eph. 2:1) in the same way that he delights to answer the prayers of those who, by faith, have been welcomed into his family as adopted children. Whereas we whom God draws near through Christ have confidence to "draw near the throne of grace, that we may receive mercy and find grace in our time of need" (Heb. 4:16), those who persist in rebellion have no such confidence. Notice that it is not the mere *presence* of sin in one's life that affects God's response to prayer, but rather open persistence in sin, praying in keeping with sinful desires, praying from a nature controlled by sin rather than a nature that has been made new in Christ.

Summary

Though God may, at times, hear and answer the prayers of unbelievers, he has not bound himself to do so in the same way that he has promised to hear the prayers of his saints, to account their prayers as pleasing incense, and to grant them the same near access as beloved children. As we saw in Part 1 above, prayer is a gift tied intimately to the gospel of Jesus Christ. Those living apart from union with Christ lack confidence that God will hear their prayers so long as they persist in unbelief and rebellion.

REFLECTION QUESTIONS

1. How do John 9 and Proverbs 28 inform our understanding of prayers that God hears?

2. Why did God hear the prayers of Noah and Job but perhaps not of others in their generations?

3. How should we assess the popular notion that God hears all prayers?

4. How does the gospel give us greater confidence in prayer?

5. How might our conversations with unbelievers use prayer as a bridge to the gospel?

If God Is in Control, Why Should We Pray?

"The secret things belong to the LORD our God, but the things that are revealed belong to us and to our children forever, that we may do all the words of this law" (Deut. 29:29). Moses's words remind us of the limits of understanding. Prayer spans a gulf between that which has been revealed and that which remains mysterious. In this chapter and the next, we touch the edges of this mystery by the light of revelation, humbly aware of our limits. This chapter considers the relationship between prayer and God's sovereign, providential care. The next chapter examines the related matter of God's complete knowledge (omniscience) and our prayers.

One mystery is the relationship between God's role as upholder of the universe and our own prayers. As theologian Millard Erickson puts it, "We need to note two facts: (1) Scripture teaches that God's plan is definite and fixed—it is not subject to revision; and (2) we are commanded to pray and taught that prayer has value (James 5:16)."[1] How can these two truths coexist? While this is a theological question, it has immediate practical consequences. Is it vanity and hubris to think that my prayers might affect the way God works in this world? If God is sovereign, and nothing happens apart from his will, then does prayer accomplish anything? Questions like these are not new, but it is important for each generation of Christians to think about such questions and answer them, for as we will see in this chapter, the way we answer them can either strengthen or undermine our prayers. In this chapter, we consider the relationship between our petitionary prayer and God's control over all created things.

---

1. Millard J. Erickson, *Christian Theology*, 2nd ed. (Grand Rapids: Baker, 1998), 430.

What Is Providence?

Saying that God is "in control" is a popular way of speaking of what theologians call God's providence.[2] Providence begins where creation rests. The Bible asserts that there is a God who has created everything that exists, and that God acts to sustain and guide all of creation according to his purposes. God "works all things according to the counsel of his will" (Eph. 1:11). Yahweh is the eternal king over creation (Ps. 10:16). God "does according to his will" in heaven and on earth (Dan. 4:35). God directs the hearts of people (Prov. 21:1), the future of nations (Jer. 18:6), and even the course of our lives (Prov. 16:9). Indeed, God is in control.

Every Christian tradition recognizes some form of this truth, though debates over the extent of God's control have divided some Christians. Some views on providence stray very far from biblical teachings to the point that they are no longer meaningfully "Christian." One such view is called "deism," which teaches that God created the world but is not actively involved in its affairs, leaving the world to run on natural laws.[3] Some views place human moral agency above God's care, such that God's "providence" is merely a ratification of human choices. Another errant view confuses providence with fate. Fate is the idea that all that comes to pass is fixed and unchangeable, controlled often by impersonal forces that constrain even God. These various errors fall short of a biblical providence, for they deny God's personal and ongoing involvement in the created order.

Within the scope of Christian teaching, theologians differ over the extent of God's involvement in the world, with some holding to a more general oversight of human affairs and others arguing for extensive (or exhaustive) and meticulous control. My own denomination's statement of faith acknowledges the latter approach, saying, "God as Father reigns with providential care over His universe, His creatures, and the flow and stream of human history according to the purposes of his grace."[4] An older Protestant catechism offers an elegant statement: "God's providence is his almighty and ever present power, whereby, as with his hand, he still upholds heaven and earth and all creatures; and so governs them that herbs and grass, rain and drought, fruitful and barren years, meat and drink, health and sickness, riches and poverty, yea, all things, come not by chance but by his fatherly hand."[5] The phrase "not by chance but by his fatherly hand" can help us better understand the doctrine of providence and its connection to prayer.

2. For a helpful summary, see Gregg Allison, *50 Core Truths of the Christian Faith: A Guide to Understanding and Teaching Theology* (Grand Rapids: Baker, 2018), 103–10.
3. For an introduction to Deism, see James W. Sire, *The Universe Next Door: A Basic Worldview Catalog*, 3rd ed. (Downers Grove, IL: InterVarsity Press, 1997), 40–51.
4. The Baptist Faith and Message 2000, "God the Father," https://bfm.sbc.net/bfm2000.
5. *The Heidelberg Catechism*, Lord's Day 10, Q. 27, https://www.rca.org/about/theology/creeds-and-confessions/the-heidelberg-catechism.

Trusting God's "Fatherly Hand"

Sometimes, we forget that God is both sovereign *and* personal. These truths must be balanced in our reflections on providence and prayer. To overemphasize God's sovereignty, his kingly rule, at the expense of his personal nature runs the risk of turning prayer into a cold, mechanical, almost fatalistic machine. To focus only on God's personal nature, at the expense of his sovereignty, diminishes our confidence in God's full and meticulous control over everything. How might we balance these two ideas when thinking about prayer?

God presently upholds all of creation (Heb. 1:3), and thus all things in it, including our individual lives, by his providence. God does not need us to pray about things in order for him to uphold, govern, sustain, or guide them. He chooses to accomplish *most* of his providential acts apart from prayer. To say that God accomplishes some of his providential upholding and directing apart from prayer also means that he chooses to accomplish *some* of his providential acts through prayer. To be clear, how God chooses to act, in response to prayer or apart from prayer, is up to his divine prerogative. He is completely powerful and wise, and does not *need* our prayers to accomplish his actions nor does he *need* to work in concert with the prayers of his people, but he *chooses* to do so. God is the creator and upholder; we are the created and upheld ones. It would, therefore, be foolish and arrogant for us to consider our prayers a sufficient condition of God's action, though they are sometimes, under God's ordering, necessary conditions.[6] It would be foolish because we are created beings who are characterized by our limitations. It would be arrogant because we simply cannot see all of the ways that God upholds his created order, and even if we could see all the ways in which he works, we could not know every particular need, for we do not know all of the ways his providence governs *our* individual lives, let alone the lives of others or even the cosmos. But Scripture gives us confidence that God does hear and act in response to our prayers.

Consider, for example, King Hezekiah's prayer in 2 Kings 19:14–20.[7] In light of almost certain defeat at the hands of the Assyrian king Sennacherib, Hezekiah asks God to save Israel (19:19) and God instructs the prophet Isaiah to reassure the king that his prayer has been heard (19:20) and sends an angel to defeat the Assyrian army at night (19:35). Here, Hezekiah's prayer was necessary because God spared Israel as a result of that prayer, but the prayer was not sufficient to cause the defeat; the defeat came through God's power demonstrated in angelic warfare. Might God have acted to spare Israel apart from Hezekiah's prayer?

---

6. See Bruce A. Ware, "Prayer and the Sovereignty of God," in *For the Fame of God's Name: Essays in Honor of John Piper*, eds. Sam Storms and Justin Taylor (Wheaton, IL: Crossway, 2010), 130.

7. This prayer is discussed more fully below in Question 15.

We want to be careful in answering this question because what we know of this prayer and God's answer is mediated through Scripture, and Scripture is clear that Hezekiah prayed, God acknowledged this prayer, and God acted in response to this prayer. God could, of course, have acted independently of the king's prayer. He was not externally constrained to respond to Hezekiah's prayer, but he chose to do so. Thus it is proper to describe Hezekiah's prayer as necessary but contingent. Here, prayer was the necessary condition of God's defeat of the Assyrians, but this condition was contingent upon God being willing to hear and respond to prayer. God's willingness to "hear" and respond to prayer is what sets him apart as the living and true God (Ps. 65:2). Hezekiah's prayer is a specific instance of the general principle that God delights to hear and answer the prayers of his people as part of his providential upholding of all things (Ps. 50:15).

A different example shows the contingency of prayer. In 2 Corinthians 12:7–10, Paul recounts a particular suffering (a thorn in the flesh) that was given to humble him. Paul prayed three times seeking relief from this situation, but the Lord did not answer Paul's request in the way Paul asked; instead he comforted Paul in this way: "My grace is sufficient for you, for my power is made perfect in weakness" (2 Cor. 12:9). We might analyze this situation in light of God's providence, seeing God's particular care for one specific person. The Lord chose to comfort Paul differently from what Paul thought was best. Paul's prayer did not bring about the change he desired (the removal of the "thorn"), but it was the contingently necessary occasion for the Lord to bring a different comfort to Paul (the assurance that his weakness was a display of God's power). Would God have reassured Paul of his care absent the prayer? Perhaps, but Scripture does not let us answer *that* question, rather, it assures us that even when God chooses not to answer our prayers, or to answer them differently than we think best, he *hears* our prayers and thus our prayers are part of his work of providence, and this work is not impersonal but personal, not mechanistic but relational.

The Importance of Prayer in God's Providence

Thus far we have said that God's providence describes the way that he personally and fully governs his creation, accomplishing his purposes. We have also seen that God has determined to accomplish some acts of providence as a result of our prayers. Though he may freely act apart from our prayers and the power to accomplish what we ask lies in God, not in us or our petitions, God accomplishes some of his works because of our prayers. The implications of this truth are very important for us to consider: God has so ordered the world that sometimes our prayers are part of his plans.

Some might object at this point. Reading that God *sometimes* answers prayers as part of his work in the world may cause them to say, "Well, if God only works this way *sometimes*, why bother praying?" It's easy to see why someone might raise this objection, for we all desire to know that our efforts are meaningful and not futile. Christians must consider objections like this in light of Scripture, though, and the Bible consistently points in the direction opposite to that of a pessimistic conclusion about prayer and providence. We pray because God is working in us "both to will and to work for his good pleasure" (Phil. 2:13).

This thought may be commonplace for those who have been Christians for some time or for those who grew up in church, but we ought to consider how profound this situation is. God invites us to participate with him in his kingly rule over creation. He calls us to pray for political leaders so that Christians might live peaceably (1 Tim. 2:1–2). He calls us to pray that other believers would be "filled with the knowledge of his will" (Col. 1:9). He exhorts us to pray for those who persecute the church (Matt. 5:44), to pray for a wavering believer's faith to remain strong (Luke 22:32), to pray for unity among believers (John 17:11), to pray for God to send laborers into the harvest, that is, those who will proclaim the message of the kingdom (Matt. 9:38), and so much more.

Our view of God's providential care encourages us to ask for these things in hope and trust because prayer is a necessary part of the way God chooses to uphold the world and our lives. It also encourages us to meditate upon the ways that God has directed our lives through prayer, whether our own or that of others on our behalf. We lack the insight to know how many of the blessings of God's care for us have come as a result of prayers offered by other Christians or to know the extent to which our own prayers for others have been the necessary means that God has used in guiding them. Thinking about the relationship between prayer and providence can also expose the consequences of our prayerlessness. If God has determined to execute some portion of his government and care for individual human lives and the whole of creation as answers to our prayers, then to ignore or neglect prayer is to reject the loving-kindness that God graciously extends.[8]

Summary

Perhaps one day we will have greater clarity in understanding how many of the kind and gracious ways that God has led us have been the fruit of prayer. Even if such clarity remains elusive, Scripture gives us confidence to say both

---

8. The doctrine of providence is closely related to the doctrine of God's decrees, the teaching that God has one eternal plan that undergirds the actions of creation, providence, redemption, etc. Though space does not permit full discussion of God's decrees in relation to prayer, suffice it to say that God has decreed that prayers and answers to prayers be effective. God's decrees also encompass our genuine moral actions, including our prayerlessness. His decree is not the cause of our prayerlessness, but God has decreed that he will create and sustain people who freely choose evil and are thus morally accountable for their own choices. God does indeed permit us to live as prayerless Christians, but what an affront this choice is to our adopting Father who invites us to pray!

that God is in control and always accomplishes his will and that our prayers are real and necessary conditions for the way in which God governs his world. Rather than discouraging prayer, the truth of God's providence undergirds our prayer, for it gives us confidence that our prayers are part of his plan; confidence to ask according to his will, for the good of the church, and in his name; and confidence to trust that God delights to answer prayer.

REFLECTION QUESTIONS

1. How would you describe God's providence?

2. What does it mean that prayer is contingently necessary?

3. How might God's providence encourage you to pray more?

4. Why should God's providence encourage, rather than discourage, our prayer?

5. What are some ways you have seen God accomplish his plans through prayer?

Does Prayer Change God's Mind?

This question is related to the previous chapter and our reflection on God's providential control: If God is indeed in control of everything and knows all things, how could prayer really mean anything? Answering this question requires us to examine several foundational areas of theology. First, we need to consider God's attributes of omniscience, omnisapience, omnipresence, and immutability. Then, we examine several biblical passages that show God responding to human prayer. Finally, we consider several theological reflections on how to put these matters together.

God's Nature Does Not Change

In light of the Bible's presentation of God, theologians often talk about God's attributes, descriptions of his traits. Some of God's attributes are uniquely divine (incommunicable), whereas other attributes correspond to human experience (communicable). Even with those attributes that are communicable (shareable), we must always remember that God made us and that he is distinct from us and from his creation. Several attributes are especially important for our question at hand: omniscience, omnisapience, omnipresence, and immutability. "Omnipresence" is the idea that God is present at all places at all times. Unlike humans, whose bodies limit their presence, God is fully present everywhere at once. God is therefore able to hear prayer—every prayer, everywhere—without limit. He is also able to be near those who pray to comfort them, wherever they may be. "Omniscience" is the doctrine that God's knowledge is complete and exhaustive. Though we possess knowledge, it is of a different kind and a different quality from God's. God is infinite and thus his knowledge is equally infinite. All human knowledge has limits, but God's knowledge is unlimited. Because God is eternal, there is no difference between past, present, and future for him, and he knows all things with equal clarity and certainty. "Omnisapience" describes God's fullness of wisdom. Wisdom involves knowledge, but it is directional knowledge; knowledge aimed at achieving a specific purpose or goal. Humans may also be wise, but all true wisdom finds its fulfillment in God. Unlike humans, though, there is no folly in God—no wrong or improper decisions leading to the wrong outcomes or wrong goals. With regard to prayer, God's fullness of wisdom means that he always answers every prayer according to what is best for his goals of creation and redemption and according to his plan. Finally, "immutability" describes the fact that God does not change. To call something "mutable" means that it is subject to change. Plants, animals, roadways, lunches: all of these things are mutable. People are mutable; we change over time. We gain height (sometimes not as much as we would like) and weight (sometimes more than we would like); we gain knowledge and lose knowledge; we acquire skills that can be perfected or lost completely. People are always subject to change. In himself (ontologically), God is unchanging. That is, God always exists as Trinity and is always perfect in his existence. He never forgets, he is never foolish, he is never absent, and so forth. God is also unchanging (ethically) in his plan and always keeps his promises. That is, God is always holy, always condemns sin, and always fulfills his covenant obligations. Another way to consider this truth is that God is the same today as he was yesterday, and the same as he was in the year 1200, and the same as he was before Solomon was king in Israel, and the same as he was before he made the earth bring forth vegetation, and the same as he was before he spoke creation into existence. But if God is not subject to change, can prayer change God's mind? We will return to this question below.

God knows all things (omniscience) and is present everywhere (omnipresence); God's decisions are always the right decisions to accomplish his purposes, which are always wise, or directed to the best ends (omnisapience); and God does not change (he is immutable). Therefore, God testifies about himself:

> I am God, and there is none like me,
> declaring the end from the beginning
> and from ancient times things not yet done,
> saying, "My counsel shall stand,
> and I will accomplish all my purpose,"
> calling a bird of prey from the east,
> the man of my counsel from a far country.
> I have spoken, and I will bring it to pass;
> I have purposed, and I will do it. (Isa. 46:9–11)

God does not need our prayers to understand our circumstances or our hearts. God created all things, upholds all things, and directs all things according to his purpose; therefore God knows all things, including whether we will pray or not, the things we will ask for in prayer, and the desires of our hearts that prompt our asking or our silence. Though some find such testimony an affront to human freedom, Jesus teaches us otherwise.

Jesus taught his followers to pray in light of his Father's perfect foreknowledge: "Your Father knows what you need before you ask him. Pray then like this . . ." (Matt. 6:8–9). Jesus acknowledges that our prayers do not add or reveal anything to God that is hidden. What assurance rests in these words! Our Father knows us and knows our greatest needs because our hearts and our lives are open before him, and he sees more clearly than we do. This truth, however, does not lead Jesus to reject prayer as futile, rather, he teaches us how to pray to a Father who sees that which is hidden. Yet the chapter's question still remains: Does prayer change God's mind?

Prayer and Relational Change

Earlier we mentioned the doctrine of God's immutability, the teaching that God's nature and purposes are stable. God does not change but people change in relation to God. Recognizing that people change in relation to God can help us make sense of those places in Scripture that mention God seeming to change his mind. The prayers of Abraham and Jonah provide insights into relational change and prayer.

Abraham prayed for God to spare the cities of Sodom and Gomorrah from destruction based on the presence of a certain number of "righteous" persons (Gen. 18:22–33). God shares his plans for the cities with Abraham, who intercedes, asking God whether the presence of fifty, forty-five, forty, thirty, twenty, or ten righteous persons in Sodom would forestall his judgment, recognizing that God's character is such that he would not judge the guilty and righteous in the same way. God expresses a change as a result of Abraham's intercession at each point, culminating in his final announcement, "For the sake of ten [righteous people] I will not destroy it" (Gen. 18:32). As the story develops, angelic messengers arrive in the city and Lot shows them hospitality, as opposed to the other townsfolk who want to use these strangers for sexual gratification. The angels warn Lot and his family about the impending destruction, but he is slow to act. The angels intervene, compelling Lot and his family's escape, and the city is destroyed. God did not change his decree for the cities as a result of Abraham's prayer, but Abraham's prayer became the contingent occasion for the rescue of Lot's family. It seems clear that Lot and his family are the "righteous persons" whom the Lord spares, exercising sovereign power to remove them from the city by the hand of angels.

Jonah provides another example of relational change. The story is well known: God commissions the prophet Jonah to warn the people of Nineveh to repent or face destruction, but the prophet tries to run from God's call before God sovereignly corrects his path by way of a great fish. The seemingly chastened prophet delivers his message; the people, from least to greatest, repent; and "when God saw what they did, how they turned (*šā'ḇû*) from their evil way, God relented (*hāyinnā'ḥĕm*) of the disaster that he had said he would do to them, and he did not do it" (Jonah 3:10). The book of Jonah is marked with irony, and this passage is illustrative of that general literary tendency: when the sinful people "turn" from their path of wickedness, God "turns" from his path of immediate judgment. Their turn did not surprise God; this was the reason that he sent Jonah in the first place. Their turning did not alter God's character; Jonah knew that such patience and kindness was part of God's character (4:2). Nor did this change in relational status mean that God changed his plans, for he ordained the means (Jonah's preaching) to bring about the effect (the people's repentance). To ask whether God would have spared Nineveh apart from Jonah's preaching or their repentance is to go beyond the warrant of the text, which declares that God fully accomplished his will, consistent with his character.

Prayer Changes Us

Before concluding this discussion of prayer and the changes it brings, we ought to consider the way that prayer changes the one offering it. It is common for Christians to say that prayer changes us, and to some, this expression sounds like little more than pop psychology with a Christian slant. Although this approach might sometimes provide camouflage for poor theology, there are several ways in which the act of prayer itself may bring genuine change in a believer's life. One way prayer changes us is by reminding us of our limits and revealing the extent of our weakness. Prayer highlights the distinction between the Creator and the created. As we adore God in prayer in light of how he has revealed himself in Scripture (the various "omnis" mentioned in this chapter might be a good starting point), we recognize a sharp distinction between God's perfection and our imperfection, between his ability and our inability, between his strength and our weakness. Though few like to admit weakness, God has designed prayer to catechize us about our limits. Petitionary prayer also exposes this distinction, for as we ask God to do those things we are powerless to do—to change hearts of wayward family members, to create faith in lost children, to restore broken relationships, and so forth—we tacitly admit our inability to bring wholeness and health.

Prayer also changes us, at times, by causing us to consider our situation in light of God's lordship and his Word. I say "at times" not because of any deficiency with prayer, but because of our own stubbornness. It is easy for us to take the gift of prayer and use it for wrong purposes (cf. James 4). Yet praying about a situation may be the very means God uses to cause us to pursue the change we seek. As we bring our desires before God, we may consider our motives for asking and may be confronted by motives that have God's glory as their end or motives that are more self-focused. The very act of asking in prayer can be a way that God exposes the desires of our hearts, be they good or bad.

Summary

God's perfections in wisdom, knowledge, holiness, and being are the grounds of our confidence in prayer. We pray because God is uniquely able to act in a given situation from full knowledge, complete wisdom, and moral purity, and he is always present to respond. At times, our prayers are the contingent occasion for God to act in concert with our asking. It would be wrong to presume that God's sovereignty is exercised impersonally, for God is indeed personal! He relates to his children as an adopting, loving Father, inviting us to pray, inviting us to glory in his perfections, to trust his powerful hand, to marvel at his control. With this relational dynamic in mind, then, we see that prayer is part of God's providential governing of all things according to his will. He wills that we pray and that our prayers become the occasion for his acting. This situation in no way binds God to human will, for he need not answer as we ask since we always ask from a position of ignorance and limited foresight. As we consider below, sometimes God says no to our petitions for various reasons, but the fact that he might say no ought not to keep us from asking. The act of praying can be revealing as we come to express and examine our motives for asking.

REFLECTION QUESTIONS

1. What are some of the attributes of God that undergird prayer?

2. How can Jesus's confidence that God knows everything encourage us to pray?

3. In what ways does prayer change God's mind? In what way does it not?

4. How might prayer change the ones who are praying themselves?

5. What is one way that prayer has changed you and helped you grow in faith?

How Does Prayer Affect Evangelism, Revival, and Renewal?

Christianity is, at its heart, a shared faith, based upon an objective proc-lamation of the gospel of Jesus Christ and the inward ministry of the Holy Spirit, who applies the outward work of Christ upon the inner being. Throughout its history, the church has expressed its missionary impulse in a variety of ways, some more reflective of a biblical witness than others, with some Christian traditions placing more emphasis upon the urgency of pro-claiming the gospel to those outside the faith and others focusing on calling those within the faith to an ongoing, vital engagement with God. This chapter considers the role that prayer plays in these endeavors.

Prayer Surrounds Evangelism

Definitions of evangelism abound. For our purposes, long-time pastor J. Mack Stiles's definition seems fitting: "Evangelism is teaching the gospel with the aim to persuade."[1] Stiles reminds us that evangelism is communicating a particular content (the gospel) with a particular intention (to persuade). Content without persuasion misses the point. Persuasion without substance is manipulation. Together, content and persuasion are powerful, but apart from prayer they may be misguided. Prayer ought to surround evangelism.

When I suggest prayer ought to "surround" evangelism, what I mean is that prayer should come before, during, and after our intentionally persuasive teaching of the gospel. Allowing prayer to occupy this place reminds us that evangelism is our privilege but God's work. Here the apostle Paul helps shape our perspective.

---

1. J. Mack Stiles, *Evangelism: How the Whole Church Speaks of Jesus* (Wheaton, IL: Crossway, 2014), 26.

Paul travelled widely throughout the ancient Mediterranean world pro-
claiming the good news of Jesus resurrected and reigning. Even as he endured
hardship for this gospel and saw women and men converted to the faith, Paul
asked Christians to pray for him and his fellow missionaries "that God may
open to us a door for the word, to declare the mystery of Christ . . . that I
may make it clear, which is how I ought to speak" (Col. 4:3–4). This passage
shows one reason that prayer should precede evangelism. Paul asks Christians
to pray that God would remove impediments ("that God may open to us a
door") to his teaching of the gospel. Paul faced significant impediments. First,
he faced external hindrances. Paul wrote as a prisoner, unable to teach the
gospel wherever and whenever he might desire. Then, Paul recognized that
he might be an impediment, so he asked Christians to pray for clarity in his
teaching the "mystery of Christ." Through prayer, God opens doors for the
gospel, and so we pray before we speak. Each day, we might pray that God
would open for us a door to share the gospel, and that we would be sensitive
to recognize these doors, walk through them, and be clear and bold as we
proclaim the mystery of Christ. Beyond praying for ourselves, we might also
make a regular habit of praying for other Christians to have similar open-
door opportunities.

We also pray *as* we speak, asking that the God who has opened for us
a door would open blind eyes to see the "light of the gospel of the glory of
Christ" (2 Cor. 4:4). We ask God to create a hunger for the Bread of Life (cf.
John 6:35), a thirst for Living Water (John 7:37–39), and a refuge for weariness that seeks rest (cf. Matt. 11:28–30). We pray for ourselves, that we would
be compassionate and attentive listeners to the questions and objections of
fellow image-bearers; that God would give us the words "boldly to proclaim
the mystery of the gospel" (Eph. 6:19); that we would fear the Lord and not
the person to whom we are speaking and listening (Prov. 29:25); and that our
words might be a "demonstration of the Spirit and of power" (1 Cor. 2:4).
Such prayers are not magical incantations guaranteed to produce fruit in our
work; rather, they are appeals to the living God to rescue sinners. Even as we
pray silently, we might ask those with whom we are conversing *how* we can
pray for specific needs that they feel pressing upon them. As believers, we are
members of a "holy priesthood," called to offer acceptable sacrifices "to God
through Jesus Christ" (1 Peter 2:5), and among those sacrifices are prayers
offered on behalf of others. This priestly ministry, perhaps sometimes overlooked, includes offering prayers for those who are "dead in [their] trespasses
and sins" (Eph. 2:1) and thus cut off from the blessings of access to God and
confidence in prayer before his throne.

Evangelism refers to the act of persuasive proclamation, and once the occasion of evangelism ends, prayer continues. Here we pray for "seeds" of the
gospel to fall upon "good soil" (cf. Matt. 13:8) and to take root in those with
whom we have spoken, we pray for other believers to "water" those seeds, and

we pray for God to give growth (cf. 1 Cor. 3:6–7). We might continue to pray for specific needs shared by those with whom we have spoken, with genuine concern for their *felt* needs and for their spiritual state. God's answers to felt needs of others may help testify to his power and serve to reinforce the truth we have shared in evangelism. In instances where we have shared the gospel with strangers, especially if we or they are away from home, we might ask God to bring other Christians into their path. We might ask God to allow us providential opportunities for further conversations as well. Prayer following evangelism might also invite God to search *our* hearts and help us reflect on the experience of evangelism so that we might be better ambassadors in future conversations. These are some ways in which prayer surrounds evangelism.

Prayer Fuels Awakening and Revival

"Spiritual awakening" refers to the ministry of the Holy Spirit through which he convicts the world "concerning sin and righteousness and judgment" (John 16:8). For many readers, "revival" produces various reactions. For some, it surely evokes images of protracted special church services featuring itinerant preachers, intensive and emotional appeals, and calls for immediate response. As used here, "revival" refers to a special work of the Holy Spirit within the heart of someone who professes Christ but whose experiential communion with Christ has grown cold. Revival is a rekindled fire in the believer's heart for Christ and his reign. Revival and awakening are not permanent—they last but for a season.

Awakening may or may not lead to repentance and conversion on the part of sinners; it is not a synonym for effectual calling. Awakening is not evangelism nor is it a synonym for revival, though many Christians use the words interchangeably. Revival implies the presence of spiritual life whereas awakening emphasizes spiritual death. Awakening may occur among nominal Christians but often affects society more broadly.[2] Spiritual awakening is different from the contemporary language of being "woke" to social or racial inequalities, although spiritual awakenings have, historically, had important consequences for the cultures where they have occurred.[3] How is prayer connected to awakening and revival?

Since awakening is an inward work of the Holy Spirit, and not our work, prayer and awakening are connected vitally. Christians cannot bring about awakening, but they can seek this work of the Spirit as intercessors for the world around them. Praying for awakening might include praying for leaders and influencers in any culture: "First of all, then, I urge that supplications,

---

2. For these distinctions, see the classic work of J. Edwin Orr, *The Re-Study of Revival and Revivalism* (Pasadena, CA: School of World Mission, 1981), iv–v.
3. See Collin Hansen and John Woodbridge, *A God-Sized Vision: Revival Stories That Strengthen and Stretch* (Grand Rapids: Zondervan, 2015).

prayers, intercessions, and thanksgivings be made for all people, for kings and all who are in high positions, that we may lead a peaceful and quiet life, godly and dignified in every way" (1 Tim. 2:1–2). It is never wrong to desire that the leaders God has placed over us or who represent us would come to hold saving faith in Jesus, and Christians should labor in prayer and witness for such conversion, but the church ought also to seek an awakening among leaders that we might live and practice our faith in peace.

In the last three hundred years, Christians have observed the important interplay of prayer, awakening, and revival. In the spring and summer of 1727, in what is now modern Germany, members of the religious community of *Herrnhut* ("The Lord's Protection") experienced the Spirit's reviving presence and began interceding for the Spirit to do likewise among other Christians and to empower missionaries. Thereafter, members prayed every day, around the clock, for much of the eighteenth century. They revived this ministry in the nineteenth and twentieth centuries among fellowships around the world.[4]

Prayer preceded the trans-Atlantic "Great Awakening" of the middle eighteenth century as pastors in Wales, Scotland, England, and North American colonies encouraged the laity to gather for focused "concerts of prayer" for the Spirit's awakening work.[5] Sinners were awakened to their condition rapidly and in large numbers.[6] In the Second Great North American Awakening that spanned the eighteenth and nineteenth centuries, Congregationalists in the north, and Presbyterians, Methodists, and Baptists in the south and on the western frontier prayed earnestly for the Spirit to awaken sinners. On the eve of the American Civil War, in 1857, Christian laypeople engaged in weekly and daily prayer meeting throughout North America that issued in a widespread awakening and revival.[7] After the war, famed evangelist Dwight L. Moody united Christians from various denominations to pray for the conversion of sinners. Prayer preceded similar awakenings in Wales (1904–1905) and Korea (1907–1910) and was significant in the birth of Pentecostalism in the early twentieth century.[8]

---

4. See Richard F. Lovelace, *Dynamics of Spiritual Life: An Evangelical Theology of Renewal* (Downers Grove, IL: InterVarsity Press, 1979), 152. For contemporary Moravian practice, see mwatch.org.
5. The details of these concerts receive more detailed explanation in Question 36.
6. The best modern treatment on the Great Awakening is Thomas S. Kidd, *The Great Awakening: The Roots of Evangelical Christianity in Colonial America* (New Haven, CT: Yale University Press, 2009).
7. The best scholarly review of this prayer revival is that of Kathryn Teresa Long, *The Revival of 1857–58: Interpreting an American Religious Awakening* (New York: Oxford University Press, 1998).
8. See the helpful overview of the topic by Rick Ostrander, "Prayer and Revivals," in *Encyclopedia of Religious Revivals in America*, 2 vols., ed. Michael McClymond (Westport, CT: Greenwood Press, 2007), 333–38.

Undoubtedly, prayer for awakening and revival has been controversial. In the nineteenth century, Charles Finney suggested that "prayer is an essential link in the chain of causes that lead to a revival."[9] Although Finney stopped short of saying that God was *obligated* to answer such prayers, the tenor of his teaching that veered at times toward mechanistic descriptions of cause and effect, combined with his practice of naming sinners openly in public prayer, brought criticism from contemporaries. As explained in greater detail in Question 17 below, prayer is not a form of magic that manipulates God. Yet great movements of God do seem to correspond to the prayers of Christians. Prayer and fasting among the church leaders of Antioch preceded the great expansion of the gospel under the missionary work of Paul and Barnabas (Acts 13:1–4). Millennia later, the prayer meeting of five college students seems to have been the catalyst for a new work of global missions.[10] Christians who long to see God awaken sinners and stir lethargic churches must seek these special blessings in prayer, even as they devote themselves to less spectacular but equally essential prayer for daily renewal.

Prayer Fosters Renewal

"Renewal" refers to the ongoing, daily pursuit of nearness to Christ, often through the ordinary means of grace (such as reading Scripture, participating in the life of a congregation, taking the Lord's Supper, among other practices). Christian historian Richard Lovelace helpfully reminds Christians that renewal involves regularly rehearsing the truth on our union with Christ and the attendant blessings of justification, sanctification, the Spirit's indwelling presence, and our authority in spiritual conflict, among other elements.[11] Lovelace also emphasizes the place of prayer in integrating these elements within the believer's personal and congregational life. Much of this present volume in the 40 Questions series is bound up in helping Christians focus on prayer as part of daily renewal, such as learning to let the Bible shape our prayers, learning to pray the psalms, and practicing set-hour and ongoing prayers. Rather than repeat these various instructions here, it seems fitting to offer a reflection on the significance of daily prayer.

As Lovelace reminds us, "If the devil can tempt us to do evil, he can also tempt us not to do good," and prayer is one of the good things that Christians are often tempted to forego.[12] As we evaluate the state of our hearts before God, or even better, as we invite God to search our hearts and lead us in our lives (cf. Ps. 139:23–24), we must ask if we have fallen into such temptation.

---

9. Charles Grandison Finney, *Lectures on Revival of Religion* (New York: F. H. Revell, 1868), 48.
10. I refer to the "Haystack Prayer Meeting" of 1806 at Williams College which was instrumental in forming the American Board of Commissioners for Foreign Missions.
11. Lovelace, *Dynamics of Spiritual Life*, 75. See also his shorter work *Renewal as a Way of Life: A Guidebook for Spiritual Growth* (Eugene, OR: Wipf and Stock, 1985).
12. Lovelace, *Dynamics of Spiritual Life*, 155.

Summary

In this chapter we have seen how prayer is related to evangelism, awakening, revival, and renewal. Prayer surrounds evangelism as we pray for open doors to proclaim the gospel, for the will to see and walk through these doors, and for the Holy Spirit to bring about the conversion of sinners. We have seen how prayer has brought about seasons of awakening and revival in the church. Prayer is also important to daily renewal, so much so that it is often one area that the devil targets for temptation.

REFLECTION QUESTIONS

1. How have you seen God answer prayers surrounding evangelism?

2. What is the difference between awakening and revival?

3. Why ought believers to pray for awakening and revival?

4. How might you begin to pray for awakening among leaders and cultural influencers?

5. How have you experienced the temptation to forego regular prayer?

How Does Prayer Address Spiritual Conflict?

In this chapter, we will consider the relationship between prayer and our conflict with invisible spiritual powers. The Bible envisions a world under siege, beset by "the prince of the power of the air, the spirit that is now at work in the sons of disobedience" (Eph. 2:2). Christians wrestle "the rulers, against the authorities, against the cosmic powers over this present darkness, against the spiritual forces of evil in the heavenly places" (Eph. 6:12). Many books address the broader definition and scope of this spiritual "warfare" in which believers find themselves, and we cannot survey all of the perspectives on this matter within this brief chapter.[1] Our focus here is on the significant place of prayer in this unseen battle. So what role does prayer play in the believer's spiritual conflict?

The Christian Life Involves Conflict

The world we see is only part of the world that exists. In both the Old Testament and the New, an invisible world interacts with and influences our visible world. Conflict defines this interaction. In the Old Testament, Yahweh fought on behalf of his people, Israel. In the Gospels, Jesus is "the Warrior Slain, the Warrior Triumphant."[2] When we are united to Christ in faith, his enemies become ours and we enter into conflict with them. The phrase "spiritual

---

1. Three books on this topic that are especially helpful are Clinton E. Arnold, *3 Crucial Questions about Spiritual Warfare* (Grand Rapids: Baker Academic, 1997); John R. Gilhooly, *40 Questions About Angels, Demons, and Spiritual Warfare* (Grand Rapids: Kregel, 2018); and William F. Cook III and Chuck Lawless, *Spiritual Warfare in the Storyline of Scripture: A Biblical, Theological, and Practical Approach* (Nashville: B&H Academic, 2019).
2. This apt phrase comes from Tremper Longman III and Daniel G. Reid, *God Is a Warrior*, Studies in Old Testament Biblical Theology (Grand Rapids: Zondervan, 1995), ch. 8.

warfare" does not appear in the Bible but is rather a twentieth-century designation for the biblical truth of conflict of worlds.

The Gospels affirm Jesus's authority over spiritual powers. He could withstand temptation by the devil (Matt. 4:1–11). He cast out demons that had possessed people (Mark 1:21–28; 5:1–20; 9:14–29). He was uniquely able to bind the strong man (Mark 3:27). John understood Jesus's authority over the powers of darkness as a key part of his incarnation: "the reason the Son of God appeared was to destroy the works of the devil" (1 John 3:8). Jesus granted his disciples "authority over the unclean spirits" and they were able to cast them out of those who were possessed (Mark 6:7, 13). Yet Jesus warned his disciples against pride in this power (Luke 10:20). Though the Gospels affirm Jesus's grant of authority, they provide no instructions on the process or procedure of using such authority. The Bible is not a tactical handbook on such conflict, even though it affirms the existence of spiritual battles.

The Axis of World, Flesh, and Devil

Christian theologians have long considered Ephesians 2:1–3 an important text for understanding the three-fold axis of enemies arrayed against believers. Here, Paul reminds the Ephesians that both he and they had once walked "the course of this world," following "the prince of the power of the air," and had given priority to the "passions of our flesh." This axis of world, flesh, and devil, then, are part of the conflict which believers experience. Setting aside discussion of the flesh and world for the present discussion, we want to consider the role of the devil in spiritual conflict, "the spirit that is now at work in the sons of disobedience" (Eph. 2:2).

In his influential treatment of Christian spirituality, Richard Lovelace considers "authority in spiritual conflict" to be a primary element of renewal, an element as important as justification, sanctification, and the indwelling Spirit's presence.[3] He suggests that it was the European Enlightenment's relegation of the supernatural to childish fantasies that led to general disavowal of spiritual conflict in many Christian traditions, yet he recognizes that biblical Christianity took such conflict seriously. Lovelace suggests that the devil employs five strategies in his warfare against believers: temptation, deception, accusation, possession, and physical attack.[4] Through temptation, the devil seeks to discredit the church's public witness. Through deception, the devil and his fallen angels oppose truth as revealed in Scripture, strive to keep unbelievers "blinded" to such truth (2 Cor. 4:4), and prop up false religions (1 John 4:1–3). The devil accuses and slanders Christians, continually bringing to mind past sins, questioning their faithfulness, trying to confuse

---

3. Richard F. Lovelace, *Dynamics of Spiritual Life: An Evangelical Theology of Renewal*, exp. ed. (Downers Grove, IL: IVP Academic, 1979), 133.
4. Lovelace, *Dynamics of Spiritual Life*, 137–40.

and discomfort believers into silence and thus ineffectiveness in service. In some instances, the devil or his demons take control of a person (Luke 8:26–33) or cause physical or emotional illness (Matt. 9:32–33).[5] In all of these situations, prayer is the fitting defense against the devil's attacks, yet sometimes the devil tempts us to neglect prayer.

One timeless analysis of the devil's strategies is that of Puritan Thomas Brooks (1608–1680). Brooks preached a number of sermon series on these strategies that he published as *Precious Remedies against Satan's Devices.*[6] Brooks suggests that the devil works to persuade Christians that "religious performances" such as prayer are too difficult: "It is so hard and difficult a thing to pray as you should, to wait on God . . . to walk with God as you should."[7] Believers must learn to recognize such temptations for what they are: deception. God gives prayer as a gift and as a fruit of the gospel of Jesus, not as a burden. Prayer is also a key way that we stand against the devil's assaults.

Armored for Battle

Believers must respond to these conflicts by gospel-directed prayer. The classic text on this topic is Ephesians 6:10–20. Here Paul exhorts believers to "be strong in the Lord and in the strength of his might" (v. 10). The passive voice imperative "be strong" (*endynamousthe*) indicates that believers are to *be* strengthened, that is, to receive strength that is beyond their own natural fitness. The source of this strength is Jesus himself: believers are to be strengthened by the "strength of his might" (*tō kratei tēs ischyos autou*), literally his "mighty strength." By stacking terms for power here, Paul emphasizes Jesus's ability to guard and empower his people.

The next command is to "put on the whole armor of God," so that "you may be able to stand against the schemes of the devil." The "armor" is God's provision in the gospel: truth, righteousness, readiness, faith, salvation, and Scripture. This image of a Roman centurion in battle attire suggests the seriousness of the conflict in which believers stand. These elements of the gospel are all God's provisions to allow believers to resist the devil. As such, believers receive them and don them for battle. Prayer seems to be the place in which

---

5. Lovelace offers a helpful side comment on this phenomenon: "It needs to be said immediately that other factors besides demonic agency join in causing almost every aberration mentioned above and that often there may not be any direct satanic activity involved. As Puritan pastoral theory recognized, spiritual pathology can arise from four different sources: physical factors (illness, fatigue, malnutrition or what today might be recognized as glandular or chemical imbalance); psychological factors ("temperament"); fallen human nature; and demonic attack" (*Dynamics of Spiritual Life*, 140).
6. As with many Puritan works, numerous versions exist. A recent edition is Thomas Brooks, *Precious Remedies against Satan's Devices*, ed. Christopher Ellis Osterbrock (Peterborough, Ontario: H&E Publishing, 2020).
7. Brooks, *Precious Remedies*, 127.

this conflict occurs: "praying at all times in the Spirit, with all prayer and supplication. To that end, keep alert with all perseverance, making supplication for all the saints" (Eph. 6:18).

In what is likely the most thorough exposition of Ephesians 6, Puritan William Gurnall (1616–1679) devoted nearly three hundred pages to Paul's command for prayer.[8] Prayer is not a piece of the armor, but rather provides the believer with the strength to stand firm in the armor. This prayer has several features: First, it is to be ongoing, "praying at all times." Second, it is to be "in the Spirit," or prayer that follows the Spirit's leadership and power. Third, it is to include "all prayer and supplication," indicating that this prayer invites God to supply our needs in battle, but also includes all sorts of prayers such as confession and thanksgiving. Fourth, we are to "keep alert" in this prayer, always conscious of the enemy's threats and ready for his plots. Fifth, we are to persevere in this prayer, never giving up. Sixth, we are to pray "for all the saints," indicating that our battle is not a solitary one. Now, one feature easily lost in English translations is that the verbs of Ephesians 6:10–20 are plural, instructions given to the church in Ephesus and thus to our congregations today. That is, churches are to "be strengthened," to "put on" the armor, to "stand firm," and to be "praying at all times." This feature is vital: we do not stand alone against the devil; rather, we stand shoulder to shoulder with other saints who have themselves been rescued and empowered by the Lord Jesus to withstand the devil. Recognizing this congregational aspect of the text helps us to apply it in a fitting way: though we must each stand against the devil and his schemes, we do not stand alone, but as Jesus's army. We stand with other armor-clad saints to hold the line against our enemy.

Believers must resist the devil's assaults. In 1 Peter, we are told to "be sober-minded; be watchful. Your adversary the devil prowls around like a roaring lion, seeking someone to devour. Resist him, firm in your faith, knowing that the same kinds of suffering are being experienced by your brotherhood throughout the world" (1 Peter 5:8–9). The two imperatives to be "sober-minded" (*nēpsate*) and "watchful" (*grēgorēsate*) bring to mind the military readiness of Paul's command in Ephesians 6:18. Another imperative, "resist" (*antistēte*), calls believers to be active in their opposition. In times of demonic assault, Christians are not to be passive, but must rather be active in their defense against assaults. James, similarly, calls believers to "resist" the devil (James 4:7).

Summary

Christians must learn to see the world as it truly exists, a spiritually charged, dangerous place of conflict. Our enemies often are not who we think they are. Recognizing whom we fight is a vital part of warfare. Our greatest

---

8.   William Gurnall, *The Christian in Compleat Armour* (London: Ralph Smith, 1662).

enemies are unseen but real spiritual forces. Though defeated by the Lamb, the devil lashes out against his followers in order to discredit and discourage us from following our commander in victory. Like a ferocious beast he stalks believers, looking to isolate and destroy us. Prayer is the battleground upon which our conflict with the devil and his fallen angels takes place. We must resist the devil's temptation to neglect prayer, but rather, we must fight him through prayer, in the strength of Christ.

REFLECTION QUESTIONS

1. When have you been aware of spiritual conflict most often?

2. Which of the devil's five strategies have you experienced most/least often?

3. How do believers find the strength to stand firm against the devil?

4. Why does the devil try to attack our willingness to pray?

5. What role does prayer have in resisting the devil?

PART 3

Prayer in Scripture

What Can Christians Learn from Narrative Prayers of the Old Testament?

Prayer was an important aspect of Israel's devotion to God and thus an important part of the Hebrew Scriptures, what Christians call the Old Testament. In this section of the book, we will consider various questions about prayer arising from specific biblical passages. The section begins by considering prayers from the Old Testament and then moves on to the New. We devote an entire chapter to prayers found in the Psalms, the prayer book of the Bible. In the present chapter, after considering the origins of prayer, we will take soundings from select prayers found in Old Testament narratives. Though Christians may easily take prayer for granted, presuming upon a God who will hear and answer, the confidence that God would respond to human prayers helped set Israel apart from other Near Eastern nations.

Prayer's Beginning: Genesis 1–11

Genesis 1–11 presents the primeval history that provides context for the history of humanity in general and the patriarchs of Israel in particular. As the Bible opens, God creates the universe and everything within it, including man and woman, who are the pinnacle of his creation, made in his image and likeness, and set as vice-regents over the world (Gen. 1–2; Ps. 8). One aspect of being made in God's image is that God and people communicate through speech.[1]

---

1. The doctrine of the *imago Dei* (image of God) includes far more than communicative speech. For a helpful recent analysis of the doctrine, see Peter J. Gentry and Stephen J. Wellum, *God's Kingdom through God's Covenants: A Concise Biblical Theology* (Wheaton, IL: Crossway, 2015), 75–86.

Though speech makes prayer possible, some prayers go unvocalized.[2] The first prayer mentioned in Scripture is uncomfortable, embarrassing, and emphasizes the dehumanizing effects of sin: Adam and Eve conversed with God while hiding naked among the trees of Eden (Gen. 3:8–13). Though created in God's image, the man and woman acted like animals. While this initial reference to prayer seems negative, it presents a larger biblical theme: human prayer is a response to God's gracious self-disclosure.[3] This incident also introduces the prophetic declaration of the woman's seed who will crush the serpent, the instigator of sin, and promises hope (Gen. 3:15). Apart from this episode, Genesis 1–11 offers few descriptions of prayer. By overhearing his prayer, readers learn that Cain is not the promised seed as God banishes him from his presence, and the means of seeking communion with God becomes the channel of divine rejection (Gen. 4:9–16). Though Cain and his descendants are marked by sin, the line of Seth holds promise, for during his lifetime and that of his son, Enosh, "men began to call upon the name of the LORD" (Gen. 4:26). Though ambiguous, this reference to calling on God's name signals an important shift in the relationship between God and his creation, one marked by communion through prayer addressed specifically to Yahweh.[4] Both Enoch and Noah "walked with God" (Gen. 5:22; 6:9), yet many details of their prayers remain obscure. Later in Genesis, patriarchs like Abraham, Isaac, Jacob, and Joseph pray.

In the balance of this chapter, we look at several different prayers from the narrative sections of the Old Testament. Hannah's prayer for a son in 1 Samuel 1:11 allows us to overhear the pleas of a seemingly powerless woman whose trust in the Lord was genuine. Solomon's and Hezekiah's prayers let us experience the weight of leading God's people in light of our own weakness at a time of great responsibility and great threat. These are by no means the only prose prayers in the Old Testament, but they each show different facets of how we might lift our hearts to God in the varying circumstances and roles of life.[5]

Hannah's Prayer

The first prayer we examine is that of Hannah, Elkanah's first wife. First Samuel records two of her prayers.[6] Late in the time of the judges, Elkanah

---

2. For example, Hannah's prayer in 1 Samuel 1:12–16.
3. So Claus Westermann, *Elements of Old Testament Theology*, trans. Douglas W. Stoss (Atlanta: John Knox Press, 1982), 153–56; Graeme Goldsworthy, *Prayer and the Knowledge of God: What the Whole Bible Teaches* (Downers Grove, IL: InterVarsity Press, 2003), 22–24.
4. Daniel Block notes four interpretive possibilities for Genesis 4:26: (1) a general expression of spiritual allegiance; (2) a general expression for worship; (3) a plea for divine help; or (4) a doxological expression of praise. See his *For the Glory of God: Recovering a Biblical Theology of Worship* (Grand Rapids: Baker Academic, 2016), 244.
5. One brief study of similar prayers is Moshe Greenberg, *Biblical Prose Prayer: As a Window to the Popular Religion of Ancient Israel* (Berkeley: University of California Press, 1983).
6. 1 Samuel 1:10–13 and 2:1–10.

and his family would travel to Shiloh to offer worship to Yahweh. Hannah was barren—a source of continual anxiety for her, especially as her husband had taken a second wife who had borne him children. During one pilgrimage to Shiloh, Hannah prayed simply:

> O LORD of hosts, if you will indeed look on the affliction of your servant and remember me and not forget your servant, but will give to your servant a son, then I will give him to the LORD all the days of his life, and no razor shall touch his head. (1 Sam. 1:11)

Hannah's prayer is brief but filled with significance. She addresses God as "LORD of Hosts" or "Yahweh almighty" (*Yahweh Sabaoth*). This title for God appears in 1 Samuel 1:3 and 1:11 for the first time in the Old Testament.[7] It expresses confidence in God's might: if he is the Lord of armies, powerful and mighty, he can surely address the hurt of this weak supplicant. Hannah approaches God with humility when she identifies herself as Yahweh's "servant" (*'ămātekā*), a slave, three times. Her petition is that Yahweh "remember . . . and not forget" her, which has nothing to do with limitations of God's knowledge or memory, but is a way of asking God to show favor in answering Hannah's request for a son, which God does (1:19). Bergen observes the irony within this narrative, namely that a humble woman who is part of a disordered marriage shows more spiritual sensitivity than Israel's priest: "Hannah was certainly portrayed as more intimate in her relationship with the Lord than Eli, the spiritual icon of his generation."[8] Hannah's prayer is poignant; her desperation is evident, as is her sincerity. In so many ways, Hannah is powerless, yet her faith in one who is uniquely powerful is unwavering.

Solomon's Prayer

In contrast with Hannah, Solomon is anything but powerless. Scripture records several of Solomon's prayers, but we focus here on the one found in 1 Kings 3:3–15. At this point in his life, Solomon was marked by godliness (3:3), and thus God's appearance in a dream does not seem out of place. Unlike other prayers where the supplicant comes to God with a need, this prayer is reversed: God approaches Solomon with the query of how he might bless the young king (3:5). Readers of the narrative are struck by this situation: Yahweh, the living and true God, not only responds to prayers, but initiates them! The focus of Solomon's petition occurs in verse 9:

---

7. Roger L. Omanson and John Ellington, *A Handbook on the First Book of Samuel*, UBS Handbook Series (New York: United Bible Societies, 2001), 26.
8. Robert D. Bergen, *1, 2 Samuel*, New American Commentary, vol. 7 (Nashville: Broadman & Holman Publishers, 1996), 68.

> Give your servant therefore an understanding mind to govern your people, that I may discern between good and evil, for who is able to govern this your great people?

Yahweh's response is marked by graciousness: "It pleased the LORD that Solomon had asked this." This response reveals God's character with regard to prayer. He not only "puts up with it," as one continually besieged with requests, but at times prompts it and in turn delights in our requests. Solomon is the beneficiary of God's special covenant with David and his house, and experiences a nearness to God, at least at this point in his life, that anticipates the relationship that God has with believers under the new covenant, those who are his children by adoption. God shows his delight by answering Solomon's request (3:11–12) and going beyond: "I give you also what you have not asked, both riches and honor, so that no other king shall compare with you, all your days. And if you will walk in my ways, keeping my statutes and my commandments, as your father David walked, then I will lengthen your days" (3:13–14).

Though readers might be tempted to try to "reverse-engineer" Solomon's prayer by seeking to get God to bless them with riches and honor by asking for something more fitting, like wisdom, a moment's reflection shows that such an approach will not work, for God distributes his gifts as he wills, not according to formulas. Solomon's desire for wisdom appears as genuine as God's willingness to bless him beyond his requests. The Lord answered Solomon's heartfelt prayer for wisdom, and for a season Solomon walked consistently with this blessing. It was later that Solomon compromised his faith by pursuing religious and political pluralism, and by his own moral decisions, abandoned the faith of his father David, and squandered God's blessings.

Hezekiah's Prayer

The prayer of Hezekiah is so significant that it appears three times in Scripture.[9] After Israel was divided in two, Hezekiah was king in Judah (the Southern Kingdom) from around 715–687 BC. Ruling as king for nearly thirty years, Hezekiah was a reformer who sought to restore Israel's worship by destroying idols and "high places" of false worship. Hezekiah "trusted in the LORD, the God of Israel" (2 Kings 18:5) and "held fast to the LORD. He did not depart from following him, but kept the commandments that the LORD commanded Moses" (18:6). This description seems to be an oblique reference to Deuteronomy 17:18–20, that places meditative attention to the law of God as a priority to ensure godly leadership in Israel. During his reign, Hezekiah faced the threat of Assyrian invasion. A military power, Assyria had risen to regional strength. Hezekiah's prayer occurs after he receives word of a pending Assyrian invasion.

---

9.   2 Kings 19:14–20; 2 Chronicles 32:20; and Isaiah 37:14–21.

> And Hezekiah prayed before the LORD and said: "O LORD, the God of Israel, enthroned above the cherubim, you are the God, you alone, of all the kingdoms of the earth; you have made heaven and earth. Incline your ear, O LORD, and hear; open your eyes, O LORD, and see; and hear the words of Sennacherib, which he has sent to mock the living God. Truly, O LORD, the kings of Assyria have laid waste the nations and their lands and have cast their gods into the fire, for they were not gods, but the work of men's hands, wood and stone. Therefore they were destroyed. So now, O LORD our God, save us, please, from his hand, that all the kingdoms of the earth may know that you, O LORD, are God alone." (2 Kings 19:15–19)

Several elements of Hezekiah's prayer command attention. First, his prayer focuses upon the unique power of the living "God of Israel," Yahweh. A marker of his genuine faith, Hezekiah ignores generations of syncretistic religious customs and pursues God directly and personally. Next, we note his recognition of God's control: Yahweh is not only God of Israel, but is God alone "of all the kingdoms of the earth." Third, Hezekiah appeals to God's honor as the basis for action. The Assyrian king has mocked the "living God" and Hezekiah wants God to act to show God's unique authority.

Summary

Allowing the Bible to shape our prayers takes different forms. In some cases, Scripture shapes our requests, at other times, our priorities, and at still other times informs our very vocabulary. In later questions we will look at practical methods for praying Scripture, but here we want to observe God's people, under the old covenant, at prayer. Whether the one praying was a king at the height of Israel's success, a ruler facing the crisis of invasion, or a seemingly insignificant woman who simply wanted the blessing of a child, all three came, equally weak, before God, shaped by their own limits and extents of power or influence. All sorts of faithful saints in the Old Testament had confidence that God would hear and answer their prayers.

REFLECTION QUESTIONS

1. What role did prayer play in the opening chapters of Genesis?

2. What can Hannah's prayer show us about sincerity in our speech before God?

3. What can Hezekiah's prayer teach us about why we trust God in prayer?

4. What can Solomon's prayer show us about God's willingness to answer prayer?

5. What lessons about prayer have consideration of these three different Old Testament prayers taught you?

How Can the Psalms Shape Christian Prayer?

When we ask how the Psalms have shaped Christian prayer through two thousand years, it is almost impossible to overstate their influence. The Psalms have played an important role in religious life of Christians from the first century forward, even as they shaped (and continue to mark) the worship of Jews before them.[1] Sometimes this influence is obvious, but other times it is harder to see. As one example of this difficulty, it is easy for New Testament readers to encounter Mary's Magnificat (Luke 1:46–55) and miss the use of so many psalms in her prayer of teenage devotion.[2] Undoubtedly, early Christians found the Psalms so important because Jesus himself had turned to them so often: when betrayed by one of his "friends," to express his zeal for the temple, and at his hour of most intense suffering on the cross, Jesus turned to these poems.[3] After his resurrection, Jesus reminded some of his disheartened followers that when they read the Old Testament, they should expect to see him in its pages (cf. Luke 24:44), and the earliest Christians often turned to the Psalms to testify about Jesus.[4]

The ancient church continued to return to the Psalms in prayer. Egyptian bishop Athanasius (d. 373) described the Psalms as a mirror that allows people to see their own souls more clearly.[5] Macrina the Younger, sister of

---

1. William L. Holladay, *The Psalms through Three Thousand Years: Prayerbook of a Cloud of Witnesses* (Minneapolis: Fortress Press, 1993), 1.
2. See Tremper Longman, *How to Read the Psalms* (Downers Grove, IL: InterVarsity Press, 1988), 38.
3. John 13:18, quoting Psalm 41:9; John 2:17 citing Psalm 69:9; and Matthew 27:46 citing Psalm 22:1.
4. For example, Psalms 2 (Acts 4:25–26) and 110 (Acts 2:32–35).
5. Athanasius of Alexandria, *Athanasius: The Life of Antony and the Letter to Marcellinus*, ed. Richard J. Payne, trans. Robert C. Gregg, The Classics of Western Spirituality (Mahwah, NJ: Paulist Press, 1980), 111.

the famed Cappadocian theologians of the fourth century, learned the Psalms by heart and taught them to her younger brothers.[6] North African bishop Augustine (354–430) discovered the Psalms in his early thirties, after his dramatic conversion to Christianity, and preached or commented on every psalm during the course of his ministry.[7] Later, the Psalms became prominent in the rhythm of the monastery, shaping the daily and weekly cycle of prayers. Magisterial Reformers like Martin Luther and John Calvin prayed, taught, and sang the Psalms. English Reformer Thomas Cranmer included the Psalter, broken up into daily readings, in his *Book of Common Prayer*. Puritan hymn writer Isaac Watts gave English-speaking Christians a modern poetic translation of the Psalms for private and congregational devotion.[8] In the nineteenth century, the great Baptist pastor Charles Spurgeon (1834–1892) preached hundreds of sermons and wrote commentaries and devotional works on the Psalms, and found them invaluable for shaping personal and family prayers. Twentieth-century German theologian Dietrich Bonhoeffer (1906–1945) explored the ways that various kinds of psalms might help Christians deepen their prayers.[9] Contemporary Protestants continue to reflect on the importance of the Psalms for worship and prayer.[10] This long list spans two thousand years of Christian reflection and is only a small sample of thoughtful engagement with the Psalms for prayer. If we overlook the Psalms as guides, our spirituality will be shallower for it. This chapter considers why the Psalms are so significant for Christian prayer and how we can experience their depth for ourselves.

The Psalms Teach Us How to Pray

One recurring theme in this book is that we learn to pray by listening to others. In the Psalms, we have occasion to listen to inspired, authoritative, and sufficient prayers (see Question 3). Unlike any other prayers that we may speak or overhear, these prayers have been inscripturated; thus the individual psalms are prayers God gives Christians that we might give them back to

---

6. Gregory of Nyssa, *Life of St. Macrina*, trans. Kevin Corrigan (Eugene, OR: Wipf and Stock, 2001), 23.

7. For Augustine's discovery of the Psalms, see his *Confessions* Book 9. The standard English translation of his *Expositions of the Psalms* contains six volumes.

8. For a marvelous modern edition, see Isaac Watts, *The Songs, Hymns, and Spiritual Songs of the Rev. Isaac Watts, D.D.*, Old Hymns New, vol. 1, ed. M. C. Boswell (Del Frisco, TX: Doxology and Theology Press, 2016).

9. Dietrich Bonhoeffer, *Psalms: The Prayer Book of the Bible*, trans. James. H. Burtness (Minneapolis: Augsburg, 1970).

10. For a sampling, see N. T. Wright, *The Case for the Psalms: Why They Are Essential* (New York: Harper One, 2013); Gordon Wenham, *The Psalter Reclaimed: Praying and Praising with the Psalms* (Wheaton, IL: Crossway, 2013); Eugene H. Peterson, *Answering God: The Psalms as Tools for Prayer* (New York: Harper One, 1989); James W. Sire, *Learning to Pray through the Psalms* (Downers Grove, IL: InterVarsity Press, 2005).

him.[11] Scholars often group psalms together by categories based on features of the text and will often speak of "wisdom" psalms or "royal" psalms or "psalms of lament" and so forth. These groupings can be helpful, and we will return to them below, but there are also other ways to look at prayer in the Psalms. In a helpful essay, Old Testament Professor Kyu Nam Jung identifies five different kinds of prayer that appear across these textual groups, and for our purposes his classification is timely. Jung sees in the Psalms (a) petitionary prayer, (b) penitential prayer, (c) intercessory prayer, (d) thanksgiving or confident prayer, and (e) hymnic prayer.[12] Though there might actually be more than five kinds of prayer, Jung's list helps us see just how rich the Psalms are for prayer. To let them shape our prayers, though, we must read them often and read them well.

Reading and Praying

The Psalms have shaped the prayers of many well-known Christians, but they have also helped countless "ordinary" Christians deepen their prayers across the centuries. What do these eminent and ordinary Christians have in common? For one thing, those who have deepened their prayers have become regular readers of the Psalms. In many Christian traditions, clergy or laity read the Psalms liturgically as part of congregational worship, but this practice seems to be less common for many churchgoers, especially in the "free church" tradition (e.g., Baptist Churches, Bible Churches, independent churches, and other nondenominational groups). In the twentieth century, Bonhoeffer encouraged Christians whose churches no longer read the Psalms: "We must take up the Psalter that much more in our daily morning and evening prayers, reading and praying together at least several Psalms every day so that we succeed in reading through this book a number of times each year, getting into it deeper and deeper."[13]

Reading Thoughtfully

We ought to consider how the Psalter (a common name for the book of Psalms) is structured and acknowledge some differences within Christian traditions in this regard. In Hebrew Bibles, the Psalms are part of the third division known as the Writings (*Ketuvim*). The Psalms also appear in a very old Greek translation of the Old Testament known as the Septuagint. These two translations differ on where to divide the text at some points, thus the numbering of the Psalms varies. This variance is important because the Greek numbering set the pattern for the Latin Vulgate translation, used by Catholics

---

11. See Donald S. Whitney, *Praying the Bible* (Wheaton, IL: Crossway, 2015), 45–46.
12. Kyu Nam Jung, "Prayer in the Psalms," in *Teach Us to Pray: Prayer in the Bible and the World*, ed. D. A. Carson (Exeter, UK: Paternoster Press, 1990), 36–49.
13. Bonhoeffer, *Prayer Book*, 25–26.

in the West from the 400s on, which in turn led to differences in modern English Bibles based on these different translations. Most English Bibles follow the Hebrew numbering, and we will do so here.[14]

There are five internal divisions or "books" of psalms in our Bible:

Table 1—Books of the Psalter	
Book 1	Psalms 1–41
Book 2	Psalms 42–72
Book 3	Psalms 73–89
Book 4	Psalms 90–106
Book 5	Psalms 107–150

As mentioned above, many of the psalms have common themes, leading scholars to suggest various categories of psalms: hymns, laments, thanksgivings, wisdom, imprecations (cursing), and so forth.[15] Some categories have a long history, such as the seven "penitential" psalms (Pss. 6, 32, 38, 51, 102, 130, and 143). Other categories are more modern, nuanced, and largely the domain of scholars. The idea of categorization is interesting and recognizes the unity and diversity of the Psalter, but mastering it is not essential to reading the Psalms well. One skill that is required is learning to engage poetry, for as we read and pray the Psalms, we must always keep in mind that they are poetic writings and that poetic writings have their own patterns and rules for interpretation.[16]

Reading Regularly

It takes about five hours to read the entire collection of 150 psalms.[17] Spread over the course of thirty days, reading a few psalms each day will take approximately twenty minutes per day. If readers follow the common practice of reading some psalms in the morning and others in the evening, this time is shortened to accommodate even the busiest of schedules. Even the longest Psalm (Ps. 119) takes only about twenty minutes to read aloud at an unhurried pace.

---

14. For a clear discussion of the differences, see Wright, *Case for the Psalms*, 12.
15. The most influential twentieth-century categorizations come from German scholar Hermann Gunkel. The most accessible overview of Gunkel's approach is Tyler F. Williams, "A Form-Critical Classification of the Psalms according to Hermann Gunkel," available at https://three-things.ca/?p=711.
16. Among the many helpful guides for reading the Psalms in greater detail is that of Longman, *How to Read the Psalms*.
17. https://www.desiringgod.org/articles/three-tips-for-better-bible-reading.

As I grow older, I find myself returning to the Psalms more frequently and spending more time there. One pattern of reading I have found particularly helpful for more than twenty years is to read through the entire Psalter over the course of a month several times each year. There are various ways to divide this reading. The long-standing pattern from the *Book of Common Prayer* is to read sequentially through the Psalms, typically five psalms per day, reading some in the morning and some in the evening.[18] Don Whitney suggests a "psalms of the day" approach in which readers engage five psalms across the Psalter keyed to the particular day of the month.[19] Many Bible reading apps include specific reading (or listening) plans for the Psalms. Another way to approach the Psalms is by reading five psalms daily by selecting one psalm from each of the five "books" (see Table 1 above).

From Reading to Praying

How, specifically, might we move from reading the Psalms to praying them? Philosopher Jim Sire suggests a helpful sequence:

1. reading, rereading, then reading again—and again
2. clarifying the text, gaining an understanding of each of the words or phrases that seem puzzling
3. analyzing the structures in the psalm: (a) rational structure, i.e., the flow of ideas; (b) emotional structure, i.e., the flow of emotions evoked in and by the psalm; (c) rhetorical structure
4. achieving a sense of the psalmist's own often complex and changing relationship to God (e.g., calm, joyous, disturbed, turbulent, angry, depressed)
5. making the answering speech of the psalmist one's own, by repeating his words as one's own, adapting his words to one's own situation or doing some of both.[20]

It is hard to improve upon Sire's advice, but perhaps two clarifying points will prove helpful. First, when Sire speaks of the psalmist's "changing relationship to God," he seems to be speaking of a change in the psalmist's *perception* of his relationship to God, not a change in the status of that relationship. Second, Sire's structure is logical as it moves from reading (1) to analysis (2–3), to interpretation (4), and finally to prayer (5). As we begin to let the Psalms shape our prayers, we might actually start simply with the final step: letting the psalmist's words become our words, allowing prayer to deepen our

---

18. See, for example, https://www.churchofengland.org/prayer-and-worship/worship-texts-and-resources/common-worship/daily-prayer.
19. Whitney, *Praying the Bible*, 91–92.
20. Sire, *Learning to Pray*, 13.

understanding of the text. Following steps 2–4 are important, for they are part of the maturing process of striving to know the God who makes himself known in Scripture more accurately, a striving that ought to characterize followers of Christ. This sort of deepening engagement with the biblical text is part of the way that God renews our minds (Rom. 12:1–2), yet we may begin praying the Psalms even as we are learning to interpret them well.

The Psalms Fit Every Season

Those who read the Psalms regularly and thoughtfully recognize different categories or themes across various psalms. Learning to see these similarities can help us use the Psalms in prayer by giving us a reference point to turn to in various seasons of life. For example, when we are overwhelmed with personal heartache, we might find the words of David in Psalm 13 especially helpful: "How long, O Lord? Will you forget me forever? How long will you hide your face from me?" (Ps. 13:1). This psalm does not stand alone, but fits into a pattern with other psalms like Psalms 55, 77, and 142 (among many others), and recognizing this pattern can be reassuring to us: if God seemed far off from those whose prayers were privileged to become Scripture, we are not alone nor unique in our hurt and God has given us words to express our inward groaning. Conversely, if we are moved to worship and praise of God, seeing a psalm like Psalm 150 helps vocalize our inward joy, and seeing so many different ways to praise God in Psalms 8, 19, 95, 111, and 148, for example, can help us express joy in our prayers.

The following lists do not attempt to be exhaustive nor to find a niche for every psalm (some are notoriously hard to pin down), but rather to offer some starting points for common themes and words for our prayers throughout life's different seasons. As you grow in reading the Psalms for yourself over the course of your lifetime, develop your own lists as aids to prayer.

- *Prayers of Repentance*—6, 32, 38, 51, 102, 130, 143
- *Prayers of Lament*—Personal: 3, 4, 5, 7, 9–10, 13, 14, 17, 22, 25, 26, 42–43, 54–57; *Congregational:* 12, 44, 80, 85
- *Prayers of Thanksgiving*—Personal: 11, 18, 34, 63, 116, 138; *Congregational:* 65, 95, 103, 117, 145–50
- *Prayers for Public Worship*—48, 50, 82, 99, 110, 115, 122, 134
- *Prayers for Wisdom*—1, 19, 37, 73, 119, 127

Summary

Christians have used the Psalms as reliable guides for prayer from the first century onward. Reading the Psalms regularly and allowing their poetry to saturate our thinking surely affects our mindsets and praying. John Calvin's reflections on the value of the Psalms are helpful in recognizing their place in shaping Christian prayer:

I have been accustomed to call this book, I think not inappropriately, "An Anatomy of all the Parts of the Soul"; for there is not an emotion of which any one can be conscious that is not here represented as in a mirror.[21]

REFLECTION QUESTIONS

1. What are some patterns of reading the Psalms that have been helpful to you?

2. Are there particular psalms that you turn to in various times of prayer? Why?

3. How can the Psalms help give voice to different kinds of prayer?

4. What makes the Psalms different from other parts of Scripture for prayer?

5. How might we move from reading the Psalms to praying them?

---

21. John Calvin, *John Calvin: Writings on Pastoral Piety*, eds. Elsie Anne McKee and Bernard McGinn, trans. Elsie Anne McKee, The Classics of Western Spirituality (Mahwah, NJ: Paulist Press, 2001), 56.

QUESTION 17

What Kinds of Prayer Does Jesus Forbid (Matthew 6:5–8)?

Jesus wants his followers to pray, and he wants us to pray in ways that honor his Father. Jesus taught his disciples to avoid certain habits that were common at that time in religious circles and among pagans, and so as we desire to pray in ways that honor the Father, we must ask what sorts of prayer Jesus forbids. This question is the first of several dealing with what is arguably the most widely known prayer in the world, the Lord's Prayer (Matt. 6:9–13; Luke 11:2–4). While other questions address the prayer itself, this question deals with two warnings that Jesus gave in connection with prayer: genuine prayer that honors the Father requires no audience and avoids notions of magic.

The Structure of the Sermon on the Mount

Since several questions in this book arise from Jesus's prayer in Matthew 6, it will be helpful to include some preliminary observations here about the structure and features of this part of Matthew's gospel to better set it within its context. As I have written elsewhere, contemporary interpreters remain divided on whether the Sermon on the Mount (Matt. 5–7) offers ethical demands for believers in the present age, whether it emphasizes the impossibility of law-keeping for the Jews, or whether its injunctions envision eschatological obedience, among other views.[1] I believe the sermon provides

---

1. I have adapted this portion of the present chapter from my article, "The Neglected Discipline of Almsgiving," in *Journal of Spiritual Formation and Soul Care* 12, no. 1 (2019): 89–111. For a helpful recent summary of these approaches, see Charles Quarles, *Sermon on the Mount: Restoring Christ's Message to the Modern Church*, in NAC Studies in Bible and Theology (Nashville: B&H Academic, 2011), 4–11.

ethical guidance for present disciples, a view in keeping with the themes of discipleship present within the gospel and in keeping with the sermon's earliest interpreters.[2]

Matthean scholars Davies, Allison, and Pennington have offered convincing arguments for a chiastic structure to the sermon built around a series of triads.[3] Matthew 5:3–16 serves as a call to God's people and forms the "A" of the chiasmus. The body of the sermon in Matthew (5:17–7:12) serves as the center, or "B" section of the pattern. The sermon concludes with warnings regarding eschatological judgment, forming the "C" of the figure.[4] This layout was almost certainly a mnemonic device to aid the recollection and transmission of the sermon, and by following the structure of this chiasm, we see that Matthew 6, with its directions for three normative acts of first-century Jewish piety (fasting, prayer, and almsgiving), lies at the very heart of the sermon. To be sure, Jesus might just as easily have mentioned other practices, but we need to reckon with the ones that he gives here, particularly prayer, which forms the exact center of the structure.[5] Private practice and secret reward punctuate Matthew's presentation of piety (6:4, 6, and 18). The parallel language of 6:2–4, 5–6, and 16–18 regarding motive, behavior, and reward is striking and has the rhetorical effect of linking these three practices.[6]

Jesus Forbids Two Kinds of Prayers

Matthew 6:1 begins with a warning about how faithful disciples ought to practice acts of piety: "Beware of practicing your righteousness before other people in order to be seen by them, for then you will have no reward from your Father who is in heaven." This warning is a blanket statement that applies particularly to the three common acts of Jewish piety that Jesus addresses in Matthew 6, namely almsgiving (6:2–4), prayer (6:5–15), and fasting (6:16–18). For each activity, Jesus warns against practices that draw attention to the

---

2. For a well-sourced history of interpretation, see Jack R. Lundbom, *Jesus' Sermon on the Mount: Mandating a Better Righteousness* (Minneapolis: Fortress Press, 2015), 45–70. A standard work is also that of Warren S. Kissinger, *The Sermon on the Mount: A History of Interpretation and Bibliography* (Metuchen, NJ: Scarecrow, 1975). A chiastic structure is a literary technique named after the Greek letter *chi* (χ) because the text takes on this letter's shape by working from the outside to a center and then back out again.
3. See W. D. Davies and D. C. Allison, *Matthew 1–7*, International Critical Commentary (London: T&T Clark, 1988); Dale C. Allison, Jr., "The Configuration of the Sermon on the Mount and Its Meaning," in *Studies in Matthew: Interpretation Past and Present* (Grand Rapids: Baker Academic, 2005), 173–215, esp. 195–96; and Jonathan T. Pennington, *The Sermon on the Mount and Human Flourishing: A Theological Commentary* (Grand Rapids: Baker Academic, 2017), 105–34.
4. See Pennington, *Sermon on the Mount*, 132–33 for an outline of this structure.
5. On the representative nature of these pious acts, see D. A. Carson, *The Sermon on the Mount: An Evangelical Exposition of Matthew 5–7* (Grand Rapids: Baker, 1978).
6. See Allison, "Configuration," 185.

act (and the actor) rather than practice that directs attention to the Father. The word "righteousness" (*dikaiosynē*) links 5:20 and 6:1, for in both places Jesus mentions people who have an appearance of righteousness in the eyes of others, but whose righteousness is only that: an appearance.

Jesus Forbids Prayer That Seeks Human Approval

Jesus warns his listeners that they "must not be like the hypocrites" who "love to stand and pray in the synagogues and at the street corners, that they may be seen by others" (Matt. 6:5).[7] Several items deserve attention here. First, who are the "hypocrites" (*hypokritai*) Jesus envisions? Then, what does he (and presumably the Father) find so offensive about their actions and motives in prayer? Regarding the identity of the "hypocrites," it seems likely this term is a reference to the "scribes and Pharisees" of 5:20. In that passage, these well-known religious folk had a reputation for righteousness; but true disciples, Jesus insists, will have a greater righteousness. In 6:1, Jesus's statement particularizes false righteousness as the sort that comes from a desire to be *seen* practicing religious duties—and thus esteemed highly—by others. Of course, this identification need not apply only to those groups; it is equally applicable to anyone who would use prayer in this way.

The second question is what is particularly odious about their behavior? Jesus's warning seems more appropriately directed against their underlying *desire* rather than the action: these people "*love* to stand and pray . . . *that they may be seen* by others" (Matt. 6:5, italics added). At issue is not that these people pray publicly, for Jesus himself offered public prayers. Rather, the adjective of purpose (*hopōs*) indicates that the desired outcome is external approval by others. Their desire for their peers to see them as righteous makes them mere pretenders or dissemblers at prayer. Jesus's warning is stark: such people will get precisely what they desire, not the answer to those requests that they *pretend* to ask of God, but the "reward" of mere human approval.

The implied contrast between those supposed righteous people and actual righteous people is that the latter receive God's reward because their desire, though unstated, is true fellowship with God. Their desire manifests itself in different actions, specifically, praying secretly, or what the Puritans used to call "closet prayer." By praying privately, so that only God hears and sees them at prayer, true believers express a desire to please the Father alone. In prizing this sort of prayer and rejecting attention-seeking prayer, Jesus calls us to consider our motives for prayer, not only our techniques of prayer.

---

7. Jesus's prohibition is strong here: *ouk esesthe hōs hoi hypokritai*, with the future indicative (*ouk esesthe*) having the force of a command. See Daniel B. Wallace, *Greek Grammar: Beyond the Basics* (Grand Rapids: Zondervan, 1996), 452.

Jesus Forbids Prayer That Mimics Magic

Jesus's second direction in Matthew 6:7–8 also addresses people's motives in prayer by way of looking at their actions. In this second assessment, Jesus looks at "the Gentiles" and their tendency to "heap up empty phrases." Jesus criticizes their practice by way of critiquing their theology: "for they think that they will be heard for their many words." What can we know about the "Gentiles" Jesus envisions? What are the "empty phrases" Jesus mentions? Why do these people believe that a surplus of words will assure that their prayers find favor with a god?

First, the phrase *hoi ethnikoi* ("the Gentiles") is a reference to ethnic/ national foreigners. The term emphasizes this group's moral or theological differences from those of the speaker's own ethnic/national group. In this case, *hoi ethnikoi* are non-Jews, but we cannot be more specific as to which non-Jewish group Jesus envisions. Second, this group's prayers featured *battalogēsēte* ("empty phrases") that true disciples are to avoid. The term *battalogēsēte* occurs in the New Testament only here, and only rarely outside the Bible, making cross-textual comparisons difficult. The word likely envisions stammering or repetitive speech, which Jesus's later phrase "their many words" (*tē polylogia autōn*) clarifies. This sort of speech may envision a pagan view of prayer as magic; that is, as repeating certain words, phrases, or requests in order to sway a deity to action.[8] While a magical view of prayer seeks immediate relief for personal circumstances, Christian prayer recognizes tensions between immediate gratification and eternal reward, prizes community, and is always relational.[9] Verse 6:8b clarifies Jesus's rejection of the theology that undergirds this practice on such grounds: "for your Father knows what you need before you ask him."[10]

In contrast to the uncertain and repetitive attempts to sway a deity, Jesus's followers pray with confidence that God, who is their Father, already knows what they need quite apart from their activity or praying. What confidence this theology imparts! Now, the issue of God's omniscience with regard to prayer has already been addressed (see Question 12), so we will not repeat that material here, except to say that Jesus draws a different conclusion than

---

8. Ulrich Luz, *Matthew 1–7: A Commentary on Matthew 1–7*, rev. ed., Hermeneia (Minneapolis: Fortress Press, 2007), 305. See also John Nolland, *The Gospel of Matthew*, New International Greek Testament Commentary (Grand Rapids: Eerdmans, 2005), 284.

9. See David Crump, *Knocking on Heaven's Door: A New Testament Theology of Petitionary Prayer* (Grand Rapids: Baker, 2006), 171–78. Here Crump identifies seven key theological differences between magic and prayer.

10. While textual links are slim, it seems reasonable to suggest that Jesus may have had Ecclesiastes 5:2 in mind as well: "Be not rash with your mouth, nor let your heart be hasty to utter a word before God, for God is in heaven and you are on earth. Therefore let your words be few." Nolland remarks on this link as well, noting correctly the differences in context between Ecclesiastes and Matthew (*Matthew*, 285).

do many readers. While some readers see God's omniscience as rendering prayer moot, Jesus encourages us to see it as liberating. Because God knows what we need before we ask, we ought to ask! Whereas the Gentiles' theology led them to approach their deity with uncertainty and formulaic, ritual repetitions, Jesus's followers come with a filial expectation and use normal conversational speech.

Summary

Jesus wants us to pray in ways that honor the Father, and he recognizes two very common impulses that derail genuine prayer: a desire for the approval of others and a desire to control God through magic. We should not read these passages as Jesus's rejection of public prayer or even of long prayers; rather, he seeks to correct two common and natural impulses related to prayer. These verses are so common that regular readers of Scripture may overlook something at once obvious and significant: Jesus asserts the authority to tell people how to pray and how not to pray! At one level, this instruction would be commonplace for a first-century rabbi (teacher), who surely helped his followers learn to pray, yet Jesus's instruction goes deeper than technique or methodology, to our hearts. On a higher level, these warnings have an uncommon authority, for Jesus, the one who speaks unequivocally about what it means to be a citizen of the kingdom of heaven, is establishing boundaries for true devotion under his rule.

REFLECTION QUESTIONS

1. Why do we need to avoid trying to impress others with our public prayers?

2. Do you think it is wrong to be moved or impressed when hearing someone else pray in public?

3. What are the "empty phrases" Jesus warns against using in Matthew 6:7–8?

4. How might you use Jesus's teaching on prayer here to encourage a friend from a Christian tradition that emphasizes repetition and lengthy prayers?

5. How might memorized or written prayers relate to Jesus's prohibitions in this passage?

How Might We Pray the Lord's Prayer (Matthew 6:9–13)?

Though only a guess, I suspect that the King James Version of the Lord's Prayer (Matt. 6:9–13) may be the most often recited passage of Scripture in the world, or certainly near the top. For more than four hundred years, the familiar English words of "Our Father" have passed the lips of innumerable millions of people within the church and in popular culture. Some years ago, I attended an eventide service at Kings College, Cambridge, and noted that the diverse crowd of tourists and locals seemed to have no trouble reciting this prayer, though other parts of the service were clearly foreign to many assembled. From as early as the first century onward, this passage and its prayer have been a significant part of the church's daily worship. Because of the important of this prayer, Christian pastors and theologians in nearly every generation have offered commentary on it.[1] Is it possible that the Lord's Prayer might become too familiar, though? Might we recite this prayer so often that we speak the words without meaning or fail to see in their simplicity the deep riches of true prayer? This chapter considers how we might come to use the Lord's Prayer as a guide for our own prayer.

Around the turn of the first century, a handbook for Christian worship known as *The Didache* ("The Teaching of the Twelve") recommended that believers should pray the Lord's Prayer three times each day.[2] This mention of Jesus's prayer is the earliest description outside of the Bible and helps us see how early Christians approached this prayer in the past. For centuries, new

---

1. One challenge in writing this chapter is that I have been so deeply influenced by many of these works over decades of reading that I no longer easily remember the ways they have shaped me.
2. *The Didache* 8. For a recent study of this ancient text, see Shawn J. Wilhite, *The Didache: A Commentary* (Eugene, OR: Cascade Books, 2019). The date of *The Didache* has been suggested as early as AD 70 to as late as AD 140. A date in the AD 90s seems most likely.

believers have learned the Lord's Prayer as part of the basic teaching of the church, a fact well attested by the prayer's inclusion in scores of catechisms across the span of ecclesial history.[3] Yet the importance of teaching new believers the Lord's Prayer also raises questions: Is reciting the Lord's Prayer the same as praying it? Should Christians stick closely to the precise words of the prayer or is it OK to use them as guides for extemporaneous prayer? Can Jesus's words become our words?

Scripture, Prayer, and Pattern

The Lord's Prayer is Scripture, it is a prayer, and it is a pattern for prayer all at the same time. First, the Lord's Prayer is part of Matthew's gospel and as such has a specific role to play in Matthew's goals for writing and in the literary flow of the gospel itself, as part of the four Gospels, as part of the New Testament, and even as part of the larger canon of Scripture.[4] As Scripture, then, it is appropriate for Christians to read the prayer aloud in public worship, to recite the prayer, to sing the prayer, and to use it in other liturgical ways. We considered the structure of Jesus's Sermon on the Mount in the previous chapter, so it is sufficient here to say that the prayer is the fulcrum of the whole sermon and its piety the main point of the greater righteousness that Jesus preached.

Second, the prayer is actually a prayer. That is, this text includes an address to God, implicit adoration of God, and supplication. In keeping with John Bunyan's definition of prayer that we are following in this book, in the Lord's Prayer Christians ask God "for such things as God has promised, or according to his Word, for the good of the church, with submission in faith to the will of God."[5] We don't need Bunyan to tell us that this passage is prayer, but we do need to be reminded that these familiar words of the Bible are prayer before anything else.

Third, the Lord's Prayer is also a pattern. The adverb *houtōs* that begins this sentence often conveys the idea of "way" or "manner."[6] Jesus tells his disciples, "You all pray, then, *in this way* (author's translation)."[7] Luke 11:1–4

---

3. Catechisms are documents used to teach new converts the Christian faith in a systematic way. This way of teaching was ingrained in the early church until the early Middle Ages, and then revived during the Protestant Reformation. Along with the Ten Commandments and the Apostle's Creed, the Lord's Prayer appears in most catechisms. See J. I. Packer and Gary A. Parrett, *Grounded in the Gospel: Building Believers the Old-Fashioned Way* (Grand Rapids: Baker, 2010), 122–23.

4. For more information on why and how to pay attention to such aspects, see Jonathan T. Pennington, *Reading the Gospels Wisely: A Narrative and Theological Introduction* (Grand Rapids: Baker Academic, 2012).

5. See Question 1.

6. See Daniel B. Wallace, *Greek Grammar: Beyond the Basics* (Grand Rapids: Zondervan, 1996), 674–75.

7. *Houtōs oun proseuchesthe hymeis.*

presents an abbreviated version of the prayer in response to a disciple's request, "Lord, teach us to pray." We call this prayer a pattern because Jesus himself sometimes prayed in similar ways, such as addressing God as Father (John 17) and asking God to accomplish his will on earth (Matt. 26), yet in his many recorded prayers Jesus does not simply repeat the words of Matthew 6:9–13 verbatim. The syntax of the passage and the variety of Jesus's own prayers give us great freedom to treat the prayer as a pattern to guide our own prayers.

As a pattern, the Lord's Prayer might be offered as our own prayer or we might expand on elements of the prayer as we think best in a given situation. Some have likened the Lord's Prayer to playing jazz.[8] As a musical form, jazz prizes controlled improvisation. Jazz musicians will often have a simple lead sheet with a song's melody and chord changes to locate them in the same musical space, but will improvise the song, reharmonizing the melody, augmenting the chords, guided by their score. This approach to music differs from classical music, where all members of an orchestra have a detailed score that specifies the exact notes they are to play on their various instruments. As an art form, classical music features much less improvisation than jazz. The Lord's Prayer, so the analogy goes, is like jazz in that the text of Scripture is our lead sheet, supplying the main themes upon which we improvise in our actual prayers. That is, the various phrases of the Lord's Prayer are the melody that we can quote *and* provide the basis for improvisation around their themes. Although he certainly would not have understood the term "jazz," this is the way that Martin Luther has suggested we might pray using the Lord's Prayer as our guide.[9]

Finally, one easy-to-miss feature of the Lord's Prayer is that its petitions are plural, not singular: "*Our* Father . . . give *us* this day *our* daily bread . . . deliver *us* from evil." In keeping with our definition of prayer being "for the good of the church," we recognize that Jesus taught his disciples, and teaches us, that though we may be alone when we pray (Matt. 6:6), we never pray alone. It is easy—quite natural, actually—to become self-focused in our prayers, but self-focused prayer is inconsistent with how Jesus teaches us to pray.

We now want to look at the Lord's Prayer in greater detail in order to consider its various parts and how they fit together to train us to pray well. The prayer begins with an address to the Father, moves to petitions concerning our relationship to him, and then goes on to petitions focusing on

---

8. I do not recall where I first learned this analogy, but it is common in contemporary explanations of the Lord's Prayer. See D. B. Hindmarsh, "The Lord's Prayer as Jazz," https://pbcc.org/ArchivedTeachings/m_retreats/2018/FridayLordsPrayer.pdf.

9. Martin Luther, *A Simple Way to Pray*, in *Little Prayer Book, 1522 and A Simple Way to Pray, 1535: The Annotated Luther Study Edition*, eds. Mary Jane Haemig and Eric Lund (Minneapolis: Fortress Press, 2017). Luther wrote this small work of practical theology for his barber and suggested using the Ten Commandments, the Lord's Prayer, and the Apostles Creed as a framework for prayer.

our relationships and needs. I will follow this pattern in the exposition below, using the King James text because of its familiarity.

Praying to Our Heavenly Father

Our Father, which art in heaven (Matt. 6:9)
Jesus taught his disciples to approach God with reverent closeness by addressing him as "our Father." Sometimes those teaching this passage suggest that calling God "Father" was unheard of among first-century Jews and thus Jesus's address to "our Father" was unique. Studies of Jewish worship after the exile and documents surviving from this period, like the Dead Sea Scrolls, show us that faithful Jews in Jesus's day would indeed address God as "Father" in their prayers, acknowledging his unique role as creator, king, and redeemer of Israel.[10] What is also clear is that Jesus's relationship as the "only begotten Son" of the Father was unlike any of his contemporaries; he alone is the Son who knows and reveals the Father (Matt. 11:25–27) and he invites his followers to address God is the same distinctive way that he prayed.[11]

As we saw in Question 4, one message of the gospel is that God has adopted those who trust him by faith. This prayer reminds us of the Father's particular, intentional love toward us.[12] Addressing God as Father reminds us what sort of father he is: namely, that he is patient (Luke 15) and merciful (2 Cor. 1:3–4). Prayer may be the best place for us to experience the Holy Spirit's reassurance that we are indeed God's adopted children (Gal. 4:6; Rom. 8:15). Although we may intentionally or absentmindedly depersonalize God, or project distorted pictures of what it means for him to be a father, Jesus corrects us and invites us to address God in this way.

In a beautiful complement, Jesus invites his followers to pray to our Father "in heaven." If the language of "Father" emphasizes God's nearness and care, then remembering that this Father is "in heaven" evokes reverential awe (Eccl. 5:1–2). God is majestic. He sees what is done in secret as easily as he sees what happens on the street corners. He is everywhere and is present to act upon our requests. He is completely powerful so that no external force hinders him from acting. He is in heaven and knows how best to answer. He is sufficient unto himself, needing nothing, having all resources to answer every request. Before we ask anything in prayer, we look upward, beyond our present circumstances, with affection to an all-powerful, loving Father, who will listen to us. Practically, then, we might begin every prayer with this simple address, fighting

---

10. For a helpful survey of the discussion, see David Crump, *Knocking on Heaven's Door: A New Testament Theology of Petitionary Prayer* (Grand Rapids: Baker Academic, 2006), 97–104.
11. Compare Matthew 26:39; Mark 14:36; Luke 11:2; and John 17:1–26. In this last passage, Jesus addresses God as "Father" six times.
12. See John 1:11–13; Ephesians 1:3–6; 1 John 3:1.

the tendency to rush ahead to the needs of the moment, pausing to recollect the one to whom we are speaking, being reminded of his glory and nearness.[13]

Seeking God's Honor

Hallowed be thy name. Thy kingdom come. Thy will be done in earth, as it is in heaven. (Matt. 6:9–10)
Following the address, the Lord's Prayer begins with three petitions directed toward God and the disciple's life under God's rule. We might recognize a priority for prayer in this ordering: begin by acknowledging God before asking about ourselves. At first glance, these petitions seem to focus exclusively on God, but they clearly involve us too. These petitions ask God to stir us to honor him as he brings his reign as king to bear on earth. In the Greek text of the prayer, these entreaties show a pattern that is easy to miss in translation; they are imperative verbs of request and are arranged in a passive-active-passive voice sequence.[14]

In the first petition, we seek God's honor: "May your name be treated as holy."[15] The familiar expression "hallowed be" is a fine, poetic translation that may leave some who recite the prayer puzzled. What does it mean for God's name to be "hallowed"? Who, exactly, is to treat God's name in this way? In the Jewish mindset of Jesus's disciples, shaped as it was by the Ten Commandments, it would be hard not to connect this first petition with the third commandment, "You shall not take the name of the LORD your God in vain" (Exod. 20:7). Yet Jesus's prayer goes further, encouraging disciples not merely to avoid vain or "empty" uses of God's name but to treat it as sacred. The idea in this petition is that treating the Father's name as sacred ("hallowing" it) is the same as treating the Father as sacred. Among whom is the Father's name to be regarded as sacred, or treated as holy? By everyone, but particularly by the ones offering this prayer. As we noted in an earlier chapter, it can be difficult for sinners to honor God as he deserves, but this petition offers us great encouragement: the first thing we ask God to do is to help us honor him as he ought to be honored.

In the second petition, we seek God's rule. "Let your kingdom arrive."[16] The language of "kingdom" (*basileia*) is appropriate, but it seems so linked in modern minds to a geopolitical territory that we can miss its importance. We can look on a map and locate the kingdom of Saudi Arabia or the kingdom of Denmark, but where can we see the kingdom of heaven? Jesus taught his

---

13. Interestingly, one of the early prayers recorded in Acts recounts Christians addressing God as "Sovereign Lord [*Despota*]" (Acts 4:24).
14. *Hagiasthētō . . . elthetō . . . genēthētō*. Wallace identifies these verbs as "imperatives of request" addressed from an inferior to a superior. See Wallace, *Greek Grammar*, 487–88.
15. *Hagiasthētō to onoma sou.*
16. *Elthetō hē basileia sou.*

disciples to pray that God's kingdom would come, and Jesus is the one who brings God's kingdom to earth (Matt. 10:7). He tells his disciples to "seek first the kingdom of God and his righteousness" (Matt. 6:33). He warns his disciples that "whoever does not receive the kingdom of God like a child shall not enter it" (Luke 18:17). He compares the kingdom to a hidden treasure (Matt. 13:44) and hidden leaven (Luke 13:20–21), and warns how difficult it is for those who trust in their own wealth to enter it (Mark 10:25).

Here, "kingdom" is not a place but a rule, God's rightful kingly reign. Asking for the Father's kingdom to "come" or "arrive" is tantamount to asking God to redirect the allegiance of rebellious sinners away from the self-destructive anarchy that has marked us as rebels since Eden and to turn it back to its only fitting object, himself. It is asking him to turn *our* hearts to yield to his rightful rule. George Ladd offers a helpful summary of this petition: "This prayer is a petition for God to reign, to manifest His kingly sovereignty and power, to put to flight every enemy of righteousness and of His divine rule, that God alone may be King over all the world."[17]

In the third petition, we seek God's plan. "May your will come to pass."[18] This petition is really inseparable from the two that have come before it, for it is *how* God's name is treated as holy and *how* his kingdom comes, by believers yielding our will to God's. In this petition, disciples ask God to align our hearts with his intentions. Genuine disciples recognize that God's will can never truly be thwarted: "Whatever the LORD pleases, he does, in heaven and on earth, in the seas and all deeps" (Ps. 135:6). Yet, as those who have rebelled against God's reign, we recognize how often we prioritize our will over God's desires. Asking that God's will "be done" or "come to pass" does not somehow make God's will contingent upon human approval; rather, it seeks to align our desires with the Father's desires. It expresses a disciple's allegiance to God's kingdom and recognition of his name.

The theme of present and future submission binds these first three petitions. Disciples defer to God's honor over our own fame, seek God's rule now, and submit to God's plans. Though these are discrete, godward petitions, each is a systematic reversal of the curse of sin. In Eden, Adam and Eve prioritized their will over God's will and sought to be on par with God rather than yield to his rule, and thus dishonored his name. In the kingdom that Jesus announces and inaugurates, the curse of Eden is undone. Though textually there are three petitions, in essence they are one single petition expressed in three ways: "In our lives and in the world, may the curse of sin be broken and God be honored and obeyed once more." Jesus teaches his disciples to pray in

---

17. George Eldon Ladd, *The Gospel of the Kingdom: Scriptural Studies in the Kingdom of God* (Grand Rapids: Eerdmans, 1959), 21.
18. *Genēthētō to thelēma sou.*

light of the present fulfillment of God's work, but anticipates a coming final fulfillment of the kingdom as well.

This eschatological emphasis sheds light on one important question, that of how the three phrases about God's name, kingdom, and will relate to the final phrase "in earth as it is in heaven." Though it is too late to change the common English wording, a better translation of this phrase is "as in heaven, so upon earth."[19] Because the King James text places a comma in the middle of this phrase, many English Bible readers assume the phrase goes with the third petition only. Yet "as in heaven, so upon earth" serves as a fitting conclusion to all three requests:

"May your name be treated as holy,"

"Let your kingdom arrive,"   "as in heaven, so upon the earth."

"May your will come to pass,"

Seeking God's Help

Give us this day our daily bread. And forgive us our debts, as we forgive our debtors. And lead us not into temptation, but deliver us from evil. (Matt. 6:11–13)

Petitions four through six focus on the disciple's needs. These supplications remind us that we depend on God to sustain us physically and spiritually. The first of these petitions is "Give us today the bread we need to survive." Even as the earlier request for God's name to be "hallowed" pointed disciples back to the Ten Commandments, so asking for "daily bread" reminds us of God's daily provision of manna for Israel during their time in the wilderness.[20] This petition teaches us to ask our Father who is in heaven to care for us as his children by reminding us of a time when God did just that for his children Israel.

Understanding this request precisely is a bit tricky because the adjective "daily" used in relation to "bread" only appears in this prayer in Luke and Matthew and in the *Didache*, which also quotes the prayer, and nowhere else in the Bible or in literature.[21] Several possibilities exist. First, it could mean "on/upon which we exist" and thus "daily" means something like "the bread

---

19. *Hōs en ouranō kai epi gēs.* See Jonathan T. Pennington, *The Sermon on the Mount and Human Flourishing: A Theological Commentary* (Grand Rapids: Baker Academic, 2017), 223–24, for a survey of scholarship and thoughtful reflection on this phrase.

20. See Exodus 16.

21. *Ton arton hēmōn ton epiousion dos hēmin sēmeron.* See BDAG.

we need in order to survive." It might also mean "for the following day," and the request is that God would give us today the bread we need for tomorrow. Finally, the saying might simply mean "for today," thus, "Give us today the bread we need for today."[22] What remains unchanged in this petition is the disciple's request for God to provide for his physical needs and for the needs of other disciples—remembering the petition is in the second person plural— a tacit acknowledgment that in ourselves, we lack the resources to survive independent from God.

Next, disciples pray for God's spiritual provision by seeking forgiveness of our sins, expressed here as "debts" (*opheilēmata*): "and forgive us our debts as we forgive our debtors." Though our sins are forgiven in Christ, disciples seek God's ongoing forgiveness in prayer because we continue to sin. This petition ought to be a comfort for us as we realize the ongoing need to be experientially reconciled to our Father in heaven. It should also challenge us, for Jesus teaches us to seek forgiveness with the condition: "as we forgive our debtors." The small conjunction "as" (*hōs*) expresses comparison and is very important. As we will see in greater detail in Question 19, the disposition of the one praying matters. In fact, this petition helps bind several of our questions about Jesus's teaching on prayer together. Prayer is not a magical spell that forces God to do our bidding, nor is it a self-focused litany of requests that ignores the needs of others, nor can it request blessings for us that we are not willing to extend to others. Consider a paraphrase: "Father . . . to the extent that I have forgiven those who have sinned against me, in that way, forgive my sins." This is a challenging petition, not because its wording is tricky but because the righteous disposition it requires is so foreign to our natural inclinations. Through this request, Jesus teaches those who would follow after him that true disciples recognize their need to receive and extend forgiveness for sins committed by and against them.

The prayer ends with a request for spiritual protection: "do not lead us into temptation, but rescue us from evil." Three considerations affect the way we understand what Jesus is teaching disciples to pray here. First, is Jesus speaking of "temptation" or "testing"? Second, is he speaking of testing/tempting in general or more specifically? Third, does Jesus teach us to seek deliverance from "harm," "evil," or "the evil one," i.e., the devil? We consider each question in turn because they have important implications for the way in which disciples pray.

The noun translated as "temptation" (*peirasmon*), along with its related verb (*peirazō*), can convey both "testing" and "tempting" depending on the context of the passage.[23] In brief, God "tests" disciples for their own good, to

---

22. See Pennington, *Sermon on the Mount*, 225 n. 38 for a survey of current discussion.
23. In Matthew 16:1, the "Pharisees and Sadducees came to *test* (*peirazontes*) [Jesus]," by asking for some heavenly sign, yet readers of Matthew's gospel know that the Pharisees had

reveal to them experientially the soundness of their faith. Our own "desires" (*epithymias*) tempt us to seek satisfaction apart from God. Satan "tempts" disciples to entice them to their spiritual ruin, to alienate them experientially from the blessings of sonship with the Father. What is clear in Matthew's gospel is that Jesus's disciples will endure times of testing because of their allegiance to their Lord (Matt. 5:10–12; 10:17–18), who was himself tested. Since Jesus himself says that his followers will face testing, it would be odd for him to teach his disciples to pray that they not experience testing. Matthew's readers recall that the Spirit led Jesus into the wilderness to be "tempted" (*peirasthēnai*) by the devil (Matt. 4:1), clearly an attempt at enticement to sin. Is Jesus teaching his disciples to pray that God protect them during similar times? Jesus's wilderness experience shows that he is the greater Adam who successfully endured the devil's traps, something the first Adam failed to do. Jesus's disciples do not endure temptation to the same extent or for the same outcome. Considering Jesus's warning in Gethsemane (Matt. 26:41) that his followers "watch and pray that you may not enter into temptation," this reading may have merit, but whether it is the best approach or not, the emphasis seems to envision "temptation" rather than "testing."[24]

Avoiding "temptation," though, is only part of the petition. Disciples ask for the Father's active deliverance or rescue from "evil." How should we understand "evil" (*tou ponērou*) in Matthew 6:13? Is Jesus speaking of "evil" in general? Is Jesus describing the harm that we experience from evil?[25] Might Jesus teach us to pray that God deliver us from the presence of the devil? In light of the links between Matthew 4:1 and Matthew 26:41, this reading is possible. Because the Greek text in Matthew 6:13 has a definite article, the NIV translates this petition as "deliver us from the evil one"; however, use of the title "the evil one" for Satan has scant support in Judaism, though it is probably the common reading among New Testament scholars today.[26] In this light, it seems better to understand the petition as a general request for God to

---

already determined to kill Jesus (Matt. 12:14). In this context, we might understand "test" as "entrap." In 1 Peter 1:6–7, *peirasmois* are God-ordained "trials" that reveal the genuine character of a believer's faith. The passage that shows how flexible this word can be is James 1:12–15, especially verses 13–14. Here, when a believer is being "tempted" (*peirazomenos*) to sin, they cannot blame God for "tempting" (*peirazomai*) them, because God "tempts no one" (*peirazei*); that person's own desires are the source of temptation.

24. Pennington, *Sermon on the Mount*, 227–28, suggests that "testing" is in view and points to the great eschatological judgment of Matthew 24:4–29 as the period of testing. While there is an eschatological emphasis in the prayer, it seems less clear that this specific period of testing is meant.

25. John Nolland, *The Gospel of Matthew*, New International Greek Testament Commentary (Grand Rapids: Eerdmans, 2005), 293.

26. Ulrich Luz, *Matthew 1–7: A Commentary on Matthew 1–7*, rev. ed., Hermeneia (Minneapolis: Fortress Press, 2007), 323.

see us through the evil that generally attends temptations or to guard us from Satan's attacks.[27]

In sum, the final petition of the Lord's Prayer teaches disciples to ask God for ongoing spiritual protection. Taken together, the final three petitions train disciples to be true citizens of the kingdom, those who rely on God to sustain and protect them. Asking regularly that God would care for us and other believers in these ways reinforce the fact of dependence. Though addressing another matter, John Calvin's comments about the foolishness of not recognizing our weaknesses seem fitting:

> Unless our own weaknesses are regularly displayed to us, we easily overestimate our own virtue, being by nature inclined to attribute all good things to our own doing. We don't doubt that our virtue will remain whole and unconquered in the face of whatever difficulties may come. Thus, we're drawn into a foolish and inflated view of our flesh. And then, trusting our flesh, we brazenly exalt ourselves before God Himself, acting as if our own abilities are sufficient without his grace.[28]

Summary

The poetic words of the King James Version of the Lord's Prayer are deeply embedded in many minds and in Western culture. Jesus was a man of prayer. His followers noticed this aspect of his devotion and sought his instruction. Rather than withhold this teaching, assuming for himself a private piety that none could emulate, Jesus made prayer the focal point of his teaching about the nature of what it means to be his disciple. Jesus's disciples pray. They pray as their Lord teaches them, and the way that they pray is itself part of the path of transformation. Though we have spent some time deciding the best way to understand some of the petitions, the prayer is beautifully simple. Jesus does not give directions on when or how often disciples ought to pray, but rather that whenever we pray, we are to pray in submission to our Father in heaven and to ask him to care for our needs and those of others, both physical and spiritual. The very way that Jesus teaches us to ask helps form us into the kind of people that he calls us to be: people who honor God's name, submit to his rule and will, and seek his provision, his mercy, and his protection. Whether we pray these words exactly, without variation, or expand upon one or more petitions, the Lord's Prayer is a reliable and beautiful framework for all prayer.

---

27. Luz, *Matthew*, 323, suggests that 2 Timothy 4:18 serves as a commentary on this petition of the Lord's Prayer: "The Lord will rescue me from every evil deed and bring me safely into his heavenly kingdom. To him be the glory forever and ever. Amen."
28. John Calvin, *A Little Book on the Christian Life*, trans. Aaron Clay Denlinger and Burk Parsons (Orlando: Reformation Trust, 2017), 60.

REFLECTION QUESTIONS

1. In what ways can the Lord's Prayer serve as a template for your prayers?

2. What is the "kingdom" that we ask about in this prayer?

3. How does the Lord's Prayer form disciples who trust and submit to God?

4. Which petition is the most natural for you to make of God? Why?

5. Which petition is the most difficult for you to pray? Why?

QUESTION 19

Must Christians Forgive Others Before They Can Pray (Matthew 6:14–15)?

As we continue thinking about Jesus's teaching on prayer in his Sermon on the Mount, we encounter this statement that comes directly after the Lord's Prayer:

> For if you forgive others their trespasses, your heavenly Father will also forgive you, but if you do not forgive others their trespasses, neither will your Father forgive your trespasses. (Matt. 6:14–15)

The text immediately reminds us of what we have just heard Jesus teach about prayer in 6:12: "And forgive us our debts, as we forgive our debtors." Writing in the 200s, Origen, an early Christian theologian, took this text at face value: "Nor is it possible for one praying to gain forgiveness of sins unless from his heart he forgives the transgressor and thinks his brother worthy to gain pardon."[1] Origen reflected on praying "as we ought." Was he correct in this reading? What is the relationship between our willingness to forgive and God's willingness to hear and act on our prayers? Why did Jesus use this aspect of his prayer as a condition and not something more practical, say giving bread to others or not tempting others? Must Christians forgive others before they can pray?

The Ethical Priority

It might be better to ask our question in this way: Must Christians forgive others who have sinned against them before God will answer their own

---

1. Origen, *Origen: An Exhortation to Martyrdom, Prayer, and Selected Works*, ed. Richard J. Payne, trans. Rowan A. Greer, The Classics of Western Spirituality (Mahwah, NJ: Paulist Press, 1979), 97.

prayers for forgiveness? Yes. Matthew 6:14–15 takes the form of conditional sentences in Greek: "For if you forgive" (*ean gar aphēte*) . . . "but if you do not forgive" (*ean de mē aphēte*).[2] Conditional sentences use "if . . . then" statements to indicate that a situation may or may not happen. In this passage, the condition is "if you forgive . . . then your heavenly Father will forgive you" and "If you do not forgive . . . neither will your Father forgive your trespasses." Luz is right to point out the intentional parallelism of this memorable statement.[3] Jesus's message is challenging, but straightforward: his disciples must forgive the sins that others have committed against them before they can expect God to answer their own prayers for forgiveness.

Jesus's statement also prioritizes our ethical response to other people over other responses. The link with the fifth petition of the Lord's Prayer is obvious, and it is interesting that the text mentions this petition exclusively. On the one hand, were he to condition forgiveness on our physical care for others or perhaps on doing them no spiritual harm, we might agree with his conditions more readily. Rather than calling on his followers to feed the hungry or avoid leading others into temptation to sin, Jesus requires what may be the most difficult response: forsaking our natural bent for revenge.

Were this teaching found only in Matthew 6:14–15, we might feel easier about disregarding it, but Jesus taught it elsewhere. Mark 11:25 reads, "And whenever you stand praying, forgive, if you have anything against anyone, so that your Father also who is in heaven may forgive you your trespasses." Though the wording varies between passages, the ideas are clearly the same: we ought not to expect God to receive our confession of sin and act to restore us to a right relational nearness while we remain consciously unwilling to forgive others. I say "consciously unwilling" because it best captures the sense of these passages. These texts do not create a situation where we might have some unconscious grudge that serves as a barrier to our prayers, nor does it mean that we must probe our memories to find some long-forgotten trespass that we overlooked at an earlier time, for it would be practically impossible for our finite minds to remember every offense we have accumulated (although some people seem quite talented in such memories). No, Jesus is teaching that we may not hold grudges against those who have wronged us. Neither should this passage convince us that such forgiveness is a prerequisite to justification. In the Sermon on the Mount, Jesus is describing the greater righteousness required of those in his kingdom, not of those on the outside. The "trespasses"

---

2. The use of *ean* with a verb in the subjunctive mood (*aphēte*) typically indicates a third-class condition in which varying degrees of certainty exist.
3. Ulrich Luz, *Matthew 1–7: A Commentary on Matthew 1–7*, rev. ed., Hermeneia (Minneapolis: Fortress Press, 2007), 327. "The logion has the form of a two-part *mashal* with excellent parallelism."

of Matthew 6:12 seem to be sins committed by Jesus's followers that disrupt our sense of relational nearness to God.

A Difficult Teaching

This word is surely hard because our natural impulse is to withhold forgiveness and to exact revenge. The current "cancel culture" movement illustrates this point. In a politically correct climate obsessed with words and perceptions, to say something that popular consensus deems insensitive or abhorrent can lead to "cancellation," a public shunning. Say something out of step with current orthodoxy and you can expect tremendous social consequences delivered with zeal. Yet a cancel culture is antithetical to the gospel that recognizes the existence of sin and preaches forgiveness and restoration to sinners.[4]

It is worth asking why else this text makes many Christians feel a bit uncomfortable. The thought process of some readers might go like this: "I didn't do anything to earn God's forgiveness, I simply exercised faith in Christ. How can it be right for me to have to 'do something' to earn God's hearing of my prayer for forgiveness?" Jesus's words can seem like a form of legalism, a stipulation, prayer with a price tag. Jesus is indeed calling his disciples to "do something" that is out of the ordinary: imitate their heavenly Father in extending forgiveness. The demands of discipleship here are deep indeed.

Summary

Jesus teaches us that we must forgive those who have trespassed against us before we confess our own sins to God and seek his forgiveness. Early in the church's history, the theologian Origen recognized that this passage, following immediately after the Lord's Prayer in Matthew's gospel, requires believers to prepare themselves for prayer by practicing the gospel that they profess. No disciples who would presume to call upon an adopting, heavenly Father to forgive their trespasses can persist in withholding forgiveness to others who have sinned against them. No, the hard call of those who would follow Jesus is to pray from a heart overflowing with mercy, which is the same heart of the Father.

---

4. A clarifying word may be pastorally helpful. Forsaking *revenge* for forgiveness is not identical to abandoning *justice*. Those who have "trespassed" against us might, in due course, face judicial consequences for their sins. A willingness to forgive a transgressor does not mean a refusal to identify sin or to provide honest testimony in such circumstances. Nor does forgiveness require an immediate restoration of trust where trust has been broken. Neither does forgiveness mean an identical restoration to circumstances before the transgression occurred. Rather, it entails us extending forgiveness to those who have legitimately wronged us.

REFLECTION QUESTIONS

1. Why is it so difficult for us to forgive sins that others have committed against us?

2. What might an unwillingness to forgive the trespasses of others indicate about our own hearts?

3. In what way is Matthew 6:14–15 conditional?

4. What might Jesus's choice of forgiveness over physical or spiritual care teach us about the gospel?

5. Whom do you need to forgive in response to Jesus's teaching?

Why Don't We Always Receive What We Request in Prayer (Matthew 7:7–8)?

The thrust of this book thus far has been to encourage Christians to pray. In this chapter, we consider two seemingly incompatible ideas: Christians should pray expecting God to answer yet recognize that God sometimes chooses not to answer our prayers in the exact way we ask them. How can Christians pray expectantly if God might say no? Might the fact that God could say no or leave a prayer unanswered undermine our confidence in prayer?

Christians Should Pray Expectantly

In Matthew 7:7–11, Jesus encourages us to pray expectantly.

> Ask, and it will be given to you; seek, and you will find; knock, and it will be opened to you. For everyone who asks receives, and the one who seeks finds, and to the one who knocks it will be opened. Or which one of you, if his son asks him for bread, will give him a stone? Or if he asks for a fish, will give him a serpent? If you then, who are evil, know how to give good gifts to your children, how much more will your Father who is in heaven give good things to those who ask him!

Jesus offers three imperatives for his disciples regarding prayer: "ask" (*aiteite*), "seek" (*zēteite*), and "knock" (*krouete*). In each case, the disciples should expect a positive response: they will be given what they ask for, they will find what they seek, and the door will be opened to those who knock.[1] According to Luz, the three verbs "have a religious dimension in Jewish-Christian usage.

---

1. The responses follow a passive-active-passive voice pattern.

One asks or seeks God, one knocks on the 'gates of mercy.'"[2] A double parable about imperfect human fathers being willing to give that which is necessary to their children illustrates from a greater-to-lesser argument that Jesus's Father, whom we have been taught to address in prayer in the Sermon on the Mount, stands ready to answer. Even our experience with earthly fathers is inadequate for God's willingness to hear and answer our prayers. One interpretive key may lie in the parable, for here the child asks his father for "fish" or "bread," those things which are necessary for life. Such a view is in keeping with our request for "daily bread" in the Lord's Prayer earlier in the sermon. In light of the great confidence Jesus suggests should characterize prayer, we want to consider why we don't always receive what we ask for in prayer.

Common Answers for Unanswered Prayer

Every culture and age proposes to answer the mystery of unanswered prayer. Before exploring the chapter's question exegetically, it may be helpful to mention common reasons contemporary Christians give for unanswered prayer.[3] Some believers suggest that prayers go unanswered because we have not prayed "correctly." That is, our prayers do not follow a specific template or format. Failing to address God as "Father" or omitting "in Jesus's name" from our prayers voids them, according to this perspective. Some believe that God answers prayers in three ways: yes, no, and not yet. Others believe God answers every prayer and that speaking of "unanswered prayers" is illusory. We will evaluate these common reasons at the end of the chapter.

We Hinder Our Prayers by Cherishing Our Sin

We must pray expectantly, for Jesus encourages us to do so, but we ought also to consider several biblical explanations for unanswered prayers.

> I cried to him with my mouth, and high praise was on my tongue.
> If I had cherished iniquity in my heart, the LORD would not have listened.
> But truly God has listened; he has attended to the voice of my prayer.
> Blessed be God, because he has not rejected my prayer or
> removed his steadfast love from me! (Ps. 66:17–20)

In this anonymous psalm, the writer praises God for hearing his prayer of praise, but envisions a scenario where God might have done otherwise: "If I

---

2. Ulrich Luz, *Matthew 1–7: A Commentary on Matthew 1–7*, rev. ed., Hermeneia (Minneapolis: Fortress Press, 2007), 358.
3. These answers are so common that I feel the freedom to avoid footnoting examples; if you are reading this book, you have heard someone offer one of these reasons for unanswered prayer.

had cherished iniquity in my heart, the LORD would not have listened." The ESV's rendering of verse 18, "If I had cherished" (*'im-rā'î'-ṭî*), points to an internal volitional decision to "regard" or "choose to look at" something,[4] in this case, "iniquity." The psalmist is not describing the mere presence of inward sin, for in that case God would hear no prayers. Rather, he seems to be describing a situation where people choose to look upon their iniquity favorably, preferring to regard their sin over righteousness or even over the one to whom they are praying. The psalmist is describing a form of idolatry. Here, one's inward disposition toward sin affects that person's prayers. To "cherish" or "regard" (NASB) iniquity or wickedness may dispose God not to listen to our prayers. We might ask a further question: What allowed the psalmist to know that God had heard his prayers? Verse 20 indicates that the twofold experience of God's steadfast love (*ḥě'sěḏ*), sometimes described as covenant loyalty, and answered prayer (the situation of "has not rejected") gave the psalmist confidence.

We Hinder Our Prayers by Our Sinful Actions

Sin, allowed to take root, hinders prayer. The Lord, through the prophet Isaiah, warned the people of Israel directly that their wickedness hindered their prayers:

> When you spread out your hands,
> I will hide my eyes from you;
> even though you make many prayers,
> I will not listen;
> your hands are full of blood. (Isa. 1:15)

This warning came in the context of an indictment against Israel for going through the motions of ritual worship while forsaking Yahweh (Isa. 1:4), evidenced by their moral failure to pursue justice for the marginalized members of Jewish society, namely orphans and widows (Isa. 1:23). Israel maintained the outward motions of worship: sacrifices continued, festivals celebrated, assemblies convened, prayers offered; yet God would not abide it.

We Hinder Our Prayers by Our Doubts

Turning to the New Testament, the epistle of James furthers our discussion. "If any of you lacks wisdom, let him ask God, who gives generously to all without reproach, and it will be given him. But let him ask in faith, with no doubting. . . . For that person must not suppose that he will receive anything from the Lord" (James 1:5–7). James echoes Jesus's confidence in prayer. God is the giver of good gifts (1:17); here "wisdom" is that gift believers should

---

4. See BDB, "*r'h*."

ask for. Wisdom allows believers to see blessing in the midst of their suffering (1:2–4), a perspective that God delights to impart. Yet in the midst of confident prayer, James describes a situation in which one might ask for wisdom yet not receive it. As in Psalm 66, the reason James gives for unanswered prayer lies with the one asking.

What does it mean that we should ask "in faith, with no doubting"? Tempting as it is to compare "faith" in James 1:6 with the famously provocative passage on "faith" in 2:14–26, a faith that shows its genuineness through works, the role of faith in regard to prayer appears to involve someone unwilling to trust God completely.[5] James describes this person as "double-minded" (*dipsychos*) and "unstable" (*akatastatos*), like a wind-driven wave. James's point is that to ask something of God, while actively doubting that God can or will actually answer the request, reveals a divided loyalty. In James's view, divided loyalty is no different from disloyalty.[6] Our disposition to trust God or not to trust God affects our prayers.

We Hinder Our Prayers by Our Wrong Motives

Prayers that we never offer, or prayers offered from selfish motives, remain unanswered. "You do not have because you do not ask. You ask and do not receive because you ask wrongly, to spend it on your passions" (James 4:2–3). In James 3:13–4:10, the author considers the way individual ambition affects prayer within a congregation.[7] The situation he addresses is a mess, marked by "quarrels" and "fights" driven by selfish desires—not an idyllic picture. James describes the root of strife within a specific church, yet his description is applicable for *any* church: competing "passions" (*hēdonōn*). Different things gave pleasure to different members of the congregation, and these competing pursuits of individual worldly "passions" produced conflict. James uses strong language of rebuke, calling the parties "adulterous people," accusing them of covetousness and of being friends of the world (and thereby enemies of God). Members' "strong desires" (*epithymeite*), shaped by personal ambition and devoid of the Holy Spirit's leading (3:15), were tearing this church apart and hindering the church's prayers.

Looking at James's indictment backwards, the factious congregation seems to be praying without effect: "You ask and do not receive, because you ask wrongly, to spend it on your passions" (4:3). "You ask wrongly" (*kakōs aiteisthe*) might also be translated "you all ask *wickedly*," indicating that the problem with their prayers is moral, not structural. That is, the things these members were asking for in prayer were motivated by their competing,

---

5. Peter H. Davids, *The Epistle of James*, New International Greek Testament Commentary (Grand Rapids: Eerdmans, 1982), 73.

6. Davids, *James*, 75.

7. Nearly all of the verbs and pronouns in this passage are second-person plural references.

worldly desires, and thus the wrong things to ask for. It is not that the *way* they were asking was wrong and if they merely changed the form of their prayer, then they would have received what they sought from God. Rather, it was that the *substance* of what they sought was wrong—worldly, opposed to God—and they should not have been shocked when God did not answer them. This warning reminds us of the relational nature of prayer. Asking earnestly for a wicked desire or from selfish motives does not move God to fulfill our wishes. It also seems that some in the church were so caught up in their individual pursuits of "desires" that they simply failed to pray: "You do not have because you do not ask" (4:2). There is, however, hope for restored communion with God and renewed confidence in prayer.

Though not necessarily a scripted sequence, James offers a path for restoration. James grounds his path in the "meekness of wisdom" (3:13) by quoting Proverbs 3:34, "God opposes the proud but gives grace to the humble" (James 4:6). This text from the Hebrew Bible introduces a series of restorative movements that Christians whose desires have become entrapped by the world, and thus whose prayers are unanswered, should take:[8] "submit" (*hypotagēte*) to God, "resist" (*antistēte*) the devil, "approach" (or "draw near to") (*engisate*) God, metaphorically "cleanse" (*katharisate*) sin-stained hands, "sanctify" (*hagnisate*) double-minded (divided) hearts, "lament" (*talaipōrēsate*) and "mourn" (*penthēsate*) and "weep" (*klausate*), "turn" (*metatrapētō*) laughter and joy into mourning and dejection. All of these actions are summed up in the command to "humble (*tapeinōthēte*) yourselves before the Lord, and he will exalt you" (4:10). James is describing a path to restored interpersonal fellowship with Christians and with God, and this latter renewal also entails restored prayer.

We Hinder Our Prayers by Our Disordered Relationships

A final way that we might hinder our own prayers involves another kind of disordered relationship, this between husbands and wives.[9] In 1 Peter 3:7, the apostle warns husbands, specifically, that their prayers might be "hindered" or "thwarted" (*enkoptesthai*) if they fail to honor their wives appropriately.[10] The idea seems to be that a husband's prayers might go unanswered based upon his attitude toward his wife. Peter's description of wife as "the weaker vessel" reflects a Mediterranean view of physical strength and weakness. Within the context of a household code, that is, instructions given to

---

8. The restorative steps are a series of ten aorist imperative verbs in the Greek text.
9. Achtemeier suggests that the passage might include all women living within the household, not wives only, based on Peter's use of the adjective *tō gynaikeiō* rather than the typical noun for wife/wives. The larger context of 3:1–7, though, seems clearly focused on both parties within a marriage. Paul J. Achtemeier, *1 Peter: A Commentary on First Peter*, Hermeneia (Minneapolis: Fortress Press, 1996), 217.
10. The verb is passive, indicating that it is God who is hindering the husband's prayers.

wives and husbands, Peter tells husbands to be living "with your wives in an understanding way" (*synoikountes kata gnōsin*).[11] This "understanding way" or "knowledge" is that husbands ought to be honoring them "since they are heirs with you of the grace of life." This view of physical difference and spiritual equality is rooted in the created order (Gen. 1:27) and reaffirmed in the gospel (Gal. 3:26–29). Husbands who refuse to honor their wives according to God's design should expect unanswered prayers.

The Mystery of Prayer

While Scripture reveals multiple reasons that God might leave our prayers unanswered, and several of these reasons involve sin on our part, we must recognize that sometimes God does not answer our prayers because our prayers are contrary to his plan. Jesus's experience in Gethsemane illustrates this difficult truth. Matthew 26 and Luke 22 recount the scene. Jesus withdraws from his disciples, kneels, and prays: "Father, if you are willing, remove this cup from me. Nevertheless, not my will, but yours, be done" (Luke 22:42). As we consider in the next chapter, God did not remove the cup of his wrath; Jesus drank it in full. Yet, in God's inscrutable plan, it was by means of this unanswered prayer that Jesus "was declared to be the Son of God in power according to the Spirit of holiness by his resurrection from the dead" (Rom. 1:4). In a similar way, Paul's thrice-repeated request that Jesus restore him and remove his "thorn" went unanswered in the way he hoped; yet he received consolation that his suffering provided the ascended Lord occasion to display his power in a way different from what Paul had thought best: "My grace is sufficient for you, for my power is made perfect in weakness" (2 Cor. 12:9). In these cases, God said no to sincere requests, but he did not abandon Paul or Jesus, showing his power and wisdom in ways better than what they sought. At times, God may say no to our requests because his plans for us are better than what we know to ask.

Sometimes God may reveal his answers to our prayer to others before he reveals them to us. Prior to the examples of Ananias and the elders of Antioch in Acts 9 and 13, respectively, the enigmatic example of Zechariah's conversation with the angel of the Lord illustrates this principle: "Then the angel of the LORD said, 'O LORD of hosts, how long will you have no mercy on Jerusalem and the cities of Judah, against which you have been angry these seventy years?' And the LORD answered gracious and comforting words to the angel who talked with me" (Zech. 1:12–13). The angel then reassures Zechariah of God's love for Jerusalem. Similar to this instance, the answer to King Hezekiah's prayer for rescue from Assyria comes through the prophet Isaiah: "Then Isaiah the son of Amoz sent to Hezekiah, saying, 'Thus says the LORD, the God of Israel: Your prayer to me about Sennacherib king of Assyria I have

---

11. "Living with" is a present tense participle.

heard'" (2 Kings 19:20). These instances show us that sometimes God uses others to assure us that God is present and answering our prayers. They also indicate that sometimes God might make us aware of the way he is working in the lives of others, and that we have a role to play in communicating this work to them. This last aspect is why participation in the life of the Christian community is so vital, for God may use others to confirm his ministry and he may use us to encourage others that he has heard their prayers.

Summary

We need to acknowledge the wonder that God answers *any* of our prayers. We began this chapter by listing some common reasons contemporary Christians give for why our prayers might go unanswered, why we do not always receive what we ask for in prayer. In light of our biblical reflection, we can dismiss the notions that all prayers are always answered or that failure to receive what we ask is simply a matter of asking with bad form. Bad concepts like these provide no comfort because they provide no path for restoration. However, when we cherish sin, harbor doubt, or pursue selfish motives, we should not be surprised if God refuses to answer us when we pray; in these situations God may refuse to answer our prayers for a season, so long as we persist in open rebellion to him, but there is hope that he will listen and act if we repent and trust him once more. But this knowledge of good theology may offer small comfort when we have pleaded with the Father to restore a cancer-stricken child, to sustain a husband of decades, to heal fractured marriages, to save wayward family members. Sometimes we do not receive what we ask for in prayer and we must simply trust in his Fatherly care, even when our hearts are broken.

REFLECTION QUESTIONS

1. What is the Christian's confidence in prayer?

2. How might Jesus's parable in Matthew 7 about the human father focus our attention on the kinds of things we might ask for in prayer?

3. What are some ways that we might hinder our own prayer?

4. Why can we trust God even when we do not receive what we ask for?

5. How might we pray with confidence and yet without presumption?

How Might Jesus's Experience of Prayer Encourage Us?

One of the most magnificent truths of Christianity is that Jesus, the God-man, prayed.[1] This fact is so commonplace that we may easily over-look it, yet the four Gospels portray Jesus as a man of prayer. In this chapter, we want to consider how Jesus's example and experience of prayer can encourage us in our own prayers.

Jesus Was a Man of Prayer

Jesus would frequently rise early and seek seclusion to pray (Mark 1:35; Luke 5:16). Jesus also prayed before or during important events such as his baptism (Luke 3:21), before calling his disciples (Luke 6:12), after the beheading of his cousin John (Mark 6:46). Jesus prayed at his transfiguration

---

1. Several significant treatments of prayer in the life of Jesus include J. D. G. Dunn, "Prayer," in *The Dictionary of Jesus and the Gospels*, eds. Joel B. Green and Scot McKnight (Downers Grove, IL: InterVarsity Press, 1992), 617–18; I. Howard Marshall, "Jesus—Example and Teacher of Prayer in the Synoptic Gospels," in *Into God's Presence: Prayer in the New Testament*, ed. Richard N. Longenecker (Grand Rapids: Eerdmans, 2001), 113–31; N. T. Wright, "The Lord's Prayer as a Paradigm of Christian Prayer," in *Into God's Presence: Prayer in the New Testament*, ed. Richard N. Longenecker (Grand Rapids: Eerdmans, 2001), 132–54; Andrew T. Lincoln, "God's Name, Jesus' Name, and Prayer in the Fourth Gospel," in *Into God's Presence: Prayer in the New Testament*, ed. Richard N. Longenecker (Grand Rapids: Eerdmans, 2001), 155–80; Graeme Goldsworthy, *Prayer and the Knowledge of God: What the Whole Bible Teaches* (Downers Grove, IL: InterVarsity Press, 2003), 27–38, 39–52, 68–84, 85–105; M. M. B. Turner, "Prayer in the Gospels and Acts," in *Teach Us to Pray: Prayer in the Bible and the World*, ed. D. A. Carson (Exeter, UK: Paternoster Press, 1990), 58–83; and Oscar Cullmann, *Prayer in the New Testament*, trans. John Bowden (London: SCM Press, 1995), 15–68, 89–110.

(Luke 9:28–29) and his crucifixion (Luke 22:41–42).[2] Jesus looked up to heaven and prayed before healing a deaf man with a speech impediment (Mark 7:34); when blessing loaves of bread before his miraculous feedings (Mark 6:41); before raising Lazarus from his tomb (John 11:41); and as he prayed for his disciples before his execution (John 17).[3] Jesus laid his hands upon children and prayed over them (Matt. 19:13). Following his resurrection, Jesus blessed his disciples while lifting up his hands (Luke 24:50). The accounts of Jesus's prayer in Gethsemane present perhaps the most significant description of Jesus's prayer. In these accounts, faith and surrender meet in the act of prayer.

The Night of Betrayal

The Synoptic Gospels each recall Jesus's prayer of desperate trust in God's providence in the hours before his arrest and execution (Matt. 26:36–46; Mark 14:32–42; Luke 22:39–46). Luke records that Jesus knelt and prayed (Luke 22:41), Mark states that Jesus fell on the ground and prayed (Mark 14:35), while Matthew alone recalls that Jesus "fell on his face and prayed, saying, 'My Father, if it be possible, let this cup pass from me; nevertheless, not as I will, but as you will'" (Matt. 26:39). While this pericope addresses vigilance and prayerfulness, it also illumines Jesus's understanding of coming events in light of his unique role as redeemer. Jesus prays as the great intercessors of Israel before him have prayed, in humble submission before God, and like Moses he is willing to die on behalf of his people (Exod. 32:30–32), yet no other intercessor has faced the prospect of divine abandonment and wrath as does Jesus here. Frederick Leahy's description seems appropriate: "Here, in Gethsemane, we see the sinless, finite humanity of Christ in deep and terrible distress."[4] Within hours, Jesus will die cursed, hanging on a tree (cf. Gal. 3:13; Deut. 21:23), his arms upraised, held firmly in place by metal spikes, praying

---

2. O'Brien asserts that in Luke's gospel, "The examples of people at prayer, especially Jesus, do not simply have a biographical or paraenetic function. The Third Evangelist employs this motif [of people praying] at critical moments in his history of salvation, indicating that petitionary prayer is an important means by which God has guided His people." See Peter T. O'Brien, "Prayer in Luke-Acts," *Tyndale Bulletin* 24 (1973): 111–27, especially 121.

3. See D. A. Carson, *The Gospel according to John*, The Pillar New Testament Commentary (Grand Rapids: Eerdmans, 1991), 418. Carson's comments that Jesus's prayer in John 11:41–44 "seeks to draw his hearers into the intimacy of Jesus' own relationship with the Father" seems appropriate.

4. Carson demonstrates that the "cup" refers not only to suffering and death, but also to God's wrath. D. A. Carson, *Matthew*, in vol. 8 of *The Expositor's Bible Commentary*, eds. Frank E. Gaebelein and J. D. Douglas (Grand Rapids: Zondervan, 1984), 542–44. See Frederick Leahy, *The Cross He Bore: Meditations on the Sufferings of the Redeemer* (Carlisle, PA: The Banner of Truth Trust, 2007), 8.

the words of the psalmist, "My God, My God, why have you forsaken me?" (Matt. 27:46; Ps. 22:1). How might Jesus's experience of prayer encourage us?

One way Jesus's experience can encourage us is the sheer fact that his life was marked by prayer. In important times and in ordinary times, Jesus prayed. Leslie Hardin expresses this truth helpfully when he writes, "[Jesus's] very life and practice—of spending hours in prayer, not minutes—goes against the grain of the fast-paced culture in which Americans live and work . . . Jesus' long sessions of prayer make us rethink our own practice of prayer and give us hope that this greater fellowship with the Father is humanly possible if we would only take time to engage him."[5]

Another way Jesus's experience of prayer can encourage us is that his experience mirrors ours in that while Jesus often saw the Father answer his prayers, in Gethsemane God did not answer his prayer in the way he had hoped. In a passage we have noted above in Question 7, the author of Hebrews describes Jesus as a high priest marked by mercy and faithfulness because of what he suffered (Heb. 4:14–16), and part of Jesus's experience is not receiving what he sought in prayer. In an earlier chapter, we saw that sometimes our own sin hinders our prayers, yet this was not the case with Jesus, who was the "lamb without blemish or spot" (1 Pet. 1:19). This dimension of Jesus's experience lets us trust that he can indeed understand us with great sympathy and thus minister mercy toward us in our times of need. A third way that Jesus's experience of prayer can encourage us also arises in his Gethsemane experience: Jesus shows us how to resign ourselves to the Father's will even when the Father chooses to act differently than we want. Jesus shows us how it is possible to trust God when God tells us no.

Summary

Jesus prayed. We may be tempted to (unintentionally) adopt perspectives about Jesus and the reality of prayer that the church, in earlier generations, has rejected. If Jesus is divine, why does he need to pray? Was Jesus simply talking to himself? Jesus's prayers are part of his genuine humanity, part of the way he experienced the charismatic leadership of the Holy Spirit, part of the way he sustained fellowship with the Father, and part of the way he sought direction, withstood temptation, and resigned himself to follow his Father's will in giving his life as a ransom for many on the cross. Jesus prayed, his prayers were as real as ours, and his prayers were part of the pattern of godliness that we must follow.

---

5.   Leslie T. Hardin, *The Spirituality of Jesus: Nine Disciplines He Modeled for Us* (Grand Rapids: Kregel, 2009), 36–37.

REFLECTION QUESTIONS

1. What are some of the ways Jesus experienced answers to his prayers?

2. How might Jesus's response to answered prayers teach you how to respond?

3. How did Jesus respond in Gethsemane when the Father chose to answer his prayer "No"?

4. Why is Jesus's prayer experience in Gethsemane valuable for his ministry on our behalf?

5. What comfort might we draw from Jesus's experiences of prayer?

How Did Paul Pray for Early Christian Communities? (Part 1)

One way that the Bible helps guide our own prayers is by allowing us to listen in to early Christian leaders praying for churches, and Paul's prayers offer rich examples for us to consider. In answering the above question, we will see that Paul's prayers provide worthy models for imitation and communicate enduring themes that ought to characterize maturing prayers among Christians today. After considering the role of prayer in Paul's life, we summarize several themes and explore one prayer in greater detail.[1] Because prayer is so significant a feature of Paul's writings, this question is divided into two parts.

Prayer Shaped Paul's Life

Many readers will know of Paul's conversion, the most famous testimony in the ancient world, yet others may not recall the details and thus it is worth summarizing here. Paul's Jewish name was Saul (*Paulos* was his name in Greek) and he was from the northern Mediterranean town of Tarsus. Trained as a Pharisee, Paul was zealous to honor God according to the old covenant law—zeal that motivated him to approve the execution of one of Jesus's followers named Stephen and, subsequently, to search for men and women who had converted to the Way (the earliest name given Christianity) that he might bring them to religious trial, likely to persuade them to renounce their faith (Acts 7:58; 9:2; Phil. 3:5–6). When Paul encountered the glorified Jesus in the early 30s AD, his life was transformed (Acts 9:3–9). The Lord also appeared to a believer in Damascus named Ananias and sent him to encourage and bless Paul, describing Paul simply: "Behold, he is praying" (Acts 9:11). Paul's

---

1. Readers who want to focus more deeply on this subject should consider the excellent study by D. A. Carson, *Praying with Paul: A Call to Spiritual Reformation*, 2nd ed. (Grand Rapids: Baker Academic, 2015).

religious life had been shaken at a foundational level and his instinct was to pray. This instinct, no doubt shaped by his religious background, marked the rest of his life and ministry. Soon after this experience, Paul began to bear public witness for Jesus as Messiah (Acts 9:20).

Using descriptions from the book of Acts, we can surmise the importance of prayer for Paul. The beginning of his formal ministry came after a time of intentional prayer and fasting by the elders of the church at Antioch (Acts 13:1–3). When imprisoned in Philippi, Paul and his fellow missionary Silas prayed and sang to God (Acts 16:25). In a scene filled with emotion, Paul prayed at Miletus with the elders from Ephesus—leaders convinced that this was their last visit (Acts 20:36–38). He prayed before embarking on a journey by sea (Acts 21:5). He prayed at the temple in Jerusalem (Acts 22:17). Paul prayed over the father of Publius on Malta (Acts 28:8). The common thread of these accounts is how unremarkable they are. In Acts, Luke presents Paul as a devout man whose life and ministry were marked by prayer.

Two aspects related to Paul's prayer life have proven controversial, and although full analyses are beyond the scope of this chapter, they are nevertheless worth considering briefly here. First, what should we make of Paul's commentary regarding the practice of speaking/praying in tongues (1 Cor. 14:1–40), and second, how might Paul's description of spiritual rapture (2 Cor. 12:1–10) relate to prayer?

In 2 Corinthians 12:1–10, Paul uses intentionally oblique language as he describes a spiritual experience of being "caught up to the third heaven" and receiving direct revelation from God, the content of which "cannot be told."[2] Here Paul engages in "foolish boasting" in order to address critics of his ministry. With regard to prayer, here we simply observe that Paul does not say that this experience came (1) as a response to prayer or (2) in the context of prayer. Prayer arises *after* or *in response* to this experience, when Paul seeks deliverance from a divinely imposed "thorn" meant to humble him. We consider Paul's experience of receiving a response to prayer below (Question 27), but here we may simply conclude that we lack sufficient evidence to conclude that Paul's revelatory experience was normative, that it came through prayer, or that similar experiences might come through prayer today.

Paul addressed the issue of tongues in a different way, devoting a significant portion of a letter (1 Cor. 12–14) to the matter. In chapter 12, Paul explains how the Holy Spirit gives believers gifts (*charismatōn*) for the "common good" of the church (12:4–7). Among the various gifts Paul lists are "tongues" (*glōssōn*). The Spirit distributes gifts according to his prerogative (12:11). Paul compares the church with its variously gifted members to a human body with

---

2. On Paul's use of the third person to refer to himself, see Murray J. Harris, *The Second Epistle to the Corinthians*, New International Greek Testament Commentary (Grand Rapids: Eerdmans, 2005), 834–35.

its various constituent parts (12:12–26), arguing that just as an individual body is unified yet diverse in its members, so too the church is unified yet its members possess various gifts. A series of rhetorical questions underscores the point that the Spirit gives different gifts to different Christians (12:29–30). Rather than complaining about the Spirit's sovereign gifting, the Corinthians ought to pursue the "more excellent way" of self-denying and others-exalting love (13:1–13) even while they "earnestly desire the spiritual gifts" (14:1). Much of Paul's instruction in the remainder of chapter 14 involves balancing spiritual gifts that edify the congregation with gifts that edify the individual. With this focus, Paul compares two particular gifts: prophecy and tongues.

Table 2—Value of Tongues and Prophesy	
Tongues	**Prophesy**
"Speaks not to men" (14:2)	"Speaks to people" (14:3)
"Speaks to God; for no one understands him, but he utters mysteries in the Spirit" (14:2)	"for their upbuilding and encouragement and consolation" (14:3)
"builds up" the speaker (14:4)	"builds up the church" (14:4)

It seems clear from context that both gifts refer to manifestations of *public speech*. Prophecy is public speech in language intelligible to the hearers whereas tongues is public speech in language that God alone understands. As Table 2 shows, Paul affirms the value of both prophecy and tongues, but for different reasons. Both types of speech "build up" (*oikodomei*, "strengthen" one's life) Christians: prophecy strengthens the hearers whereas tongues strengthen the speaker. Paul can even express a wish that the whole Corinthian congregation could speak in tongues (14:5a), affirming the value of this gift, although he has been clear that only some can exercise this gift. Prophesy, though, is generally more desirable (14:5b), because it edifies more hearers (14:12).

For clarity, we should note that "speaking" and "praying" in tongues are related, but really are two separate issues. Thus far, Paul seems to have focused on tongues as public speech, perhaps ecstatic expressions of worship offered when the church meets. In 1 Corinthians 14:13–19, Paul shifts his instruction to prayer, yet his focus is clearly on *spoken*, public prayer, for his caution involves the "unfruitfulness" of praying aloud in a way that is of no benefit to the larger church (14:16). The issue is not that the speech is offered, but that it does not "build up" those who hear it. Paul, who apparently has the gift of tongues (14:18), expresses thankfulness to God for this gift while subordinating it to prophetic teaching. Hans Conzelmann states the situation well: "Again, [Paul] does not bind the community to his own person and his own abilities. He does not exploit these in order to kindle religious experiences."[3] These experiences of heavenly rapture and prayer in tongues were divine gifts, beneficial *for Paul*, but not experiences he preaches as tests for genuine faith nor standard expressions of mature spirituality. Rather, Paul prizes intelligible speech that consoles, encourages, and strengthens other believers. His prayers offered on behalf of churches are examples of such speech.

Paul's Prayers for Churches

Having considered prayer in Paul's own practice, we turn our attention to the content of his prayers. Because Paul's letters are occasional (written or "occasioned" by a certain need), we shouldn't expect to form a systematic picture of Paul's prayer life. Paul wrote letters of encouragement and correction for churches, not a handbook on prayer. However, his occasional letters offer "real life" pictures of how Paul prayed for churches.

In this chapter, I want to explore Paul's prayers in two ways. First, a thematic approach helps us identify specific concepts that were important for Paul and thus warrant our attention. Second, an in-depth analysis of one prayer will show how Paul's theology shaped his prayers and might help us pray.

Common Themes in Paul's Prayers

Paul's writings contain around forty prayer texts.[4] Some texts are only fragments of a sentence while others are several paragraphs long. Some prayers show literary artistry while others are short exclamations of praise. Scholars classify Paul's prayers variously as "wish-prayers," "prayer reports," prayer requests, and so forth.[5] "Wish-prayers" frequently use the Greek optative mood to express Paul's desire that God answer a request.[6] "Prayer reports" summarize how Paul has been praying for churches prior to writing a particular letter. The classifications are interesting but unnecessary for this chapter's purpose. We have no way of knowing how often Paul prayed for churches, nor should we consider his prayer reports or wishes exhaustive as much as summative.[7] Nearly all his prayer texts can be read aloud in a matter of seconds. It seems likely for one who prioritized prayer that

3.   Hans Conzelmann, *1 Corinthians: A Commentary on the First Epistle to the Corinthians*, Hermeneia (Philadelphia: Fortress Press, 1975), 239.
4.   Romans 1:8–10; 10:1; 12:12; 15:5–6, 13, 30–33; 1 Corinthians 1:4–9; 16:23; 2 Corinthians 1:3–7; 2:14–16; 9:12–15; 12:7–9; 13:7–9; Galatians 6:18; Ephesians 1:3–14, 15–23; 3:14–21; 6:19–20; Philippians 1:3–6, 9–11; 4:6–7, 23; Colossians 1:3–14; 4:2–4; 1 Thessalonians 1:2–3; 2:13–16; 3:9–13; 5:23–24, 28; 2 Thessalonians 1:3–10, 11–12; 2:16–17; 3:1–5, 16; 1 Timothy 1:12; 2:1–3; 2 Timothy 1:3–7, 16–18; Titus 3:15; Philemon 4–7, 25.
5.   One critical study of Paul's prayers is that of Gordon P. Wiles, *Paul's Intercessory Prayers: The Significance of Intercessory Prayer Passages in the Letters of St. Paul*, Society for New Testament Studies Monograph Series 24 (Cambridge: Cambridge University Press, 1974), 297–302. Wiles rejects several prayer passages above as non-Pauline, but his assessment is by no means universal.
6.   In Greek, the optative mood expresses a wish or a desire as opposed to a command or a request.
7.   We consider Paul's prayer habits for churches more fully in Question 24.

these shorts texts are just summaries of the main themes of his actual prayers, though there is certainly no harm in using his actual words in our own prayers. Paul may have even written some of them for this purpose.[8]

One way to benefit from Paul's prayers for churches is to consider themes that appear in multiple prayers. This approach omits some details, but allows us to see patterns we might otherwise miss. Some clear themes are a focus on human weakness, an awareness of God's grace, a celebration of God's work, a burden for the needs of others, and a clear attentiveness to the work of the Father, Son, and Spirit in prayer.

Focus on Our Weaknesses

Paul is acutely aware of his weakness and that of those to whom he is writing and for whom he is praying. For Paul, Christians ask God to work in us and the world because our strength is inadequate and our knowledge is incomplete. Paul's occasional requests for prayer are one indication of this focus:

> I appeal to you, brothers, by our Lord Jesus Christ and by the love of the Spirit, to strive together with me in your prayers to God on my behalf, that I may be delivered from the unbelievers in Judea, and that my service for Jerusalem may be acceptable to the saints, so that by God's will I may come to you with joy and be refreshed in your company. (Rom. 15:30–32)

> Continue steadfastly in prayer, being watchful in it with thanksgiving. At the same time, pray also for us, that God may open to us a door for the word, to declare the mystery of Christ, on account of which I am in prison—that I may make it clear, which is how I ought to speak. (Col. 4:2–4)

These requests would be superfluous, perhaps a rhetorical ploy calculated to gain sympathy, unless Paul genuinely recognized his own weakness and thought that God would hear and answer the prayers of Christians. Yet it seems clear that Paul really did see his human limitations. Paul did not only ask for strength for others; his own prayers included thankfulness to Christ for strengthening him, rescuing him, and appointing him apostolic authority (1 Tim. 1:12). Perhaps the classic text for considering's Paul's perspective on weakness and prayer is 2 Corinthians 12:7–9:

> So to keep me from becoming conceited because of the surpassing greatness of the revelations, a thorn was given me in the flesh, a messenger of Satan to harass me, to keep me from

---

8. Wiles, *Paul's Intercessory Prayers,* 22, 42–44.

becoming conceited. Three times I pleaded with the Lord about this, that it should leave me. But he said to me, "My grace is sufficient for you, for my power is made perfect in weakness." Therefore I will boast all the more gladly of my weaknesses, so that the power of Christ may rest upon me.

In this passage, Paul acknowledges his weakness and celebrates it as a divine gift that enables him to experience the sustaining power of Christ in answer to his own prayers for deliverance.[9] A positive acknowledgment of weakness offers a glimpse into this theme in Paul's prayers. Our natural absence of spiritual resources is another way this theme emerges.

Paul prayed for supernatural empowerment for his recipients.

> For this reason I bow my knees before the Father, from whom every family in heaven and on earth is named, that according to the riches of his glory he may grant you to be strengthened with power through his Spirit in your inner being, so that Christ may dwell in your hearts through faith—that you, being rooted and grounded in love, may have strength to comprehend with all the saints what is the breadth and length and height and depth, and to know the love of Christ that surpasses knowledge, that you may be filled with all the fullness of God. (Eph. 3:14–19)

> And so, from the day we heard, we have not ceased to pray for you, asking that you may be filled with the knowledge of his will in all spiritual wisdom and understanding, so as to walk in a manner worthy of the Lord, fully pleasing to him: bearing fruit in every good work and increasing in the knowledge of God; being strengthened with all power, according to his glorious might, for all endurance and patience with joy. (Col. 1:9–11)

Here, Paul tacitly acknowledges the presence of weakness by asking God to provide inward strength, spiritual comprehension, spiritual wisdom and understanding, and strength to endure trials joyfully. His prayers affirm that left to ourselves, we will often miss the grandeur of God's work within us and fall under the pressures of external hardship. Our natural resources are inadequate to flourish spiritually. God must strengthen us. Recognizing this theme in Paul's prayers provides a helpful diagnostic for our own prayer lives. Are we increasingly aware of our weakness? Do we perceive others as spiritually stronger than us? Will we pray for those leaders within the church whom God

---

9. Paul's language that he will "boast" (*kauchēsomai*) in his weakness (2 Cor. 12:5) is celebratory.

has placed over us? For our leaders, our brothers and sisters, and we ourselves share a common weakness and have a common need for God's strength.

Awareness of God's Grace

Paul's prayers overflow with mention of God's unmerited favor, his grace. Take time to read and consider the following prayers:

> I give thanks to my God always for you because of the grace of God that was given you in Christ Jesus, that in every way you were enriched in him in all speech and all knowledge. (1 Cor. 1:4–5)

> The grace of the Lord Jesus be with you. (1 Cor. 16:23)

> The grace of our Lord Jesus Christ be with your spirit, brothers. Amen. (Gal. 6:18)

> In love he predestined us for adoption to himself as sons through Jesus Christ, according to the purpose of his will, to the praise of his glorious grace, with which he has blessed us in the Beloved. (Eph. 1:4–6)

> The grace of the Lord Jesus Christ be with your spirit. (Phil. 4:23)

> The grace of our Lord Jesus Christ be with you. (1 Thess. 5:28)

> Now may our Lord Jesus Christ himself, and God our father, who loved us and gave us eternal comfort and good hope through grace, comfort your hearts and establish them in every good work and word. (2 Thess. 2:16–17)

> The grace of the Lord Jesus Christ be with your spirit. (Philem. 25)

Paul's prayers contain other mentions of God's grace, but this representative sampling shows that Paul lived with an awareness of God's grace. He recognized that his conversion to Christianity and his ministry as apostle were by God's grace (1 Cor. 15:10).

"Grace" opens and closes Paul's first letter to the Corinthians, as was his custom, but this was uncommon among other first-century letter writers.[10]

---

10. In technical terms, it forms an *inclusio* that treats as bookends the letter's first and final verses. Regarding this customary approach, "Occasionally in Jewish letters one finds

The frequent prayer request for recipients to experience "the grace of the Lord Jesus Christ" at the end of Paul's letters was a standard letter closing for him as well as his genuine wish. Grace and weakness go hand in hand. When we, like Paul, learn to see our weakness and depend on God for strength, we may grow more aware of God's grace in our own lives. In what ways are we showing in our prayers a growing awareness of God's grace? The absence of grace in our prayers may reveal a proud heart.

Summary

In this chapter, we have considered key prayer texts in Paul's letters and noted the importance of prayer in the apostle's life and ministry. Paul's letters show a dependence upon God's grace with a genuine awareness of his human weakness, and his prayers join these themes. These two themes help explain why prayer seems so important for Paul and can help us understand its place in life and ministry as well. Christian ministers serve in churches with various culturally defined expectations. For some, to admit weakness and request prayers from their congregations is normal and welcomed, but other ministers in different settings might be reticent to make such admissions. Considering Paul's prayers and prayer requests can free ministers and laity alike to seek grace in light of weakness through prayer.

REFLECTION QUESTIONS

1. What are ways Paul requested prayer from other Christians?

2. How might the fact that Paul asked other churches to pray for him encourage ministers and other leaders to do the same?

3. What might the frequent mention of prayer in Paul's relatively short letters teach us about its importance to him?

4. What are some ways that prayer shaped Paul's ministry?

5. How would you summarize the role of human weakness and the importance of prayer for Paul?

'mercy' (ἔλεος) alongside 'peace' (εἰρήνη), but never 'grace' (χάρις)." Eduard Lohse, *Colossians and Philemon: A Commentary on the Epistles to the Colossians and to Philemon*, Hermeneia (Philadelphia: Fortress Press, 1971), 5.

How How Did Paul Pray for Early Christian Communities? (Part 2)

This chapter continues the reflection on Paul's prayer for early churches from the previous chapter. There, we noted how important prayer was in Paul's life and began exploring key themes that appear in Paul's prayers, mentioning his recognition of human weakness and an awareness of God's grace. Here we take note of three additional themes in Paul's prayers and examine one prayer in greater detail.

Common Themes in Paul's Prayers

Celebration of God's Work

Celebrating God's work among the congregations to whom he wrote is a third theme in Paul's prayers.

> First, I thank my God through Jesus Christ for all of you, because your faith is proclaimed in all the world. (Rom. 1:8)

> I thank my God in all my remembrance of you, always in every prayer of mine for you all making my prayer with joy, because of your partnership in the gospel from the first day until now. (Phil. 1:3–5)

> We give thanks to God always for all of you, constantly mentioning you in our prayers, remembering before our God and Father your work of faith and labor of love and steadfastness of hope in our Lord Jesus Christ. (1 Thess. 1:2–3)

> But we ought always to give thanks to God for you, brothers beloved by the Lord, because God chose you as the firstfruits to be saved, through sanctification by the Spirit and belief in the truth. (2 Thess. 2:13)

Perhaps the most extended and magnificent celebration is found in Ephesians 1:3–14, which is a *berkah* (blessing) celebrating the work of the Father, Son, and Spirit in planning, effecting, and applying deliverance from sin. The paragraph is sublime. It is no wonder one theologian mentions the healing that came from meditating on it daily for half a year.[1]

Paul interpreted his apostolic calling as a divine vocation (2 Cor. 1:1; Gal. 1:1). He was willing to boast of those whom had been converted under his ministry (2 Cor. 1:14). He had a fatherly affection for churches he had planted and individuals God saved under his ministry (1 Cor. 4:15; 1 Thess. 2:11–12; Philem. 10). He even describes himself as a mother in the pains of labor (Gal. 4:19) and a "nursing mother" (1 Thess. 2:7) in relation to his converts. By using these parental metaphors, Paul expresses his pride in the growing faith and virtues (faith, hope, and love) of young believers, but in his prayers, he is quick to offer thanksgiving to *God* for these changes. This theme is noteworthy and important for our own prayers.

Paul's celebration of God's work ought to challenge us to consider our own gratitude to God in prayer. Are we quick to recognize the fruit of God's work and to return thanks, privately and publicly? This consideration is important for all readers, but may be especially meaningful for those involved in vocational ministry, whether as pastors, teachers, counselors, missionaries, worship leaders, or other areas of kingdom work. If "success" in ministry is measurable, how might it be measured? One possible measurement would be the inward and outward growth in faith, hope, and love in those we touch. Like Paul, we ought to feel a responsibility to nurture these virtues and should be delighted to see them flourish within our charges. But Paul teaches us to minimize self-congratulation and to prioritize thankfulness to God. As he reminded the Corinthians, those who minister cannot take credit for work that belongs to God:

> What then is Apollos? What is Paul? Servants through whom you believed, as the Lord assigned to each. I planted, Apollos watered, but God gave the growth. So neither he who plants nor he who waters is anything, but only God who gives the growth. He who plants and he who waters are one, and each will receive his wages according to his labor. For we are God's fellow workers. You are God's field, God's building. (1 Cor. 3:5–9)

---

1. See John Jefferson Davis, *Meditation and Communion with God* (Downers Grove, IL: IVP Academic, 2012), 7.

A Burden for Others

Paul's prayers reveal a priority of praying for others. Don Carson calls our attention to this others-focused orientation when he writes, "If we follow Paul's example, then, we will never overlook the monumental importance of praying for *others*."[2] One striking imbalance in Paul's correspondence is the rate at which he reports prayers for others versus the frequency with which he requests prayer from others. We should not make too much of this difference simply because of the nature of occasional letters, but neither should we ignore nor minimize it. If we will listen to Paul at prayer, we will surely hear his heart: true growth in the virtues of faith, hope, and love are the work of God in the lives of his saints, and the prayers of others, especially leaders, is a vital part of this work. Perhaps we might see here that much growth in our lives comes as the result of answered prayers that we know only in part, or perhaps we never know at all. How might God use our prayers offered on behalf of Christians we know and those we know only by reputation (here I am thinking of missionaries that we "know" only through distant affiliation or of nameless pastors and Sunday school teachers of churches we pass on our daily commute). Will we pray for their growth in Christlikeness and virtue, even if we never know the fruit of these prayers? Paul prayed for Christian communities that he had played a direct role in evangelizing, like Philippi and Corinth, yet he also prayed for many Christians he had not met personally, Christians in Rome, Colossae, and elsewhere. His burden was for their growth and maturity and recognizing this focus may help us pray in a similar way.

Trinitarian Attentiveness

One striking feature of Paul's prayers is how naturally and frequently he seeks the work of the Father, Son, and Spirit in his prayers. In the following examples, notice Paul's various mentions of the Godhead:

> First, I thank my *God* through *Jesus Christ* for all of you, because your faith is proclaimed in all the world. (Rom. 1:8)

> May the *God* of hope fill you with all joy and peace in believing, so that by the power of the *Holy Spirit* you may abound in hope. (Rom. 15:13)

> I appeal to you, brothers, by our *Lord Jesus Christ* and by the love of the *Spirit*, to strive together with me in your prayers to *God* on my behalf. (Rom. 15:30)

---

2. D. A. Carson, *Praying with Paul: A Call to Spiritual Reformation*, 2nd ed. (Grand Rapids: Baker Academic, 2015), 55 (italics original).

> For this reason I bow my knees before the *Father*, from whom every family in heaven and on earth is named, that according to the riches of his glory he may grant you to be strengthened with power through his *Spirit* in your inner being, so that *Christ* may dwell in your hearts through faith. (Eph. 3:14–17)

> Now may our *God and Father* himself, and our *Lord Jesus*, direct our way to you, and may the *Lord* make you increase and abound in love for one another and for all, as we do for you. (1 Thess. 3:11–12)

> Now may our *Lord Jesus Christ* himself, and *God our Father*, who loved us and gave us eternal comfort and good hope through grace, comfort your hearts and establish them in every good work and word. (2 Thess. 2:16–17)

In Questions 5 and 6 above, we reflected on the Trinitarian nature of theology, namely that we pray to the Father, *through* the Son, *in* the Spirit's power. John Bunyan's definition of prayer (offered "to God, through Christ, in the strength and assistance of the Holy Spirit," Question 1) expresses a similar idea to that which we see in Paul's prayers. Attentiveness to the distinctive work of each person of the Trinity is one way by which believers can honor God. Why? This attentiveness causes us to think deeply about God as he reveals himself through Scripture, and such focused attention shifts our perspective from a self-orientation to a godward look. The more we behold God, the more captive our minds and hearts will be to his distinctive excellence. This sort of captivating refocus just may warm our hearts to worship. Are we, like Paul, attentive to the Trinity in our prayers?

Paul's Prayer in Depth

A second way of letting Paul's prayers for early Christian communities shape our own prayers is by examining each prayer in depth. Space here necessitates offering a single example, and Paul's prayer in Ephesians 1:15–23 offers a rich reflection. More than twenty years ago, a professor in an exegetical class on Ephesians asked a question of this text that I have never forgotten: "How do you pray for Christians when everything in their life seems to be going well?"[3] It is a wise question. Many (most?) of our prayers arise from the difficulties that we or others face: financial strain, relational struggles, indecision, suffering, and so on. These situations have a way of focusing prayer, but

---

3.   That professor was the late Charles Draper. I mention his name here to communicate his legacy of biblical and practical scholarship to a generation that will never know him personally. I thank God for his instruction!

prayer is broader than our immediate needs. In this passage in Ephesians, Paul prays for a *genuine* need that may not be a *felt* need and thus shows us how to pray for ourselves or others when things seem to be going well.

Prayer Motivated by Love

We have mentioned Paul's burden for others as an important theme, and his prayer in Ephesians 1 demonstrates this burden: "For this reason, because I have heard of your faith in the Lord Jesus and your love toward all the saints, I do not cease to give thanks for you, remembering you in my prayers" (1:15–16). Paul offers no rebuke or correction here; he celebrates the recipients' growing inward trust ("faith in the Lord Jesus") as well as their own care for others ("your love toward all the saints"). One way Paul's prayers can teach us is by asking if we too are willing to thank God for the evidence of faith and love that we see in other Christians.

Prayer to the Triune God

We have also noted Paul's attentiveness to each person of the Godhead in his prayers, and this prayer highlights this theme: "[asking] that the God of our Lord Jesus Christ, the Father of glory, may give you the Spirit of wisdom and of revelation in the knowledge of him" (1:17). Paul prays *to* the Father ("the God of our Lord Jesus Christ, the Father of glory") *asking for* an inward work by the Holy Spirit, namely that the Spirit will teach the Ephesians to navigate life well ("wisdom") and that he will show them the truth that is found in Jesus ("revelation in the knowledge of him").[4] We need not reach the conclusion that every prayer we offer must demonstrate the same degree of theological precision in order to be heard, yet as we grow in our knowledge of the Word of God and in our theological reflection on Scripture, it seems fitting to give particular glory and honor to each member of the Trinity for his distinctive work. Where Scripture gives us clarity in these details, let us pray according to this knowledge. We see in this passage the particular work of the third person of the Trinity displayed.

Prayer for a Deeper Awareness of God

Paul offers a summary of three petitions that he has been praying on behalf of these Christians, and these petitions revolve around a deeper awareness of the gospel: "[I am praying that,] having the eyes of your hearts enlightened . . . you may know what is the hope to which he has called you, what are the riches of his glorious inheritance in the saints, and what is the immeasurable greatness of his power toward us who believe" (1:18–19). In theological parlance, Paul is praying for the Spirit to illumine these believers ("having

---

4. Paul's pronouns in Ephesians 1 are notoriously challenging to follow. The pronoun "him" might refer to either the Father or the Son.

the eyes of your hearts enlightened").[5] Paul wants them to be able to perceive with greater clarity three aspects of God's work in their lives: (1) the hope of God's calling, (2) the riches of Jesus's inheritance among Christians, and (3) the unmeasurable power of God that is at work in believers.

Hope is a forward-looking virtue that anticipates the future work of God. As one older writer described it, "Hope is the fruit of the Holy Spirit whereby we look forward with patience and endurance to the fulfillment of God's promises."[6] In modern sloganeering, "hope" is a nebulous desire for something better to happen in the future. Here, Paul tethers "hope" to God's call in the gospel. The Ephesians had "heard the word of truth" (1:13a), "believed in [Christ]" (1:13b), and "were sealed with the promised Holy Spirit" (1:13c). Jesus is the one on whom all history hinges, and Paul wants the Ephesians (and us!) to wait patiently with a Spirit-wrought anticipation of the summing up of all things in Christ (1:10).

In his introductory blessing, Paul acknowledges that God has blessed believers with "every spiritual blessing" (1:3), that he has lavished "the riches of his grace" upon them (1:7–8), and that "in [Christ] we have obtained an inheritance" (1:11). Later, Paul describes Christ's riches as "unsearchable" or "incalculable" (*anexichniaston*, 3:8). Paul emphasizes this theme in other letters as well.[7] *Having* these manifold blessings and *being conscious* of them seem to be two different matters, which explains Paul's second prayer request.[8]

What are these riches? Pausing to meditate on the "riches" of Christ may seem like a digression, but such meditation deepens our prayers. After all, Paul prays that these believers would "know" the riches of Christ that are ours as an inheritance. Puritan Thomas Brooks offers a helpful summary: Jesus is the "heir of all things" (Heb. 1:2); Jesus is willing to give pardon and spiritual sustenance freely to all who ask of him (Isa. 55:1); he gives treasures to all parts of every believer: mind, will, conscience, heart; Jesus has given grace in every generation and thus his supply is inexhaustible; and with the Father, Jesus gives the Spirit in his fullness to every believer.[9] God has put "all things under his feet" (Eph. 1:22). These spiritual riches belong to Christ but also to Christians: "He who did not spare his own Son but gave him up for us all,

---

5. Paul may be echoing Psalm 13:3 or 19:8 here.
6. Godefridus Udemans, *The Practice of Faith, Hope, and Love*, trans. Annemie Godbehere, ed. Joel R. Beeke, Classics of Reformed Spirituality (Grand Rapids: Reformation Heritage Books, 2012), 26. Udemans was part of the Dutch *Nadere Reformatie* (New Reformation) movement. See Question 40.
7. See Romans 2:4; Philippians 4:19; and Colossians 2:3.
8. I am indebted to Peter T. O'Brien, *Ephesians*, Pillar New Testament Commentary (Grand Rapids; Eerdmans, 1999), 136, for noting this connection. With sadness I note that this commentary has proven controversial because of plagiarism, yet it has been a helpful, if flawed, guide.
9. Thomas Brooks, *The Unsearchable Riches of Christ*, in *The Works of Thomas Brooks*, vol. 3, ed. Alexander Balloch Grosart (Edinburgh: James Nichol, 1866), 150–55.

how will he not also with him graciously give us all things?" (Rom. 8:32). Thus Paul prays that Christians would have an increasing knowledge of the riches in Christ that are also our inheritance.

Paul's third request is that these believers would know "what is the immeasurable greatness of his power." Longtime Bible readers can easily overlook the wordplay Paul uses here. If Jesus's power is "immeasurable," how can Christians "know" the greatness of it? Similar to meditating on Christ's "unsearchable" riches, a growing knowledge and reflection on Christ's "immeasurable" power emboldens us to pray. To illustrate this immeasurable power, Paul mentions the singular events of Christ's resurrection, ascension, and enthronement (1:20–21). When Paul prays for Christians, and when we pray, the same power that God displayed when he raised Christ from the dead, brought him into heaven, and set him as sovereign over "all rule and authority and power and dominion" (1:21) is at work. Paul asks that the Spirit help believers perceive this power. Though we may look at the power, wealth, and spiritual darkness of the world, in Christ we pray with hope, resources, and power.

Summary

In this chapter and the one before, we have considered the prayers of the apostle Paul and have seen how his own devotion to prayer translated into regular prayers for churches he planted, as well as churches he knew mainly by reputation. We have noted important themes in his prayers and explored one prayer more deeply. It seems clear that a growing independence and maturity, particularly in the theological virtues of faith, hope, and love, was one of Paul's priorities for young churches. Gordon Wiles offers an incisive reflection about this priority in Paul's prayers as a whole: "He wanted his churches to grow rapidly toward maturity and to become less dependent on his pastoral care. Constantly he is giving thanks for the continuing victories of his converts, praying that they increase in the graces of faith, hope, and love, and urging them to take their full share in the wider life of the whole church."[10] We can learn much about mature prayer from Paul.

REFLECTION QUESTIONS

1. What are some specific ways Paul prayed for churches?

2. What are some common themes in Paul's prayers?

---

10. Gordon P. Wiles, *Paul's Intercessory Prayers: The Significance of Intercessory Prayer Passages in the Letters of St. Paul*, Society for New Testament Studies Monograph Series 24 (Cambridge: Cambridge University Press, 1974), 3.

3. What encouragements do Paul's prayer requests offer you?

4. How might you integrate Paul's prayers into your own prayer life?

5. What are ways you might pray Ephesians 1:15–23 for members of your own congregation?

What Does It Mean to Pray "Without Ceasing" (1 Thessalonians 5:17)?

In the previous question we saw several ways in which Paul prayed for the early churches and we learned how his prayers might shape our own. In considering this chapter's question, we will look specifically at two exhortations Paul gave these communities regarding their own habits of prayer, so that from the apostle's example *and* instruction we might better learn to pray. The particular lesson we need to learn is to let prayer become part of the regular rhythm of our lives rather than a mere aspect of our religion.

Pray Always (1 Thessalonians 5:17)

Paul's letter to the Thessalonians is among his earliest correspondence, likely written in AD 50.[1] This early date is important because it places the letter approximately twenty years after the resurrection and ascension of Jesus, and one of the letter's major themes is Christ's imminent return. As scholar Charles Wanamaker notes, this theme is especially important in 1 Thessalonians 5:1–11,[2] which makes the closing exhortations in 5:12–22 so pressing. If Jesus might return for his church at any moment, like an unexpected thief (5:2) or like the sudden onset of labor pains (5:3), then Christians ought to live alert, expectant, and vigilant lives. When he was with them, Paul had taught these Gentile converts to "walk in a manner worthy of God" (1 Thess. 2:12). He ends his letter with a series of staccato exhortations intended to help this recently planted church (Acts 17:1–9) do just that: to practice a new pattern

---

1. Leon Morris, *1 and 2 Thessalonians*, Tyndale New Testament Commentaries, vol. 13 (Downers Grove, IL: InterVarsity Press, 1984), 22.
2. Charles A. Wanamaker, *The Epistles to the Thessalonians*, New International Greek Testament Commentary (Grand Rapids: Eerdmans, 1990), 62.

of living that reflects the transformation the gospel brings (1 Thess. 1:6; 2:13) and prepares them to meet Christ.

Paul's exhortation to pray unceasingly is one of fourteen imperatives (commands) found in verses 14–22. As commentator Gene Green observes, the three commands of verses 16–18 deal with the cultivation of inward devotion or "habits that characterize Christians' relationship with God."[3] Taken in turn, the three commands are to "rejoice," "pray," and "give thanks." The associated adverbs and phrases "always," "without ceasing," and "in all circumstances" (lit. "in everything") show that these habits are new dispositions of the heart that give evidence of lives transformed by the gospel. The three commands are intertwined for believers, as constant prayer is one way we express continual joy and offer ongoing thanksgiving.

Looking more closely at the question of what it means to "pray without ceasing," or to "constantly pray" (*adialeiptōs proseuchesthe*), Paul's own example helps us better understand this command. Constant prayer serves as bookends and encouragement through the whole letter. As Paul exhorts these Christians to pray in 5:17, he has already told them that he prays for them "constantly" at the letter's beginning (1:2), that he and his fellow missionaries "also thank God constantly" for the Thessalonians' faithful acceptance of their preaching (2:13), that they "pray most earnestly night and day" to see these young Christians again (3:10).[4] That Paul prayed for the Thessalonians "constantly" need not mean that he prayed for them "exclusively" nor that he did no other activity but pray, but rather that their young church was continually on his mind and, although apart from them physically, he could nevertheless seek God's care for them through prayer.

Pray Steadfastly (Colossians 4:2)

When Paul wrote to the young church in Thessalonica, he was writing to Christians whose faces and stories he knew, for he had lived with them, encouraged them, and prayed with them, but the letter to the Colossians was different. Epaphras, one of Paul's fellow missionaries, brought the gospel of Jesus to this strategic city, and what Paul knew of this church came secondhand from his friend (Col. 1:7–8). Epaphras was himself a man of prayer. Paul described his friend as "struggling" on behalf of the young church in his prayers, and these prayers were focused on spiritual growth and assurance of God's will (Col. 4:13). While Paul had not started this church, he nonetheless prayed for the congregation's spiritual health (Col. 1:9–14), encouraged them to pray steadfastly, and invited them to pray for his own missionary labors (Col. 4:2–4). For Paul, prayer united Christians who had never met in a

---

3. Gene L. Green, *The Letters to the Thessalonians*, Pillar New Testament Commentary (Grand Rapids: Eerdmans, 2002), 257.
4. See also 2 Timothy 1:3, which uses the same language of "constant" prayer.

common mission: the preaching of the gospel. Though separated by distance and freedoms (Paul wrote from prison), prayer bound Christians together and continues to do so today.

Paul exhorts the Colossians to "continue steadfastly in prayer, being watchful in it with thanksgiving." Three noteworthy elements appear here. First, Paul insists that the Colossians must be "devoted" to prayer (*tē proseuchē proskartereite*). This language is intense, as it suggests the need to give great personal effort to prevent disruption or distraction. The language is also familiar, for it is almost identical to what Paul has also told Christians in Rome (Rom. 12:12) and Ephesus (Eph. 6:18). In each of these three places, Paul encourages diligence and persistence in prayer.

Second, Paul encourages ongoing alertness (*grēgorountes*) in prayer, something he has encouraged among the Ephesians (Eph. 6:18) and Corinthians (1 Cor. 16:13) also. Jesus had used similar language in his Olivet discourse (Mark 13:35, 37)[5] and in Gethsemane (Matt. 26:38, 40–41), and while we cannot be certain that Paul had these incidents in mind, they surely share a similar idea: Christians must never lower their guard when it comes to prayer.

The third element of note here is the instruction to pray "with thanksgiving" (*en eucharistia*). Thanksgiving is an important theme in this short epistle, appearing in every chapter. Paul and his fellow missionaries "always thank God" when they pray for these believers (1:3). They ask God to give the Colossians an inward disposition of thanksgiving as a response to the gospel (1:12, 2:7) and as an overflow of their congregational unity and worship (3:15, 17). Thanksgiving is also a common bond between Colossians 4 and 1 Thessalonians 5: Christians are to pray always, being devoted to it, watchful in it, and thankful through it.

Summary

To pray without ceasing is to develop the practice of praying as a normal part of our daily lives. This practice does not replace intentional, formal times of prayer that we might set aside specifically to seek God, but it stems from a growing recognition of how desperately we need God in every aspect of our lives. Praying without ceasing need not mean only offering petitionary prayers, but might include regular thanksgiving or adoration of God, pausing frequently to give thanks as a natural part of our days and nights. Praying unceasingly or praying steadfastly means that we develop a tenacious habit of praying in all circumstances and about everything.

---

5.   See also parallel passages in Matthew 24:42 and 25:13 and in Luke 12:37 and 39–40.

REFLECTION QUESTIONS

1. How might you grow in praying "without ceasing"?

2. Why must Christians "be alert" as we pray often?

3. How might praying in these ways help us fight sin?

4. How would you summarize Epaphras's prayer?

5. How does a renewed heart equip Christians to pray unceasingly?

What Is the "Prayer of Faith" (James 5:13–16)?

In this chapter, we want to consider a very specific question about "the prayer of faith" mentioned in the New Testament epistle of James:

> Is anyone among you suffering? Let him pray. Is anyone cheerful? Let him sing praise. Is anyone among you sick? Let him call for the elders of the church, and let them pray over him, anointing him with oil in the name of the Lord. And the prayer of faith will save the one who is sick, and the Lord will raise him up. And if he has committed sins, he will be forgiven. (James 5:13–15)

What is this prayer? Who may offer this prayer? What are its effects? How does it differ from other sorts of prayer?

Context

James concludes his epistle with a call to prayer, common in other New Testament correspondence.[1] The passage envisions three situations, the first two in 5:13 are general and the third (5:14) is specific. James has addressed the whole epistle to a church, and assumes his readers possess faith in Christ. How should believer, people who takes their faith seriously, respond to the general situation of "suffering" or "cheerfulness" in light of their Christian practice? The first general situation is negative, the experience of "suffering" (*kakopathei*), or hardship. No particular kind of suffering (physical, emotional, spiritual) is in view here. The correct way to respond to this difficulty is by "praying" (*proseuchesthō*). The second general situation is one's experience

---

1. Ephesians 6:18–20; Philippians 4:6; Hebrews 13:18–19, etc.

of being "cheerful" or "happy" (*euthymei*), and the response is that this person should sing psalms of praise (*psalletō*).[2] The third situation is more specific and James provides more detail about the response.

What sort of sickness is in view in 5:14? The word is *asthenei*, which almost always describes a physical illness.[3] With modifying words, the word some-times means something like a spiritual weakness, such as being weak because of fear (2 Cor. 13:3) or uncertainty in making choices (Rom. 14:2), but no such qualifier is present here.[4] Dibelius suggests the "sickness" is rooted in demonic possession and thus the ritual anointing and praying is an exorcism, but this suggestion is unlikely based on the text itself.[5] If a member of the church finds himself too ill to gather with the assembly, he is to summon the "elders of the church"—that is, the congregation's recognized leaders—who are to pray over him and anoint him with oil. As mentioned below in our consideration of posture and prayer, the reference to the elders praying "over" the sick person envisions that the elders have responded to the person's summons, that is, they are physically present and able to apply oil and pray for the ill one.

We need not assume from James's instruction that only ministers have the responsibility and calling to pray over those who are experiencing sickness, but we ought to recognize that the calling to ministry does include care for those who are suffering from illness. Those called to pastoral ministry who have no inclination to visit the sick and suffering need to discern their calling carefully. Neither should we presume that *only* the elders may pray, and not the people themselves who are ill or other Christians within the church. James's response simply explains what the elders are to do without reference to others. With this context established, we now turn to our main question of the chapter, what is the "prayer of faith" in James 5:15?

Prayer That Trusts God

The "prayer of faith" seems to be prayer offered by sincere believers that trusts God to respond. First, the elders of the church are the ones offering this prayer, since the conjunctive particle "and" links 5:14 to 5:15. Presumably the reason that the sick person has summoned them to pray is that these be-lievers have sincere faith in God. We remember that in James 1:6–8, James has warned this church that asking without faith or with doubting does not lead

---

2.   This second instruction does not mean that one must sing the Old Testament psalms, but neither does it stop one from doing so. It is the generic term for a song of praise.

3.   Matthew 25:39; Luke 4:40; John 4:46; Acts 19:12, among other places.

4.   Douglas J. Moo, *The Letter of James*, The Pillar New Testament Commentary (Grand Rapids: Eerdmans, 2000), 237. "When *astheneō* refers to spiritual weakness, this meaning is made clear by a qualifier ('in conscience' in 1 Cor. 8:7; 'in faith' in Rom. 14:1, 2) or by the context."

5.   Martin Dibelius and Heinrich Greeven, *A Commentary on the Epistle of James*, Hermeneia (Philadelphia: Fortress Press, 1976), 252.

to answered prayers. Perhaps the one who is ill has a weak faith or perhaps he is simply too ill to pray for himself at the moment. The text does not allow us to answer with certainty, but recognizing that the sick person has summoned the spiritual leaders of the church to pray is an indication that they are surely among those who trust God's ability and willingness to answer prayer.

The phrase "prayer of faith" (*euchē tēs pisteōs*) uses a rarer New Testament word for prayer, but the word does not indicate a special sort of prayer as distinct from James's more typical term *proseuchē*. The genitive expression "of faith" might also be translated "the faithful prayer" or "the prayer offered in faith." This is to say that there is not a special sort of prayer, denominated as "the prayer of faith," that elders are to use in this circumstance. Such a view would make prayer something more like a conjurer's spell, where the right words themselves bring about the desired result. Rather, James is speaking of ordinary prayer, speech petitioning God for the desired outcome, offered in faith that God hears and can act.

Faithful Prayer's Result: Wholeness

What is the outcome of the "prayer of faith?" We might characterize the three different outcomes of James 5:15 under the general term "wholeness." First, James suggests that prayer offered in faith "will save the one who is sick." The future-tense indicative verb *sōsei* expresses James's confidence that God *will* respond to faithful prayer. The term may simply mean "heal" as it does in a variety of New Testament passages where physical illness in view.[6] This sense seems to be preferable in light of the second outcome, "and the Lord will raise him up." In this particular instance, one who is too ill to attend the gathering of believers requests that the gathering's elders come to him and pray over him. The phrase "raise him up" points to physical restoration, and the immediate cause seems to be God's response to prayer, for it is "the Lord" who will raise him up. The third outcome is spiritual. "And if he has committed sins, he will be forgiven."

We ought not to assume that all illness is a manifestation of a particular moral transgression. That is, our sickness is not always the result of a particular sin we have committed (cf. John 9:3). In the Christian worldview, "sin" does lie behind all illness inasmuch as sickness and death entered the world as a result of Adam and Eve's sin, but in this passage, James does not suggest that the sick person is in such a state because of a particular transgression, for he uses the conjunctive *kan* ("and if") to express the possibility that sin might be present, not the certainty that it is. What is certain is that faithful prayer can bring about spiritual restoration, even as much as physical healing. The term "wholeness" expresses both the physical and spiritual restoration that this passage envisions. Prayer is able to accomplish this because it places believers

---

6. See Matthew 9:21; Mark 5:34; Luke 8:48.

in communion with the God who heals, restores, and forgives. The power of prayer is not inherent in the practice itself, but its power is the power of a living, personal God who hears and responds. The "prayer of faith" is prayer that trusts the faithful God who acts in human history to act in a particular situation. Now, is this passage speaking of the deliverance of one who is spiritually lost, that is, a non-Christian, or the restoration of a believer?

Without going beyond the text itself, we can suspect that this situation involves a person who is a believer: First, he is part of the church but physically unable to attend. Second, he has the inclination to call for the church's elders, presumably because of their faith. Third, he has the elders pray over him and anoint him with oil as the pathway to restoration. Fourth, James offers a conclusion in 5:16 of the power of confession and prayer for the restoration of believers: "Therefore, confess your sins to one another and pray for one another, that you may be healed." We consider the implications of interpersonal confession more fully in Question 36, but here we can suppose that the one who is sick may also confess specific sins to the elders, if there are specific sins to confess, and that their prayer would include petition for forgiveness. Regardless of whether the suffering is natural or spiritual, prayer offered in faith is the response James envisions.

Summary

The "prayer of faith" in James 5:15 seems to be faithful prayer offered by the elders of a church on behalf of someone who is suffering. This prayer expresses confidence, or "faith," that God is able and willing to heal the person being prayed over. The person's illness may have natural or spiritual causes, but prayer can address both situations. A broader question is the place of healing within the will of God. Douglas Moo addresses this question well and his response is worth quoting in full:

> The faith exercised in prayer is faith in the God who sovereignly accomplishes his will. When we pray, our faith recognizes, explicitly or implicitly, the overruling providential purposes of God. We may at times be given insight into that will, enabling us to pray with absolute confidence in God's plan to answer as we ask. But surely these cases are rare—more rare even than our subjective, emotional desires would lead us to suspect. A prayer for healing, then, must usually be qualified by a recognition that God's will in the matter is supreme. And it is clear in the NT that God does *not* always will to heal the believer. Paul's own prayer for his healing, offered three times, was not answered; God had a purpose in allowing the "thorn in the flesh," that "messenger of Satan," to remain (2 Cor. 12:7–9). . . . The faith with which we pray is

always faith in the God whose will is supreme and best; only sometimes does this faith include assurance that a particular request is within that will.[7]

REFLECTION QUESTIONS

1. How have you heard the "prayer of faith" explained before?

2. What is the role of faith in answered prayer?

3. Why does James suggest a sick person call the elders of the church to pray?

4. In what way is "sin" involved in all illness? Is a specific sin always behind a specific sickness?

5. What does this passage teach about the place of praying with others?

---

7. Moo, *The Letter of James*, 244–45.

PART 4

Prayer in Practice

How Does Prayer Relate to Other Spiritual Disciplines?

Prayer . . . [is] the soul in paraphrase, [the] heart in pilgrimage."[1] The great Anglican poet George Herbert (1593–1633) captured the act of praying insightfully, for prayer is the soul's speech and the heart's journey, and is indeed a great mystery and source of wonder. But there is another side to prayer that we must consider: the actual activity of praying. In this part of the book, we will take up several questions about the act of prayer itself, learning by doctrine and example how we might grow in our praying.[2] This chapter's focus is how prayer intersects with other spiritual disciplines, especially solitude, fasting, and journaling.

The spiritual disciplines are Spirit-empowered activities, practiced by Christians and guided by renewed minds, that cultivate godliness, fellowship with God, and conformity to Christ. The disciplines are not thoughts but activities, actions that we undertake that are responsive to the grace of God (cf. Titus 2:11), actions that dispose us to an awareness of God's love for us in Christ. God does not love us more when we diligently practice the disciplines nor less when we neglect them. These are not spiritually meritorious works, but they are part of the way that we yield our bodies as "living sacrifices" to God as part of our "spiritual/reasonable" worship (cf. Rom. 12:1–2). Prayer is both God's gift to us and our activity to undertake. While the Son and the Spirit may pray on our behalf in heaven and other Christians lift up

---

1. George Herbert, *The Country Parson, The Temple*, eds. John N. Wall Jr. and Richard J. Payne, The Classics of Western Spirituality (Mahwah, NJ: Paulist Press, 1981), 165.
2. Jonathan Edwards reminds readers of his *Life of David Brainerd* that "there are two ways of representing and recommending true religion and virtue to the world, which God hath made use of: the one is by doctrine and precept; the other is by instance and example: Both are abundantly used in the holy Scriptures." See Jonathan Edwards, *The Life of David Brainerd*, in The Works of Jonathan Edwards, vol. 7, ed. Norman Pettit (New Haven, CT: Yale University Press, 1985), 89.

our names in intercession here on earth, we must engage our bodies, minds, souls, and strength in prayer; no one else can do this for us. As we engage in the discipline of prayer, we will find that the Bible and the experience of Christians who have lived out a biblical faith commend to us the practices of solitude and fasting along with prayer.

Prayer and Solitude

Many spiritual-discipline handbooks written since Richard Foster's influential *Celebration of Discipline* (1978) have included the practices of silence and solitude as normative spiritual habits that help believers grow in godliness. Christians practice solitude by breaking for a season the normal pattern of fellowship and engagement with the world, that they may draw closer to God. The normative biblical pattern for the Christian life is clearly one of community (cf. Acts 2:42–47) and thus solitude is occasional and temporary. Even though some very careful New Testament scholars have raised questions about the role of solitude as part of Christian spiritual practice, the clearest biblical witness for this practice comes from the life of Jesus.[3]

All four gospel writers remembered Jesus's tendency to withdraw from the crowds, and even from his own disciples, for prayer. This tendency is present, although less obvious in John's gospel, but has abundant witness in the three Synoptic Gospels (Matthew, Mark, and Luke). A summary of relevant passages shows the shape of Jesus's practice.

Table 3—Jesus's Practice of Solitude and Prayer				
Text	**Time**	**Place**	**Duration**	**Activity**
Mark 1:35	"very early in the morning, while it was still dark"	"a desolate place" in Galilee	unspecified	"there he prayed"
Matthew 14:23	"when evening came"	"up on the mountain"	from afternoon through approx. 3 to 6 a.m. (Matt. 14:25)	"he went up . . . by himself to pray"
Luke 6:12[4]	"all night"	"out to the mountain"	unspecified, but overnight	"he went out . . . to pray"
Luke 9:18	unspecified	unspecified	unspecified	"he was praying alone"

---

3. Robert L. Plummer, "Are the Spiritual Disciplines of 'Silence and Solitude' Really Biblical?" *Journal of Spiritual Formation and Soul Care* 2 (2009): 101–12.

4. Other Lucan passages are likely references to this practice but lack enough detail for certainty. See Luke 4:42–44.

As Table 3 summarizes, the first three Gospels all record Jesus's withdrawal for extended times of prayer as part of his personal piety. Luke 5:16 offers a clearer detail that this activity was regular or habitual: "But Jesus Himself would *often* slip away to the wilderness and pray" (NASB 1995). The NASB translators italicized the word "often" to show its absence from the Greek text, yet why did they include it at all, especially since many other English translations omit it?[5] The reason for this dynamic translation is a grammatical function where two participles (*hypochōrōn*, "withdrawing" or "going away" and *proseuchomenos*, "praying") are used with the imperfect form of the verb "to be" (*ēn*) to express iterative, or habitual, action.[6] Perhaps Jesus's own habit shaped his admonition to his disciples to seek seclusion, rather than publicity, when they prayed (Matt. 6:6) and helps explain his desire for semi-solitude in Gethsemane before his betrayal and arrest (cf. Matt. 26:36–46). Following Jesus's example, believers are right to seek occasional opportunities to withdraw from the normal routines of life and ministry for seasons of prayer in solitude, be it on a mountain, in the wilderness, or in a closet.[7]

Developing the habit of praying always means that Christians will train themselves to pray at times they find inopportune or not ordinarily conducive to conversation and fellowship with God. Yet if short, hurried prayers offered in the midst of life's demands become the only occasion for our prayers, our prayers will likely become focused only on our immediate circumstances and thus will ignore other important, long-term matters. For example, a crisis in a child's schoolwork may indeed be a fitting occasion for parents to pray, yet parents should also take occasion to pray for the long-term spiritual health and growth of their child, which may not come to the forefront of their prayers apart from a disciplined approach. Similarly, a husband might respond to a text message from his wife that she is having a hectic day by stopping to pray for her in the moment, yet surely he will also want to pray not only for a calm spirit in the midst of a hectic day but also for her continued growth in grace and in her walk with God, and for her to manifest the Spirit's fruit in every circumstance. Both prayers matter. Seeking time and space for solitude is indeed a discipline, for it requires us to be proactive in identifying and maintaining our temporary distance from community (such as family, work, or church). Solitude is also the context in which the discipline of prayer can deepen and flourish in rich soil.

---

5. KJV, NRSV, and ESV omit any word of frequency, yet NIV includes the word "often."
6. Joseph A. Fitzmyer, *The Gospel according to Luke (1–9)*, Anchor Bible (New York: Doubleday, 1981), 575.
7. Andreas J. Köstenberger, *Excellence: The Character of God and the Pursuit of Scholarly Virtue* (Wheaton, IL: Crossway, 2011), 74.

Prayer and Fasting

Few Christians love fasting. At the school where I teach, my colleagues and I receive many questions about fasting each year from students preparing for ministry. One of the most common questions is, Do I really *need* to fast? This question reveals much, for if students preparing for ministry are unsure of the role and importance of fasting, how widespread might questions be within their churches? When was the last sermon you heard on fasting? I suspect fasting is unpopular because it is uncomfortable. Since we pray and practice the disciplines as whole people, meaning our minds, souls, and bodies are involved in our exercise, we *feel* fasting perhaps more acutely than other disciplines. Defined simply, fasting is the temporary abstention from food, and sometimes water, that we might seek God more intently. When we fast, we break for a season the normal patterns of eating and contentment. This season might be only a matter of hours (such as skipping one meal), or it might be slightly longer (avoiding more than one meal), or considerably longer.[8] Many books on the spiritual disciplines cover the biblical arguments for fasting, the steps for fasting, and other information such as kinds of fasts, duration, health considerations, and so forth, and we will not repeat all those details here. Jesus's statement in Matthew 6:16–18 begins, "when you fast," implying that fasting is a normal act of devotion that disciples follow until Jesus returns (Luke 5:34–35). In this part of the chapter, we want to focus on the relationship between prayer and fasting. Where are these disciplines linked in Scripture? How might fasting strengthen our prayers?

Fasting and prayer are connected in Scripture. At the news of Jerusalem's plight, Nehemiah "continued fasting and praying before the God of heaven" (Neh. 1:4). Daniel sought God's mercy on behalf of the exiled Jews "by prayer and pleas for mercy with fasting and sackcloth and ashes" (Dan. 9:3). The leaders of the Antiochene church fasted and prayed before commissioning Barnabas and Saul as missionaries (Acts 13:3), and these same leaders followed this pattern in setting apart other elders in other churches (Acts 14:23). Fasting and prayer were hallmarks of devotion in first century Palestine, attested by the practice of John the Baptist's disciples as well as of the disciples of the Pharisees (Luke 5:33) and of the godly widow Anna (Luke 2:37). One disputed reference involves Jesus's teaching to his disciples that they failed to exorcise a demon because they did not fast and pray (Matt. 17:21).[9] Other

---

8. From a physiological standpoint, fasting changes our bodies. If you are concerned that fasting might damage your health, or if you are unsure about how it might affect you, consider asking a medical doctor or nutritionist their perspective. Some readers may be unable to fast for various reasons, but being unable is different from being unwilling.

9. Scholars raise questions about the authenticity of this verse because of its absence in the oldest manuscripts.

examples could be added.[10] Clearly there are examples of fasts where prayer is not mentioned, just as there are examples of prayer where fasting is not discussed, but these two practices are found together often enough to see a connection. Why?

Fasting is a humbling experience, for it reminds us quickly that we are not self-sufficient. Deprived of food, even temporarily, we are aware of our frailty. Our heads ache; our stomachs growl; our bodies feel faint; our tempers may flare. Fasting reminds us that we are not God, an act that sometimes exposes sins that remain hidden to us in our normal contented lives. Who we are when we are hungry and weak may be a better reflection of who we truly are. One reason that fasting and prayer are so closely related is that fasting can help bring to light sins that we do not ordinarily see, offering us occasion to repent of these sins through prayer. Bringing humility, fasting can also help us to see God as truly other: he does not hunger nor does he grow weary; his temperament is not affected by food or its absence; he needs nothing, he possesses all; he is worthy of worship. Thus fasting can prompt prayers of adoration and thanksgiving toward the God who need not fast.

Prayer and Journaling

Although the practice of maintaining a journal appears regularly in spiritual-discipline handbooks, its absence from Scripture means that it is a different sort of practice than meditation or fasting; a helpful practice but not an obligatory one.[11] In an age where we are accustomed to reading the personal thoughts of friends and strangers on our phones instantly, remembering that such access is less than two decades old can be difficult. The practice of keeping a personal written record of one's life has some precedent in the ancient world, such as Augustine's *Confessions*, yet much information about people's interior reflections or prayers went unwritten, or was consigned to letters shared among friends. By the seventeenth century, personal writings were becoming more common, and numerous diaries and journals survive from the eighteenth century on that allow readers a glimpse into the prayer lives of the women and men who kept them. Though we often use the labels "diary" and "journal" interchangeably, those who study such writings tend to differentiate a "diary," which was personal writing rarely intended for publication, from a "journal," which contained private reflections that one might release to the public. One well-known author of both was the Presbyterian missionary David Brainerd, who published a serial journal of his missionary work among Native Americans yet also maintained a private diary that was far more introspective. Puritan and evangelical pastors often maintained

---

10. For example, 1 Samuel 7:6; 2 Chronicles 20:3; Ezra 8:21–23; Psalm 35:13; 69:10; Isaiah 58:3–6; Joel 2:12–15; 1 Corinthians 7:5; among others.
11. See Donald S. Whitney, "Do I Have to Keep a Journal?" (2009), biblicalspirituality.org.

journals and diaries, and many lay members within their congregations did so as well, and we can learn much about the daily religious life of such men and women from their personal writings.

How might journaling or diary-keeping relate to prayer? One way is by preserving a reminder or memorial for ourselves of God's work in our lives. Keeping a record of the things we pray about and the way God has answered them is so very helpful. It is very easy for us to forget the myriad of petitions we make of God and the innumerable ways that he cares for us through prayer. In your own life, can you recall exactly what you asked of God six months, two years, or ten years ago? How did God answer those requests? Do you remember times where your experiential awareness of the love of God was connected with times of adoration or thanksgiving in prayer? Maintaining a record of our prayers and God's answers might foster more thankfulness towards God and can increase our faith as we see reminders of his ongoing care over the course of months, years, or decades.

Another way that journaling and prayer intersect is by way of testimony, leaving a record for others of God's faithfulness in answering prayer. Though my own grandmother had only a sixth-grade education and rarely travelled more than a few hundred miles from the small community where she had been born over a century ago, her letters to family members serve as a journal inasmuch as she mentioned specific things she was praying for and testified to God's goodness in answering her prayers. By reading them, I am encouraged that she and I pray to the same God, one who delights to hear prayer, and I am encouraged that her prayers were answered, even as my own are. In this way, my grandmother's faith is still bearing fruit decades after her death; she is shaping me spiritually through her ordinary record of prayers. In a similar way, our own prayer journals might provide our family members with an enduring witness to God's faithfulness that will survive long after our own deaths. German Baptist George Müller's (1805–1898) written prayers offer a good example of this, for during his lifetime, Müller recorded more than fifty thousand answers to his prayers.[12]

Yet another way that journaling can aid prayer is by forcing us to concentrate on what we want to say or ask. The act of writing has a way of making abstract thoughts more concrete. That is, many times we are burdened with numerous things about which we want to pray, but naming and expressing these desires can be overwhelming. As we have mentioned above, one of the greatest blessings in such times is to remember that the Holy Spirit prays within us and for us when we do not know how to pray, yet journaling can also be a practical aid to help us untangle our burdens. Some folks find it

---

12. For an introduction to Müller, see Donald S. Whitney, https://www.crossway.org/articles/what-george-mueller-can-teach-us-about-prayer/.

helpful simply to list their prayers while others find the act of writing down specific needs and requests aids them in articulating their petitions to God.

What are some ways that we might maintain such a prayer journal? Considering how we might keep such a journal can be very helpful, for accessibility, portability, and longevity all affect approaches we might take. Our journals might be handwritten, electronic, or a hybrid of both. An inexpensive spiral-bound notebook or a leather-bound book might serve the purpose of maintaining a journal equally well. Paul Miller suggests using 3" by 5" index cards to record prayer requests as these are very inexpensive and easily portable.[13] I have found that small side-stapled notebooks that are 3.5" by 5.5" are very helpful because they can be tucked inside a Bible or in a shirt pocket easily and thus be nearby when needed. A variety of journaling applications exist for computers or smart phones, and such applications often feature daily reminders or easy integration with cloud storage systems to make journaling easier. More general note-taking software is also widely available for numerous computing platforms and devices. Word-processing software might also be a way to keep such a record. A hybrid approach is to maintain a written journal and, using widely available scanning applications for smart phones, to capture a picture for storage in a note-taking system. This hybrid approach makes it less likely that we will lose our record of prayers if we misplace a physical notebook.

Summary

Prayer is closely related to many spiritual practices or disciplines, and we have considered only three here. Solitude is the temporary withdrawal from community to seek God more intentionally. Solitude is both a discipline and the context in which prayer might flourish. We can, of course, pray at all times, wherever we might be, and do not need to seek a special place for prayer to be effective, yet we should also recognize that our familiar surroundings may make us prone to distractions and less focused on our prayers. We see that Jesus was often withdrawing to secluded places for prayer. Fasting is the temporary abstention from the regular rhythm of eating and contentment that we might seek God more intensely. Journaling is the intentional act of keeping a record of God's work in our lives and our reflections on this work. We might pray without ever keeping a record of it, but often, keeping a record of our prayers can help us express our prayers more clearly and allows us (and others) to see God's faithfulness in answering our petitions.

---

13. Paul J. Miller, *A Praying Life: Connecting with God in a Distracting World* (Colorado Springs: Navpress, 2009), 225–33.

REFLECTION QUESTIONS

1. How might Jesus's practice of solitude and prayer inform our own practices?

2. What are some ways that fasting might aid prayer?

3. How can journaling encourage us to continue in prayer?

4. What are some ways you might begin journaling your prayers?

5. What are some ways you can incorporate these disciplines into your own prayer life?

Why Does God Sometimes Seem Absent in Prayer?

Throughout this book, one common theme has been the unique role that prayer plays in sustaining relational nearness between believers and God. Reading Scripture, we find expectations that prayer makes real communication with God possible. David experienced God's nearness in prayer: "I call upon you, for you will answer me, O God; incline your ear to me; hear my words" (Ps. 17:6). "In the day of my trouble I call upon you, for you answer me" (Ps. 86:7). "On the day I called, you answered me; my strength of soul you increased" (Ps. 138:3). Jeremiah received this prophetic assurance from Yahweh, "Thus says the LORD who made the earth, the LORD who formed it to establish it—the LORD is his name: Call to me and I will answer you, and will tell you great and hidden things that you have not known" (Jer. 33:2–3). Jesus expressed great confidence that God heard his prayers: "And Jesus lifted up his eyes and said, 'Father, I thank you that you have heard me. I knew that you always hear me, but I said this on account of the people standing around, that they may believe that you sent me'" (John 11:41–42). The author of Hebrews repeatedly exhorted Christians to "draw near" to God in confidence (4:16; 7:19, 25; 10:1, 22; 11:6). James implored Christians, "Draw near to God, and he will draw near to you" (James 4:8). Countless saints across two millennia add their voices to the vital place of prayer in their experience of closeness to God. With such a common refrain, we might feel unwilling to admit that sometimes, perhaps many times, this experience is not our own. Why does God sometimes seem absent in prayer?

Answering this question requires us to examine our expectations of what it means for God to *be* present and for us to be *aware of* God's presence. It requires that we consider what it means to "hear" God, how God speaks to people, and how we experience the Spirit's leadership. These questions are big and others have asked them before us. We can only sketch brief answers here, but considering them just may help us become more sensitive to hearing God and being more aware of his presence when we pray.

We Trust That God Is with Us

Though God may seem absent, we have confidence that he is with us. Jesus promised his disciples, "I am with you always, to the end of the age" (Matt. 28:20), a promise that Yahweh had made to Joshua after the death of Moses and at the outset of Israel's campaigns to take the land of promise (Josh. 1:9). King David echoed the words of Joshua to his son Solomon: "Then David said to Solomon his son, 'Be strong and courageous and do it. Do not be afraid and do not be dismayed, for the Lord God, even my God, is with you. He will not leave you or forsake you, until all the work for the service of the house of the Lord is finished'" (1 Chron. 28:20). These proclamations of God's presence occur at key points in the biblical narrative and are tied to God's various covenants with his people. Elsewhere, we have mentioned the biblical teaching of God's omnipresence, the truth that he is always present everywhere, and the facts of our union with Christ and the indwelling presence of the Spirit, hallmarks of the new covenant between Jesus and his people. By faith, we take God at his word, that even when we feel he is absent he is indeed with us. We are not alone, though, in our experience of God's absence in prayer.

While Scripture presents God as present and answering, some in the Bible have lamented their inability to hear him. David cried out, "How long, O Lord? Will you forget me forever? How long will you hide your face from me?" (Ps. 13:1). Asaph asked, "O Lord God of hosts, how long will you be angry with your people's prayers?" (Ps. 80:4). Ethan the Ezrahite asked, "How long, O Lord? Will you hide yourself forever?" (Ps. 89:46). The words of the prophet Habakkuk say, "O Lord, how long shall I cry for help, and you will not hear? Or cry to you 'Violence!' and you will not save?" (Hab. 1:2). Notice that these laments come from godly people, from prophets, kings, and poets who walked with God; from those through whom God wrote Scripture. Using a similar lament from Job 23:3, Austen Phelps, nineteenth-century professor at Andover Theological Seminary, summarized this situation well: even if one maintains consistent devotion, "a consciousness of the *absence of God* is one of the standing incidents of the religious life."[1] To be sure, some people experience God's absence in prayer because they are truly separated from God by their sin, because they refuse to let go of sin, because they do not trust God, or for many other reasons. Yet what of truly faithful Christians, who pursue godliness, who love the Lord and desire to follow him? Why does God sometimes seem absent even to them?

---

1. Austen Phelps, *The Still Hour: Or Communion with God* (Boston: D. Lothrop, 1893), 7–8 (italics original). Phelps's small book is a classic treatment of this topic.

Dark Night of Desertion

In the Old Testament, faithful believers sometimes experienced a sense of God's absence. In the New Testament, the most striking example of God's seeming absence is Jesus's cry from the cross, "My God, my God, why have you forsaken me?" (Matt. 27:46; Mark 15:34), his words a quotation of Psalm 22:1. The New Testament seems quiet on experiences of God's absence, but we must always be cautious in establishing positions based on silence since much of the New Testament is made up of occasional documents and is not a catalog of every possible experience. We ought to recognize, though, that the New Testament does present a fairly strong testimony of the Spirit's indwelling presence as a decisive difference from the Old Testament. God is indeed with his people in a different way than under the old covenant.

Two Christian traditions did give attention to this experience of God's absence from very different perspectives. One tradition is that of mysticism and the other is Puritanism. Full discussion of either approach would go beyond this book's boundaries, but a sketch of some important hallmarks and writers, as well as some cautions, is appropriate. Like prayer, mysticism exists in many religions and has numerous definitions, but generally it is an ineffable experience, an encounter with God that cannot be captured in words. Three common hallmarks are purgation, illumination, and unification, known as the *triplex via* or "threefold way."[2] Mystical writers recognize sin as a barrier to communion with God and encourage the faithful to cultivate holiness and self-denial. Illumination involves gaining a clearer awareness of God and his presence which, paradoxically, involves greater awareness of how mysterious God is. Unification, a stage mystical writers suggest only some believers will attain, involves a strong awareness of union with God that foreshadows a future heavenly experience. Mysticism transcends denominational labels and exists within Protestantism, Orthodoxy, and Roman Catholicism, but it is more representative of these latter two ecclesial families. In the ancient church, writers like Gregory of Nyssa and Pseudo-Dionysius represent this approach. One Catholic mystic writer who explored God's seeming absence in prayer was John of the Cross (1542–1591). A member of the Carmelite monastic order, John was a poet and author, and is probably best known for the phrase "dark night of the soul." One modern interpreter sums up the idea of dark nights in this way:

> Dark nights of the soul are those seasons and times in the spiritual life in which God initiates a profound work of purging or purifying the human spirit of sins and vices of

---

2. For a balanced assessment of the threefold way from a Protestant perspective, see Tom Schwanda, "Threefold Way," in *Dictionary of Christian Spirituality*, ed. Glen G. Scorgie (Grand Rapids: Zondervan, 2011), 798–800. For a critical assessment, see Winfried Corduan, *Mysticism: An Evangelical Option?* (Grand Rapids: Zondervan, 1991).

the heart that hinder union with God and the Spirit's characterological filling of the believer. The experience is of the felt absence of God (desolation) in contrast to the felt presence of God (consolation). Whereas consolation is intended by God to encourage the believer with the experience of God's presence and direct the heart to God through the spiritual disciplines, desolation is intended by God to be a mirror revealing what is in the heart of the believer.[3]

As writers in this vein interpret the experience, God works during these seasons to wean believers away from growth that is in their own power, to help expose lingering patterns of sin, or to cause them to pursue deeper faith and love.

Puritan authors represent a different approach to the issue of God's absence in prayer. We devote an entire chapter to Puritans and prayer in Question 40 and thus forego here an introduction to the diverse groups of Protestants who bore that title. Though some Puritans address similar themes as mystical writers, their focus on the experience of life in God's presence is deep and worth the time to explore.[4] Joseph Symonds's *The Case and Cure of a Deserted Soul* (1642) presents nearly forty chapters to help Christians understand and overcome the sense of God's absence.[5] Thomas Goodwin's *A Child of Light Walking in Darknesse* (1659) is an extended sermonic meditation on Isaiah 50:10–11 intended to encourage believers to persevere in faith when God seems distant.[6]

According to Symonds, one reason that God may seem absent is that believers may have "grieved" the Holy Spirit (cf. Eph. 4:30). As considered above, the Holy Spirit is God and the Spirit is personal. Because he is personal, we may live in such a way that honors his presence and work or that dishonors him. Believers may grieve the Spirit through dishonor or disobedience.[7] We dishonor the Spirit by rejecting his fruit, comforts, and leadership. We disobey the Spirit when we openly choose to sin in spite of a clear command of God or ignoring a clear responsibility enjoined in Scripture. Yes, the Holy Spirit is God and thus sovereign, but the Spirit is also personal and the person of the Godhead "nearest" to us and thus perhaps the first one that we honor

---

3. John H. Coe, "Dark Night," in *Dictionary of Christian Spirituality*, ed. Glen G. Scorgie (Grand Rapids: Zondervan, 2011), 389.
4. Puritanism, because of its diversity, included authors who addressed a spectrum of spiritual experiences. In general, Puritans fostered spiritual practices more intentionally linked to Scripture than did Roman Catholic or Orthodox mystical writers. Readers wishing to go deeper might find David Chou-Ming Wang, "The English Puritans and Spiritual Desertion: A Protestant Perspective on the Place of Spiritual Dryness in the Christian Life," *The Journal of Spiritual Formation and Soul Care* 3, no. 1 (2010): 42–65, a helpful starting place.
5. Joseph Symonds, *The Case and Cure of a Deserted Soul* (Edinburg: Robert Bryson, 1642).
6. Thomas Goodwin, *A Child of Light Walking in Darknesse* (London: 1659).
7. Symonds, *A Deserted Soul*, 154.

or dishonor, that we obey or disobey. When God seems absent in our prayers, we may be tempted to forego prayer altogether, yet this is certainly a wrong choice. Instead, we should seek God's grace all the more, inviting the Spirit to search our hearts and repenting when he makes us aware of grieving him.[8]

Goodwin explores several efficient causes of these times of darkness: First, the Holy Spirit, while not actively *causing* our sense of distance, may withdraw a felt sense of his presence for a season. Then, our own hearts may also cause a sense of God's absence. Even though our hearts are renewed by the Spirit, sin's presence is not removed during believers' lives, and thus our affections are still susceptible to weakness. Satanic temptation is the third efficient cause of a sense of divine absence. Goodwin notes that Satan "hath a special inclination and a more peculiar malicious desire to vex and molest the Saints with this sort of temptations, of doubts and disquietnesse that God is not their God."[9] According to Goodwin, Satan's angelic power gives him advantage over human nature, allowing him to tempt humans to doubt God's nearness and love, and thus to cloud our vision of God, through both outward and inward suggestions.[10] Goodwin devotes about one hundred pages to analysis of Satan's methods, culminating in seven "advantages" that Satan has in tempting believers to doubt God's presence and nearness.[11]

Though born too late to be a "Puritan," British pastor D. Martyn Lloyd-Jones (1899–1981) was deeply influenced by Puritan authors and in his preaching had a Puritan-like expository ministry. Lloyd-Jones was a pastor, not an author, but many of his sermons have been turned into books in the twentieth and twenty-first centuries, and one work that addresses the perceived absence of God in prayer is his *Spiritual Depression*.[12] Himself influenced by Puritans and Lloyd-Jones, Pastor John Piper's *When I Don't Desire God* explores the experience of God's absence, including a helpful reflection on the practice of prayer during these seasons.[13] One thing these authors have in common is a commitment to exploring the sense of God's absence among those who have been born again, that is, those who have experienced new spiritual life flowing from the gospel and thus the fruits of true prayer. This approach is indeed a contrast to the "dark night" view, though the latter is undoubtedly influential and more well known.

Lloyd-Jones and Piper both emphasize the place of the Psalms for understanding the experience of God's absence. Lloyd-Jones believes Psalm 42:5 provides believers a model for persevering through these seasons:

---

8. Symonds, *A Deserted Soul*, 241.
9. Goodwin, *Walking in Darkness*, 68.
10. Goodwin, *Walking in Darkness*, 78–85.
11. Goodwin, *Walking in Darkness*, 168–77.
12. D. Martyn Lloyd-Jones, *Spiritual Depression: Its Causes and Cure* (Grand Rapids: Eerdmans, 1965).
13. John Piper, *When I Don't Desire God: How to Fight for Joy* (Wheaton, IL: Crossway, 2004).

Why are you cast down, O my soul, and why are you in turmoil
within me?
Hope in God; for I shall again praise him, my salvation and
my God.

Though many psalms contain prayers directed to God, here the psalmist
speaks to himself, dialoging with his own soul. The psalmist "asks" and "reminds" himself of several things: First, using poetic parallelism, he asks his
soul why it is dejected and in turmoil. Then, he reminds himself to hope in
God, anticipating a future time of restored worship. Piper finds David's experience of "waiting patiently on Yahweh" in the midst of a "miry bog" in Psalm
40 a help when God seems distant.[14] In our own dark times, we also need to
learn how to listen to God.

We Learn to How Listen to God

One reason God may seem distant is that we might be unaccustomed to listening to him. Learning to hear God and considering the ways that God speaks
to his children can help us recognize his presence in our lives and in our prayers.
In Scripture, God sometimes spoke audibly or directly to people. Although
some in Scripture "heard" the voice of God in response to prayer, or perhaps
equally as often *apart* from prayer at God's initiative—such as Moses's experience at the burning bush (Exod. 3:5), Samuel's bedtime summons (1 Sam. 3),
or even Saul's conversion on the road to Damascus (Acts 9)—it is eye-opening
to consider how few individuals in Scripture heard God's voice directly. Some
did, to be sure, yet many did not. We might assume that the Bible contains more
descriptions of this sort of fellowship than it actually does, and thus presume
that what the Bible presents as occasional and rare is the normal experience.

Scripture sometimes presents Jesus as speaking to his people in prayer. In
Acts 9, Jesus speaks to Ananias and directs him to search out and commission
Saul (9:10–16). Here, Luke writes as an omniscient observer of visionary dia-
logue between Ananias and the Lord. Similarly, the Lord speaks to Paul, comforting him (Acts 18:9–10), directing him (Acts 22:10), and encouraging him
(Acts 23:11). Luke also describes the Holy Spirit as speaking and guiding the
church. For example, when the leaders at Antioch were fasting and praying,
"The Holy Spirit said, 'Set apart for me Barnabas and Saul for the work to which
I have called them'" (Acts 13:2). We ought not to overlook the strategic importance of these incidents in the life of Paul and in Luke's presentation of the
church's mission; they validate Paul's ministry. Yet we should not ignore Luke's
inspired testimony that Jesus and the Spirit sometimes lead Christians directly
in prayer. Elsewhere, Paul recounts Jesus's comforting presence in prayer.

---

14. Piper, *When I Don't Desire God*, 214–15.

In 2 Corinthians 12:1–10, Paul, arguing for the authority of his ministry, recounts a divine impediment to his ministry, one for which he sought relief. Paul pleaded with Jesus several times that this "thorn" might be removed, "But he said to me, 'My grace is sufficient for you, for my power is made perfect in weakness'" (2 Cor. 12:9). Paul's language is straightforward: he "pleaded" (*parekalesa*) with the Lord, but the Lord "said" (*eirēken*) that his grace was sufficient. This description is of conversation.

The fact that these instances involve the Son and Spirit are important. Jesus speaks with God's voice: "Long ago, at many times and in many ways, God spoke to our fathers by the prophets, but in these last days he has spoken to us by his Son" (Heb. 1:1–2). While the "speaking" of this passage surely refers to Christ as the ultimate Word of God, the one to whom all history points, it has significance for our prayers and the ways that we hear God. For one thing, unlike the ways and people through whom God spoke in previous days, the Son is himself God (1:2–3), and thus no higher or further prophet can arise, no new revelation can surpass what God has said through Jesus. Then, the Son who speaks is also the Son who intercedes on behalf of his people (7:25) and leads his people. We remember Jesus's statement that "my sheep hear my voice, and I know them, and they follow me" (John 10:27).

Another way that God is present in our prayers is through his Word, the Bible. We have mentioned the vital place of the Bible in many other places in this book and need not rehearse all of these matters here, but this may be the most common way that we experience God's presence in response to our prayers. At this point, some readers may be tempted to sigh, "Not the Bible again," yet there is no better way to hear God than to listen to him speak through his Word. I recall a former colleague who once lamented that, while ignoring their Bibles, so many Christians prayed that God would speak to them. His point was that God does speak clearly and if we neglect to read the Word, we might simply be unable to hear God because we aren't satisfied with or perhaps even aware of the conversation.

Summary

If you feel that God is sometimes absent in your prayers, take heart: you are not alone. God might indeed withhold his comforting, consoling presence at times—perhaps to cause us to seek him all the more or maybe in response to our active pursuit of sin and rebellion against the Spirit—or perhaps he *is* present and we would rather him speak directly than hear him through his Word. It is through God's Word that we hear his promises never to leave or forsake us; thus, by faith, we trust his promise even as we seek him more. If God seems far off, dear Christian, pray as did David: "You have said, 'Seek my face.' My heart says to you, 'Your face, LORD, do I seek'" (Ps. 27:8).

REFLECTION QUESTIONS

1. What confidence do believers have that God is present, even if he seems absent?

2. How would you explain the idea of a "dark night of the soul"?

3. What role does the Bible play in helping us be aware of God's presence in our prayers?

4. Is it comforting to know that believers in Scripture sometimes felt God's absence?

5. How does the ministry of the Holy Spirit relate to our experience of God's absence or presence in prayer?

Should We Argue with God in Prayer?

Sometimes in Scripture prayer seems to be less about asking and more about persuading. Take for example Abraham's prayer for Sodom in Genesis 18. After learning that God intended to destroy the city, Abraham intercedes, asking whether God will follow through with his plans if fifty righteous people can be found in the city, to which God says he will spare the city if fifty righteous people can be found therein. Abraham continues to plead down the number: forty-five, forty, thirty, twenty, and finally ten. Each time, God promises to stave off his destruction for the sake of the righteous. Or consider the example of Moses's prayer after the people grumbled about entering the Promised Land in Numbers 14. The Lord threatened to disinherit the people, strike them down, and raise up a new people from Moses's family. Moses prayed on Israel's behalf, reminding Yahweh that the fame of his name was connected to the success of Israel, and God relented. What are Christians to make of these texts, and what are their implications for prayer? Should believers argue with God in prayer?

Arguments Are Not Always Disagreeable

Many readers will understand the word "argue" as something like "heated debate," or an "angry disagreement," which is all too often our experience. Negatively, the word can connote these things, but I am using the term a bit more broadly as a shorthand way of saying "offering persuasive reasons" for our ideas. Arguments might be sound or unsound, valid or invalid, persuasive or unpersuasive. Sometimes arguments (and prayers) start with the right facts but reach the wrong conclusion. The classic example of this mistake is Jonah, who refused to preach repentance to the citizens of Nineveh precisely because he *knew* God's gracious and merciful character (Jonah 4:2) and that Yahweh was likely to forgive this people whom the prophet despised. In the examples of Abraham and Moses above, and elsewhere in Scripture, we find God's people offering arguments for their requests in prayer.

Persuasive Prayers

Considering Abraham's situation in Genesis 18, God appears in a theophany (a temporary appearance of God in a human form) as three men. We learn that two of the men are angels. Abraham receives the men with hospitality and the men reveal that Sarah will bear a child in her old age. Afterward, the men leave to travel to the cities of Sodom and Gomorrah to see the wickedness that has been spoken of them and the Lord announces his intention to destroy these cities because of their sin. Abraham intercedes, asking the Lord to consider the presence of the righteous in the city among the wicked, and then offers an argument based on God's character: "Far be it from you to do such a thing, to put the righteous to death with the wicked, so that the righteous fare as the wicked! Far be it from you! Shall not the Judge of all the earth do what is just?" (Gen. 18:25). Abraham appealed specifically to God's justice, intimating that it is proper to punish the wicked but not those who are just.

In Numbers 14, after Moses's spies return to report on the fortifications and strength of the people whom they will face in the promised land, the people complain about God's deliverance from Egypt: "Why is the LORD bringing us into this land, to fall by the sword?" (Num. 14:3). In the larger narrative, Israel has already complained about God's rescue and Moses's leadership with the incident of the golden calf in Exodus 32. With this latest complaint, God proposes to smite them and begin again with Moses's family to set apart a new people. Moses intercedes on Israel's behalf, offering God several reasons to relent: First, because the Egyptians might hear of this situation and interpret it as weakness on God's behalf: "Now if you kill this people as one man, then the nations who have heard your fame will say, 'It is because the LORD was not able to bring this people into the land . . . that he has killed them'" (Num. 14:15–16). Second, Moses argues based on God's character:

> And now, please let the power of the LORD be great as you have promised, saying, "The LORD is slow to anger and abounding in steadfast love, forgiving iniquity and transgression, but he will by no means clear the guilty, visiting the iniquity of the fathers on the children, to the third and the fourth generation." Please pardon the iniquity of this people, according to the greatness of your steadfast love, just as you have forgiven this people, from Egypt until now. (Num. 14:17–19)

Moses offered two arguments, one for God's reputation and one for God's character. The first is that God's enemies would use the occasion of Israel's destruction to bring disrepute upon his name. The second is that God's own character is one of forgiveness and forbearance. As with Abraham's prayer, God relents from immediate, public destruction, but nonetheless promises to hold those who have sinfully grumbled to account, sparing the righteous (Num. 14:20–25).

The prospect of arguing with God in prayer may seem disrespectful or foolish: Who are we to argue with God? There might be many arguments or reasons that would indeed be foolish: presuming that we are giving God information that he lacks in order to make the best decision; presuming that God has not considered our perspective or our desires; presuming that we have more foresight than God to see the consequences or the potential good that comes from an action; and the like. Yet in the cases looked at here, God does not chastise Abraham for having the audacity to try to persuade him to a different action nor does he rebuke Moses for daring to remind him of his reputation and character. Instead, these arguments prevail without divine objection.

Guardrails for Arguing in Prayer

In our own families, jobs, and society, one reason that we argue is that we are unable to see situations from someone else's point of view. Of course, some arguments arise precisely because we *do* understand someone's side of things and think they are wrong! But we recognize that we have our limits. We all have a perspective on what we think is best for our lives, what we would like to happen, and what outcomes we think would be best; yet every person has this in common: we see our situations and needs only in part. Partial information is not inaccurate, but partial information can lead us to make bad decisions, including arguing with God, suggesting that he does not understand what we face. He does. God not only *sees*, but *declares* "the end from the beginning" (Isa. 46:10). God knows what we need before we ask him (cf. Matt. 6:8) precisely because he is our Father "who is in heaven" (v. 9). Reflecting often on these truths is so important for our prayers, for we always ask from some degree of ignorance, but God always answers from full omniscience. How might this truth shape our prayers? First, it is right for us to acknowledge our limited knowledge of any situation we bring before God and to ask him to let such limitations humble us. Second, we should ask God to give us a greater vision for our situation that we might worship him for the wisdom of his provision. We ought also to consider that we have never received an answer to prayer that was *not* the right answer at the perfect time.

Summary

For some readers, the idea of offering arguments for our prayers seems odd, perhaps because the only reason we are accustomed for seeking things is, "I want it." The examples of Abraham and Moses could be multiplied. For example, David argues with God in Psalm 143, making more than a dozen requests for this reason: "For your name's sake, O LORD, preserve my life! In your righteousness bring my soul out of trouble! And in your steadfast love you will cut off my enemies, and you will destroy all the adversaries of my soul, for I am your servant" (Ps. 143:11–12). Arguing with God—reminding him of his promises, character, and name—is a different sort of thing than arguing for our own way.

REFLECTION QUESTIONS

1. What are two ways of understanding "argue" in relation to prayer?

2. What argument does Abraham make for God not to destroy the wicked cities?

3. What argument does Moses make for God not to destroy Israel?

4. What are other arguments that we might use in prayer?

5. What are limitations we must consider when arguing in prayer?

How Does Prayer Form Character?

Those whose lives Christ has transformed through the gospel and calls on the path of discipleship recognize the distance between whom they are called to become and who they actually are. That is, Christians remain aware of the continuing presence of sin in their lives, and they desire to grow more like Christ in their actual lives, to grow nearer to the Father, and to grow through the indwelling power of the Holy Spirit. One aspect of becoming more like Christ involves moral change: living consistently with our calling. Scripture portrays Jesus as consistently obeying God's law as it was revealed in Scripture. Unlike every other man or woman, Jesus walked with impeccable integrity. In an earlier chapter we considered how Jesus's active obedience is accounted to Christians, but it is also clear that Christians are to actually strive to live obediently in light of Christ's righteousness. Another way of saying this is that Christians' lives are to come to look increasingly like that of our Lord. One aspect of our salvation is the freedom to pursue moral change as a response to the gospel. How does prayer relate to this moral transformation? What role does prayer play in long-term moral change? How might prayer help us wrestle with aspects of right and wrong that we find difficult? In this chapter, we want to consider how our prayers intersect with the ways we think about right and wrong (ethics) and affect the way we actually live (morality) on a consistent basis (character).

Ethics, Morality, Character, and Prayer

Nearly everyone has heard the terms "ethics" and "morality," and often these words seem interchangeable, but they are different. Ethics is the reflection on or study of what makes a certain choice right and an alternative choice wrong. Morality refers to the actual practice of living out our ethic, making real choices that are right or wrong, good or evil, consistent or inconsistent. When we speak of someone's "character," we are often talking about the consistency of their moral choices. Prayer affects our character, morals, and ethics.

At the highest level of our reflection, prayer should govern our ethics, because without it we may fail to trust the goodness and rightness of God's commands. This failure is hardly new; it has followed us from Eden forward. Adam and Eve's moral failure (eating from the tree of the knowledge of good and evil) grew from an ethical failure, namely doubting God's motives for proscribing this fruit. The biblical narrative is filled with bad choices (morals) flowing from bad principles (ethics).

Prayer also directs our moral choices. In Colossians 3:5–10, Paul identifies a pattern of living that characterizes a mind that is set on the things of the earth:

> Put to death therefore what is earthly in you: sexual immorality, impurity, passion, evil desire, and covetousness, which is idolatry. On account of these the wrath of God is coming. In these you too once walked, when you were living in them. But now you must put them all away: anger, wrath, malice, slander, and obscene talk from your mouth. Do not lie to one another, seeing that you have put off the old self with its practices and have put on the new self, which is being renewed in knowledge after the image of its creator.

The strong imperative "put to death" (*nekrōsate*) calls believers to enact decisive moral change in relationship to others. Believers must "put away" (*apothesthe*) these immoral behaviors because they are "putting away" (*apekdysamenoi*) their old way of life. The Colossians, and we, are a new sort of people who must practice a new sort of morality, one guided by the ethic of love toward others (3:14) and manifesting itself in the moral behaviors that marked Christ's compassion and must now mark that of his disciples: "kindness, humility, meekness, patience" and forgiveness (3:12–13). In the opening verses of chapter 3, Paul links moral change with spiritual knowledge and practice:

> If then you have been raised with Christ, seek the things that are above, where Christ is, seated at the right hand of God. Set your minds on things that are above, not on things that are on earth. For you have died, and your life is hidden with Christ in God. When Christ who is your life appears, then you also will appear with him in glory. (Col. 3:1–4)

Christians are to "seek" (*zēteite*) and "set their minds" (*phroneite*) on a way of living shaped by Christ's present heavenly reign and their own new identity of being "hidden with Christ in God." Prayer is a key way that we seek and set our minds on Christ and our identity in him.

If character is formed in consistency of moral choices that align with our Christ-focused ethics, then the sort of prayer Paul insists upon in

1 Thessalonians 5:17, "unceasing prayer," is urgently important. We continually face innumerable moral choices that are working to form our character in ways consistent or incompatible with our ethics, and we need continual strength and direction to seek and set our minds on the new life that is ours in Christ and to choose the good for the glory of God and the good of our neighbor.

Prayer and Gospel Character Integrated

As we draw the elements of this chapter together, we see that prayer integrates our ethics, morality, and character into a united whole. Perhaps the best way to see this integration is through a case study that shows why prayer is so valuable at each level of our character and how prayer integrates these three together through the gospel.

One case study on the integrating role of prayer involves Jesus's command to love our enemies: "You have heard that it was said, 'You shall love your neighbor and hate your enemy.' But I say to you, Love your enemies and pray for those who persecute you, so that you may be sons of your Father who is in heaven" (Matt. 5:43–45). Jesus's intention is straightforward: Christians show the reality of our adoption by loving and praying for our enemies. How might prayer integrate ethics, morals, and character here?

At the ethical level, we might pray that God would help us trust that this way of responding to those who seek our harm is part of his good plan for those whom he has saved. Praying for and loving our enemies does not make us Christian, but being Christian means loving and praying for our enemies, and these actions cut against the grain of our natural inclinations. How can these moral actions of loving and praying be in our best interest if they seem so alien to us? Even more challenging, how can these actions be the best ways of responding when the world seems to value and reward the opposite actions of hating and cursing our enemies? Prayer governs our ethics when we ask God to help us trust that this principle of love and prayer is good, right, and most consistent with what it means to be women and men who follow him in discipleship.

Then, prayer relates to morality in this example when we are faced with a real enemy whom we are to love and for whom we are to pray. There are no shortage of situations in our actual lives: complete strangers driving aggressively during our evening commute; faceless government bureaucrats who delay visa applications or adoption travel because of their antimony toward Christian faith or seemingly merely because they have the power to do so; local political leaders who take heavy-handed approaches to communities of faith while promoting secular virtues; national leaders who abuse human rights on inconceivable scales; and the list goes on. Prayer directs our morality in these instances as we are faced with the choice to live consistently with our ethic of loving and praying for these enemies or to set our ethic aside and respond as the world, the flesh, and the devil (cf. Eph. 2) would have us do. It may seem odd to pray about prayer, but in this instance it is fitting that we confess our hesitance to return good for evil and seek spiritual empower-ment to respond in a way that honors God's claims over our lives and shows the truthfulness of the gospel's message of forgiveness and reconciliation.

Finally, prayer relates to our character when we ask God to help us live in ongoing awareness of our enemies and to *consistently* love them and pray for them, not only once but in repeated ways. Character involves a pattern of moral obedience. God forms character in us through our habitual practice, and prayer sustains habitual practice as we repeatedly "with confidence draw near to the throne of grace, that we may receive mercy and find grace to help in time of need" (Heb. 4:16) and may draw upon the "riches of his grace" (Eph. 1:7) to address our spiritual poverty.

Summary

Ethics involves our reflection on what is right and wrong, and Christians set their ethics using the norm of Christ. Morality involves the actual choices to live consistently or inconsistently with our ethics. Character is the habitual practice of morality that forms us into the people God calls us to be through the gospel. Prayer integrates these three elements into our actual lives. On the formative side, prayer is a proactive way to seek Christ and set our minds on Christ and the new life to which he frees us through the gospel. Through prayer, we yield our struggles and doubts to God and seek the leadership of the Spirit. And when we make immoral choices that are contrary to our ethics (as we inevitably will), we confess our sin through prayer and seek forgiveness and restoration.

REFLECTION QUESTIONS

1. What is the difference between ethics and morality?

2. How is character related to morality?

3. How does prayer affect our ethics?

4. In what ways does prayer integrate ethics, morality, and character?

5. What is an area of Christian ethics that you need to address in prayer?

What Should We Ask For in Prayer?

The definition of prayer that we have been using throughout this book suggests that we should pray "for such things as God has promised, or according to his Word, for the good of the church." When we pray, what sorts of things ought we to pray for? One way of answering this question is to say "everything," appealing to Philippians 4:6: "Do not be anxious about anything, but in everything by prayer and supplication, with thanksgiving let your requests be made known to God." A more literal translation is "Do not be anxious, but make your requests known before God in all prayer and supplication with thanksgiving." In anxiety-producing circumstances, then, it is fit to turn to prayer. Rather than worrying, which is of no value (cf. Matt. 6:27), God brings peace by way of prayer (Phil. 4:7). Prayer (*proseuchē*), supplication (*deēsei*), and thanksgiving (*eucharistias*) do not remove us from those things which make us anxious; rather, they put us in nearer fellowship with our loving, adoptive Father who is able to bring us through these situations. Establishing this broad principle, namely that we should feel freedom to pray in any circumstance when we face the pressures of life, can help reassure us that no pressure is too small nor too large for prayer. But what specifically ought we to seek in prayer?

In the ancient church, the philosopher-teacher Origen suggested that we should pray in ways shaped by Scripture: "pray for those who abuse you" (Luke 6:28); "pray earnestly to the Lord of the harvest to send out laborers into His harvest" (Matt. 9:38; Luke 10:2); "pray that you may not enter into temptation" (Matt. 26:41; Mark 14:38; Luke 22:40); "pray that your flight may not be in winter or on a Sabbath" (Matt. 24:20; Mark 13:18); "and when you pray, do not heap up empty phrases" (Matt, 6:7).[1] More recently, Don Whitney

---

1. Origen, *Origen: An Exhortation to Martyrdom, Prayer, and Selected Works*, ed. Richard J. Payne, trans. Rowan A. Greer, The Classics of Western Spirituality (Mahwah, NJ: Paulist Press, 1979), 83.

suggests there really are only a few categories of things that we typically pray about: family, future, finances, work/school, Christian ministry, and whatever our "current crisis" happens to be (which often involves one of the other categories).[2] Over the course of our lives, we do find ourselves praying about these circumstances and needs, even if the list might be expanded. But saying that we might pray about "everything" can sometimes be overwhelming. It is impossible to list every conceivable specific prayer we might offer, but it is helpful to think briefly and categorically about our requests. I want to suggest several categories of things that we might pray for.

We Should Ask for Continuing Spiritual Growth

As we noted in an earlier chapter, salvation is by grace, through faith; it is God's gift (Eph. 2:8). God saves us from our sin, but he does not wholly remove us from the presence or effects of sin in this life and thus we continue to pursue spiritual growth (sanctification) over the courses of our lives. The apostle Paul is very clear that God wants us to experience continued growth, for as he wrote to the Thessalonians,

> Finally, then, brothers, we ask and urge you in the Lord Jesus, that as you received from us how you ought to walk and to please God, just as you are doing, that you do so more and more. . . . For this is the will of God, your sanctification. (1 Thess. 4:1, 3)

The particular path of sanctification for this church involved sexual purity and marital fidelity, but the general truth holds: "God has not called us for impurity, but in holiness" (4:7). Thus we ought to pray for continued growth in holiness: asking that God would give us a greater desire for holiness, that we would remember that our holiness is a reflection of his character (1 Peter 1:15), that we would remember that without holiness no one will see God (Heb. 12:14), that we would strive to put to death the deeds of the flesh through the Spirit (Rom. 8:13), and so forth. As we consider other kinds of prayer, we might intercede for holiness on behalf of our children, our spouses, church members, or others; we might thank God for evidence of continuing sanctification; we might adore him for his perfect holiness; we might confess our weaknesses and uncleanness before him.

We Should Ask for Growth in Virtue

A second category of things we ought to ask for in prayer involves growth in virtue. Remembering the priority of faith and God's "divine power," Peter encouraged Christians scattered throughout Asia Minor to "make every effort

---

2. Donald S. Whitney, *Praying the Bible* (Wheaton, IL: Crossway, 2015), 18–19.

to supplement your faith with virtue" (2 Peter 1:5). The participle *pareisenen-kantes* ("make every effort") shows the diligence required to pursue growth, and this deliberate pursuit surely includes prayer. The object of this effort is *aretēn*, what the ESV translates as "virtue" and what New Testament scholar Andreas Köstenberger calls "excellence."[3] As philosopher J. P. Moreland says,

> A virtue is a skill, a habit, an ingrained disposition to act, think, or feel in certain ways. Virtues are those good parts of one's character that make a person excellent at life in general. As with any skill (for example, learning to swing a golf club), a virtue becomes ingrained in my personality, and thus a part of my very nature, through repetition, practice, and training.[4]

Plato suggested that the "cardinal" virtues were courage, self-control, wisdom, and justice. Aristotle added generosity, gentleness, friendliness, truthfulness, and ambition to Plato's list. Historically, Christians have included faith, hope, and love as three "theological" virtues.[5] As with all good gifts, we recognize that the virtues are patterns of living we must walk in but that they are grounded in God's character. Thus we should pray that God would help us walk in these virtues, even as we intercede for others in light of these characteristics and praise God as the source of all virtue.

We Should Ask for the Success of the Gospel

Christians ought to pray that those who preach the gospel would have success. Paul asked Christians at the church in Colossae to pray for this purpose: "[P]ray also for us, that God may open to us a door for the word, to declare the mystery of Christ, on account of which I am in prison—that I may make it clear, which is how I ought to speak" (Col. 4:3–4). Paul sought prayer on behalf of himself and his fellow missionaries, but his request was broader than their own abilities and performance; he wanted God to provide occasions for them to declare the gospel and he wanted clarity in his own proclamation. Paul's goal in these requests is that the message of Christ would bear fruit; with God granting occasion and clarity, people would hear and some would respond. In our own prayers, we ought to pray for those who proclaim the gospel, even as we pray for our own opportunities to proclaim it. We might pray for us and other Christians to be intentional in turning conversations toward the gospel; we might ask God for courage to proclaim

---

3. Andreas J. Köstenberger, *Excellence: The Character of God and the Pursuit of Scholarly Virtue* (Wheaton, IL: Crossway, 2011), 43–44.

4. J. P. Moreland, *Love the Lord Your God with All Your Mind* (Colorado Springs: NavPress, 1997), 106.

5. Bernard Adeney-Risakotta, "Virtue," *Dictionary of Christian Spirituality*, ed. Glen G. Scorgie (Grand Rapids: Zondervan, 2011), 822.

Christ crucified, for eyes to see the opportunities that God has opened for us, and for a willingness to make the most of these opportunities. Remembering that Paul was imprisoned when he made this request might stir us to also remember Christian prisoners and ask God to give them occasion to proclaim the gospel of Christ in prison, even as we ask for their release from prison. We might pray for sensitive hearts that allow us to focus on the gospel of Christ even in the midst of our own persecution and suffering. Above all, we pray and thank God for the success of the gospel that we have beheld and believed.

Summary

While we ought to pray at all times and in all circumstances and for all things, having some general ideas of specific things we might pray about, for ourselves or others, can help us stay focused in our prayers and remind us how to pray when things are going right. We pray for continued growth in the gospel, in virtue, in holiness. We might also pray for God to care for particularly vulnerable people: orphans, widows, sojourners. We might also pray that God be glorified in our lives and in the lives of other Christians.

REFLECTION QUESTIONS

1. Which of the categories in this chapter do you pray about most often?

2. Which of the categories in this chapter do you pray about least often?

3. How does prayer affect anxious hearts?

4. Who are specific vulnerable people you are praying for?

5. Which virtues do you need to pray for growth in today?

Should Christians Use Written Prayers?

Although written prayers are a common and long-standing part of many Christian traditions, some Protestants are unsure if such prayers are helpful or even genuine. "Read prayers are dead prayers!" goes one common trope within the "free church" or "independent" tradition. Are they? In answering the question of whether Christians should use written prayers, I will sketch a very brief history of written prayers, consider some common objections to their use, and suggest some ways in which they might be used profitably in personal or corporate devotion.

A Brief History of Written Prayer

The practice of Christians writing prayers as devotional aids for other believers is quite old. Although written prayers are less common within the Eastern Church, some early examples include those found in Latin sacramentaries (handbooks with scripted church liturgies) popular in the Western Church's public celebration of the Mass, especially in the sixth through tenth centuries.

Near the end of the eleventh century, Anselm of Canterbury (1033–1109) composed a short, influential, and innovative collection of prayers for the private devotional use of Tuscan royalty. One reason that these prayers were innovative was that Anselm wrote them for *private* devotional use and another is that he wrote them for devout laypeople (notably for women) and not only for the "religious" (clerics, monks, or nuns).

During the twelfth and thirteenth centuries, increasing numbers of laypeople sought devotional helps, fueling the popularity and availability of written prayers, most notably through hundreds of editions of books of hours. These books were devotional primers that adapted Latin monastic routines for laity. Exquisite and expensive, these manuscripts were often multigenerational family heirlooms. After the advent of moveable type, however, they became popular even among the poorer members of European social classes.[1] They contained written prayers for the seven "canonical" daily hours, which were seven set times of prayer throughout the day and night (see Question 39) and their widespread use dated back to the monastic rule of Benedict in the mid-sixth century.

One very important development in the influence of written prayers came during the Reformation in England, through Thomas Cranmer's (1489–1556) *The Book of Common Prayer*. The book provided an English Protestant liturgy in place of the Latin Mass and overflowed with prayers, notably the several dozen "collects," which are brief, focused prayers, many of which Cranmer adapted from ancient sources.[2] Reminiscent of poetry like sonnets, the collects have a literary beauty and economy of words, such as the following collect drawn from the Christmas season:

> Almighty God, which hast given us thy only begotten son to take our nature upon him, and this day to be born of a pure Virgin; Grant that we being regenerate, and made thy children by adoption and grace, may daily be renewed by thy holy spirit, through the same our Lord Jesus Christ who liveth and reigneth with thee and the holy ghost now and ever. Amen.[3]

This example shows the typical structure and focus of a collect: (1) address, (2) acknowledgment, (3) petition, (4) aspiration, and (5) pleading. Some collects are longer, some shorter, some omit elements of this common structure, yet all focus on exactly one topic.

These prayers became part of the common private and public devotion in the daily worship of innumerable Christians within the English realm and abroad, but they were not received warmly among all British Christians. During Britain's Commonwealth (1649–1660), the book and its prayers were proscribed; then in the mid-seventeenth century, the newly restored monarchy mandated the use of the prayer book. Thousands of ministers whose consciences could not abide its strictures found themselves ejected, imprisoned, and labeled enemies of the state. The state church used written prayers to decimate church unity, and one effect was a rejection of such prayers by radical Protestants.

---

1. For an introduction, see Eamon Duffy, *Marking the Hours: English People and Their Prayers 1240–1570* (New Haven, CT: Yale University Press, 2006), 3–22.
2. Pronounced "*caw*-lects." Interested readers should see C. Frederick Barbee and Paul F. M. Zahl, *The Collects of Thomas Cranmer* (Grand Rapids: Eerdmans, 1999), ix–xii. Cranmer adapted, translated, and authored more than eighty collects in his prayer books of 1549 and 1552.
3. Barbee and Zahl, *Collects*, 10. This is the second collect for use on the Sunday after Christmas Day.

Yet for everyday Christians emerging from centuries of Roman Catholic rituals where extemporaneous individual prayer was largely foreign, Reform-minded pastors saw a great need to train the laity for genuine godliness, which included training in how to pray, and thus they produced manuals that included exemplary written prayers for mornings, evenings, times of family worship, and so on.[4] These written prayers were pedagogical, not liturgical, and thus different from those of the established church.

In America, written prayers began as part of Anglican worship with the Jamestown settlement in the early seventeenth century, and persisted into the eighteenth century in colonies such as Virginia and Georgia through con-tinued Anglican influence in the Episcopal Church and other anglophone groups influenced by the English Church (e.g., Methodism). Episcopalians produced their own American *Book of Common Prayer* in 1789 with signifi-cant revisions following during the nineteenth and twentieth centuries. Late in the twentieth century, Christians in various historically "independent" denominations (such as Baptists and Presbyterians) found Arthur Bennett's *Valley of Vision*, which gathered numerous Puritan and Puritan-inspired prayers, to be a helpful devotional aid.[5]

This summary of the history of written prayers is only a thumbnail sketch, yet it shows multiple approaches to written prayers coexisted histori-cally. On the one hand, Christians in power used written prayers to shape (or control) worship. On the other, leaders recognized the value of providing models for families and individuals to instruct young or immature believers in godliness.

Common Objections to Written Prayers

Though written prayers have been a common feature within many Christian traditions, equally godly believers have argued against their use. Considering some objections to written prayer seems appropriate in answer this chapter's question about whether Christians should use such prayers today. While diverse critics have offered other rejections of written prayer, the two objections treated here arose in the context of inter-Protestant persecu-tion in seventeenth-century England and are weighty and sincere.[6]

---

4. See, for example, the famous Lewis Bayly, *The Practice of Pietie: Directing a Christian How to Walk That He May Please God* (London: 1616). Interested readers might also compare Anthony Horneck, *The Fire of the Altar* (London: 1684) for written prayers preparing one for the Lord's Supper or Simon Patrick, *The Devout Christian Instructed How to Pray and Give Thanks to God* (London: 1684) for model prayers for families.
5. Arthur Bennett, *Valley of Vision: A Collection of Puritan Prayers and Devotions* (Carlisle, PA: The Banner of Truth Trust, 1975). Ironically, Bennett included prayers from many staunch critics of written prayers!
6. Other arguments against written prayers include their absence in Scripture and their being rote and thus a violation of Jesus's prohibition in Matthew 6:7–8.

Written Prayers Are Insincere

Baptist allegorist John Bunyan (1628–1688) voiced this objection while jailed for ecclesial nonconformity. Bunyan, like other independent-minded Protestants, found the prayer book to have too much Roman Catholic influence to be a reliable guide for genuine Christian worship and prayer.[7] More basic, Bunyan feared that most congregants who merely recited written prayers that mentioned the name of Jesus had no genuine faith or union with Christ himself and thus no warrant to pray in his name.[8] True prayer must be sincere, or from one's heart, not merely the lips. Sincere prayer must be heartfelt, "It is not, as many take it to be, even a few babling, prating, complementory expressions."[9] Bunyan offered an ongoing critique of written prayers throughout his short treatise, but the sketch above sufficiently captures this objection. Bunyan's status as a political prisoner does not make his assessment inherently correct, but we should listen charitably to one who suffered so unfairly.

Written Prayers Bind the Conscience

John Owen (1616–1683), the great Protestant scholar of the seventeenth century, considered this objection at length as he wrote about the Holy Spirit's work in prayer.[10] Owen allowed for written forms of prayer for private use, even though he thought them likely unhelpful, but rejected compulsory public usage. His primary focus was on the spiritual benefit of these prayers, not their lawfulness. He was sure that Christ gives his church sufficient help in prayer apart from written forms. Though some believers of "low and mean" backgrounds might need help in prayer that forms could offer, might not these same forms also be used amiss to keep such Christians enfeebled in prayer?[11] Where churches mandate written prayers to the exclusion of a Christian's free prayer, however, Owen found them "destructive of [a church's] liberty" and contrary to the gospel.[12] Owen's position is well-articulated, grounded in Scripture, and makes allowances for critics.

How Might We Selectively Use Written Prayers?

In light of these objections, it may seem odd to suggest that written prayers have a helpful place in Christian piety, but that is exactly what this

---

7. John Bunyan, *I Will Pray with the Spirit, and I Will Pray with the Understanding Also, or, A Discourse Touching Prayer, from I Cor. 14.15*, 2nd ed. (London: 1663), 11–12; 14. When quoting Bunyan, I retain his spelling throughout.
8. Bunyan, *I Will Pray with the Spirit*, 18–20, 34.
9. Bunyan, *I Will Pray with the Spirit*, 6–8.
10. John Owen, *A Discourse of the Work of the Holy Spirit in Prayer*, in *The Works of John Owen*, vol. 4, ed. William H. Goold (Carlisle, PA: The Banner of Truth Trust, 1682, repr. 1967), 338–50.
11. Owen, *A Discourse of the Work of the Holy Spirit in Prayer*, 343.
12. Owen, *A Discourse of the Work of the Holy Spirit in Prayer*, 347.

section does. The objection that written prayer is insincere is a valid objection so long as the one repeating the prayer has no genuine union with Christ. But what if the people repeating the prayer or using it as a starting point for their own prayers are indeed believers? Owen's insistence that a church must not bind believers to written prayers is on target but yet he acknowledged that, as private aids, written prayers might have some benefit to some Christians.

We all learn to pray by listening to and imitating the prayers of others. Children listen to parents, congregants listen to pastors, even criminals listen to chaplains, and we all listen to one another. If we were to hear recordings of ourselves at prayer, we would likely pick out requests, phrases, and structures that we first heard from someone else, even if they have been part of our own vocabulary for so long that we have forgotten their origin. This imitative aspect of prayer is part of the beauty and blessing of the communal nature of Christianity. God does not leave us to our own creativity or limited knowledge, but we learn how to pray from other believers. When his followers wanted to know how to pray, Jesus gave them a model, not a rebuke (cf. Luke 11:1–4). To be sure, Jesus's prayer is a pinnacle of spiritual maturity and is inspired whereas prayers that we overhear and adapt from even the godliest saints are neither. Yet the disciples' willingness to ask to be better at prayer and Jesus's willingness to teach them seems to open the possibility that learning to pray from others is viable and valuable.

So what do learning and imitation have to do with written prayers? An analogy may be helpful here. One of the blessings of short-term mission trips is exposure to Christians from different backgrounds and languages. Many Christians find their prayer lives enriched from sharing cross-cultural experiences of worship and praying with other believers from whom they are ordinarily separated by barriers such as language, culture, and distance. Now, to the extent that written prayers are genuine petitions from saints whom we can no longer overhear in audible prayer because distance, language, location, and time separate us from them, it seems odd to reject them as a source of learning. Though we may never be able to vouch for the fidelity of the person who penned such a prayer, one test is its adherence to Scripture and sound doctrine.

Written prayers from other eras of the church's history are not inherently more true or better than prayers overheard today, yet they may prove valuable in helping us identify gaps and deficiencies in our own requests. What C. S. Lewis said of old *books* might also be true of old *prayers*: they just might help us identify and thus "correct the characteristic mistakes of our own period."[13] Learning what Christians of bygone eras have prayed for might show us topics we have never included in our own prayers because we never thought to ask about them or have never heard another living Christian ask

---

13. C. S. Lewis, "On the Reading of Old Books," in *God in the Dock: Essays on Theology and Ethics*, ed. Walter Hooper (Grand Rapids: Eerdmans, 1970), 219.

concerning them. Similarly, such prayers may help confirm our own experience of praying for something that other Christians have also asked about over the centuries. In such a way, considering written prayers helps us avoid the error of "presentism," that is, assuming that our own age is inherently more spiritually mature or correct simply because it is *now*.

One common question from those unaccustomed to written prayers is what precisely we are supposed to *do* with a written prayer. Do we read it aloud? If so, do we read the whole thing? Is reading a written prayer the same thing as praying it? Are such prayers supposed to replace or supplement extemporaneous prayers? This question of mechanics is quite old, and one equally old answer worth quoting in full is that of Anselm:

> The purpose of the prayers and meditations that follow is to stir up the mind of the reader to the love or fear of God, or to self-examination. They are not to be read in a turmoil, but quietly, not skimmed or hurried through, but taken a little at a time, with deep and thoughtful meditation. The reader should not trouble about reading the whole of any of them, but only as much as, by God's help, he finds useful in stirring up his spirit to pray, or as much as he likes. Nor is it necessary for him always to begin at the beginning, but wherever he pleases.[14]

Anselm's advice remains appropriate. Written prayers help "stir up" our minds and affections to prayer. To this end, we need not read the prayer aloud or in full, nor must we feel compelled to paraphrase all (or even part) of a written prayer, but only as much as is needed to set our own minds to praying. In this way, written prayers form a sort of "kindling" to help ignite our own prayers.

Summary

Many Christians have experienced occasions, maybe even seasons, where prayer seems difficult. We know we ought to pray and may even have a desire to pray, yet numerous distractions impede the actual work of prayer. In such times, the first and best place to turn is to Scripture (see Questions 3, 18, and 35), followed by asking help of fellow Christians within the church (see Question 36). Sometimes, though, listening to the voices of Christians who have come before us can help set us to praying.

---

14. Anselm, preface to *The Prayers and Meditations of St. Anselm with the Proslogion*, trans. Benedicta Ward (London: Penguin, 1973), 8–9.

REFLECTION QUESTIONS

1. What was your experience with written prayers prior to reading this chapter?

2. How would you respond to someone who says Protestants must use (or must avoid) written prayers?

3. What are two different ways the church has used written prayers in the past?

4. What are two objections Protestants have raised to written prayers? What are the merits and weaknesses of these objections?

5. If you use written prayers devotionally, how do you assure that you also practice heartfelt extemporaneous prayer?

How Should Christian Parents Teach Children to Pray?

While some of the questions in this book have arisen from questions others have asked, this question is personal. As a father, training my own children in "the discipline and instruction of the Lord" (Eph. 6:4) is a weighty responsibility and one where I feel inadequate. As parents, my wife and I know the importance of prayer and want to see our children grow in their own prayers. Some days I am eager to seek opportunities to help my children grow in prayer, other days I am distracted, rushed, and very little thought goes into my own prayers, let alone those of my family and children. I expect I am not alone. How might Christian parents teach their children to pray?

Parents Lead in Teaching

God calls parents who are believers to make known God's instruction to their children. As Israel stood ready to enter the land of promise, Moses instructed the people to recount their own experience of God's presence to their children:

> Only take care, and keep your soul diligently, lest you forget the things that your eyes have seen, and lest they depart from your heart all the days of your life. Make them known to your children and your children's children—how on the day that you stood before the LORD your God at Horeb, the LORD said to me, "Gather the people to me, that I may let them hear my words, so that they may learn to fear me all the days that they live on the earth, and that they may teach their children so." (Deut. 4:9–10)

Those who witnessed God's deliverance at the Red Sea and trembled in his presence at Sinai were responsible for relating their encounters to their off-spring. My comparison is that Christian parents should be ready to tell their testimony of how God brought them on a new exodus through Christ. No one else can tell your story. Our experience of God's mercy in Christ is one way that we glorify God, by recounting his work in our lives. This aspect of godly leadership is the subjective side of our faith, but God also calls parents to teach their children his Word.

Moses gave Israel this unique doctrine: "Hear, O Israel: The LORD our God, the LORD is one. You shall love the LORD your God with all your heart and with all your soul and with all your might" (Deut. 6:4–5). The words Moses commanded the people to "hear" (*Shema*) were to be inscribed upon their hearts, that is, indelibly marked upon their very centers of being. These words were also for the next generation:

> You shall teach them diligently to your children, and shall
> talk of them when you sit in your house, and when you walk
> by the way, and when you lie down, and when you rise. You
> shall bind them as a sign on your hand, and they shall be
> as frontlets between your eyes. You shall write them on the
> doorposts of your house and on your gates. (Deut. 6:7–9)

Parents who have been transformed by God's Word are called to teach the transforming Word to their children. Notice that parents are to "teach" the Word, not to transform their children. Parents may make an important impression on their children and may form them with many lifelong habits and train them in many ways, or, regrettably, squander their influence through indifference or apathy, but they cannot transform their children, not spiritually. Only God, who is Spirit, can transform a living soul. But parents *can* teach their children God's Word, and they can do so in every walk of life, weaving Scripture into everyday situations every day. Moses's command presupposes that parents themselves "hear" the Word, internalize the Word, and then teach it to their children. By teaching children Scripture and telling our story, we help them hear and see God, who he reveals himself to be (Scripture) and how he works (testimony) in real lives. This twofold teaching is the foundation for training children to pray. Prayer, apart from Scripture and testimony, is only words. Testimony and Scripture, without prayer, is formality. The triad of Scripture, testimony, and prayer is piety.

A final observation about this concept seems appropriate. Parents *lead* in teaching, but parents are not the only teachers in children's lives. The *Shema* was for Israel: fathers, mothers, kin, tribe, and nation. Their collective testimony set them apart from the surrounding nations and distinguished them from the people of the earth. The first relationship was parents and children, but this relationship was not the only relationship. In a similar way, Christian parents lead in instructing their children, but Christian grandparents, aunts and uncles, neighbors, deacons, ministers, community group members, and so on, all have an influence on a child's thoughts about God.

Seek Faith, not Prayer

Parents ought to teach children to pray yet must recognize that unbelieving children will merely be learning the form of prayer and seeing the faith of others modeled for them without experiencing its relational benefits. Faith, not prayer, makes one a believer. Evangelicals have long been committed to "conversionism," the firm belief that no person is born a Christian, rather they must be born again (cf. John 3:7) or "regenerated" (Titus 3:5) by a work of God's Spirit. From at least the 300s forward, some forms of Christianity have practiced water sprinkling or ritual washing in rites involving infants as a ceremony marking the child as part of a Christian household or for other purposes. I am writing as a Baptist, a tradition that does not practice infant baptism nor christening, even though I suspect some readers will be from backgrounds that do adhere to these practices. My ecclesial background shapes my perspective on this question. Children can experience the new birth Jesus described to Nicodemus, though I may not be wise enough to discern genuine faith when I encounter it and suspect I have misinterpreted spiritual sensitivity or inquisitiveness among my children as genuine faith. Nonetheless, as English theologian John Owen wrote, "God is pleased to exercise a prerogative and sovereignty in this whole matter [of conversion], and deals with the souls of men in unspeakable variety."[1] Owen's wisdom has been so pastorally helpful on this issue because it reminds us that there is no one "typical" experience of conversion among adults, let alone children. There must, of course, be a factual and experiential grasp of the gospel for genuine conversion to happen, but the individual experience of awareness of God's holiness, personal sinfulness, and Christ's reconciling sacrifice will vary. Earlier, we considered the question of whether God hears the prayers of unbelievers and concluded that while God is aware of their prayers, he has not bound himself to act upon the prayers of unbelievers in the same way that he has promised to hear and respond to the prayers of believers. This general principle holds true for the prayers of children who are unbelievers. God may choose to act in response to the prayer of an unbelieving child just as much as he might for a lost adult, but he has not given assurance that he will do so.

---

1. John Owen, *Pneumatologia: Or a Discourse Concerning the Holy Spirit* (London: 1674) in The Works of John Owen, 24 vols., ed. W. H. Goold (Edinburgh: Johnstone & Hunter, 1850–1855), 3:360–61.

Model Regular, Simple Prayers

Christian parents should model prayer for their children. While we might pray at meal times or during times of family devotions, children also need to see us praying "without ceasing." Not the sort of prayers designed to make observers think much of us—few kids are likely to be impressed by long prayers! No, these are the sort of ordinary prayers offered up as we drive to school, notice an emergency vehicle, express thanks to God for unexpected blessings, and the like. One of the sweetest, and sometimes humbling, situations is hearing our own voices speaking through the prayers of our kids. It can be sweet as they ask God for things they do not yet understand; it can be humbling when they ask for things we should have thought to pray for but didn't.

Children of Christian parents should also find their parents at prayer. I'm not suggesting that we stage a scene so that our children will "discover" us praying, for that is hypocritical and the sort of prayer that Jesus warns disciples to avoid. Rather, we ought not to hide our prayer times from our children. There might be many embarrassing situations that children could find their parents in, but prayer is not one of them. Children need to see that prayer is a natural part of the faith life of their parents, grandparents, and other adults. They need to hear us pray about all sorts of circumstances in life, for in this way they will learn by example that the faith of their parents is relational and communicative, not formal only.

Parents should teach children to pray simply and to pray different kinds of prayer. That is, we ought to teach children to ask God for things (supplication), but also to intercede for others, to confess sin, to return thanks, to celebrate God for who he is (adoration), and so forth. Each of my children attended the same preschool, which for years has taught a simple mealtime prayer, and thus many of our dinner-table prayers had little variety for many years. Each child worked really hard to get the words of the prayer memorized and my wife and I wanted to give them the chance to lead our family in what they were learning. At some point over the years, I wrestled with this situation: on the one hand, my children were being trained subtly that prayer is formulaic and a matter of getting the words right; on the other, the prayer they were learning contained truth about God and his work in the world that I wanted them to believe. We let the school prayer stay, but also taught them to pray in different ways too. One approach that our family has used is to ask each child what is one thing that we ought to thank God for, one thing that we ought to ask God for, and one need somebody else has that we ought to ask God about, and then we pray using those guides.

We should teach children to pray Scripture. One theme throughout this book is that learning to read, consider, and make the words of Scripture our own words can deepen and expand our prayers. In the same way, praying the Bible can teach children how to pray. Many Christian parents will work on memorizing Bible verses with their children. These verses can become great starting points for prayer prompts. For example, when our middle child went through a season of great fear at night, my wife had him memorize Isaiah 41:10: "fear not, for I am with you; be not dismayed, for I am your God." In light of this verse, we might teach children to pray this way: "Lord, help me remember that you are with me and help me not be scared." There might be a dozen different ways to pray this verse, and we can teach children this practice very easily, even as we encourage children to memorize and pray passages like the Lord's Prayer or the Ten Commandments.

Learn from History

Little reflection is necessary to recognize that the twenty-first-century Western view of childhood and adolescence is significantly different from that of earlier generations, or even from present-day cultures in different parts of the world. Without longing for the "good old days" of raising children, whatever those might be, Christian parents can reacquaint themselves with some older patterns of teaching children the value of following God sincerely, including older patterns of prayer. We recall that childhood morality was often much higher in earlier generations, and thus Christian parents lived with a greater awareness that a simple fever might signal a family tragedy; thus they taught their children to seek God early, in the "morning of their lives." Among the Puritans of England and New England, we find many commendations of "early piety," "early religion," or talk of "the rising generation," common phrases in the eighteenth century for faith among children and young adults.[2]

One common sermon text that preachers used was Ecclesiastes 12:1, "Remember now Thy creator in the days of thy youth, while the evil days come not" (KJV). Jonathan Edwards preached this passage to the young people of his Massachusetts congregation, encouraging them that

> They who give their lives to God early are likely to have more opportunity to serve and glorify God. It is much more to the honor of God when persons seek Him in the first place, serving God with their first fruits.[3]

This vision of early faith leading to a life of honoring God is so desirable that it would be hard to imagine a Christian parent who is not moved to say "yes!" and affirm this goal. Jonathan and Sarah Edwards raised ten children, all of whom survived childhood diseases and accidents, though their daughter

---

2.   A quick search of one academic database returned more than eight hundred sermons or tracts printed before 1800 that addressed the topic of "early piety."

3.   Jonathan Edwards, "The Time of Youth Is the Best Time to Be Improved for Religious Purposes," in *To the Rising Generation: Addresses Given to Children and Young Adults*, ed. Don Kistler (Orlando, FL: Soli Deo Gloria Publications, 2005), 19.

Jerusha died suddenly at age 17 from a fever. The Edwardses practiced intentional discipleship of their children.[4] What sorts of things ought children and youth to pray for? According to Edwards, they should pray for the application of the fruits of the gospel:

> Thus pray that the eyes of your heart may be opened, that you may receive your sight, that you may know your self and be brought to God's feet, and that you may see the glory of God and Christ, may be raised from the dead, and have the love of Christ shed abroad in your heart. Those that have most of these things still need to pray for them; for there is so much blindness and hardness and pride and death remaining that they still need to have that work of God upon them, further to enlighten and enliven them.[5]

Summary

Christian parents must lead their children by teaching them how God has worked in their own lives and what God says about himself in his Word. Though parents are not the only religious influence or the only ones who can or should teach children about God, his work, his ways, and his Word, they are to lead in this instruction. If parents want children who will pray, they must be people of prayer themselves, building prayer into the fabric of their homes and ordinary lives. Children who hear their parents praying learn about the value of prayer. Parents can teach their children to pray simply, biblically, and often.

I have avoided a lot of detailed prescriptions about prayer that might appear in books on Christian parenting or discipleship. I have not mentioned the specific role of fathers and mothers, though I do believe that God calls both parents to model faith, though in differing roles. I have not laid out models for what family devotions "ought to" look like, exhorted parents to catechize their children, or offered lists of potential prayer topics. I have avoided all these things, as helpful as they might be, to reinforce one idea: teaching children how to pray is much simpler than we often make it and it may look different from family to family.

---

4. See the summary of their domestic life in George Marsden, *Jonathan Edwards: A Life* (New Haven, CT: Yale University Press, 2003), 321–22.
5. Jonathan Edwards, *Advice to Young Converts*, in *Jonathan Edwards' Resolutions and Advice to Young Converts*, ed. Stephen J. Nichols (Phillipsburg, NJ: P&R Publishing, 2001), 28. Edwards wrote this advice to a teenage girl named Deborah Hatheway who had sent him a letter asking for advice on following God.

REFLECTION QUESTIONS

1. What are two key ways that parents should teach their children about God?

2. What role do other believers have in training our children in the faith?

3. How might parents teach children to pray Scripture?

4. Why is modeling prayer so important in training our children to pray?

5. Why is training children to honor God so important for their lives of faith?

Does Our Physical Posture Affect Prayer?

As we have seen in other chapters, although it may take a variety of forms, prayer is a key means given to God's people to enable them to "seek [his] face" (Ps. 27:8). Prayer is both an act of the mind and of the body. Because prayer is a physical act, those who would pray must consider the relationship between body and prayer. C. S. Lewis emphasized the importance of this relationship in his *Letters to Malcolm*. Describing how frequent travel and debilitating osteoporosis hindered his preferred practice of prayer, Lewis noted, "When one prays in strange places and at strange times one can't kneel, to be sure. I won't say this doesn't matter. The body ought to pray as well as the soul. Body and soul are both better for it. . . . And but for our body one whole realm of God's glory—all that we receive through the senses—would go unpraised."[1] Others have also affirmed the importance of one's body in the practice of the prayer.[2] This chapter considers the importance of the posture of prayer using biblical theology. Does the posture of our body matter when we pray? Does the Bible command or commend certain physical postures for prayer? Do some postures enhance or hinder our experience of prayer?

The Posture of Prayer in the Old Testament

The Bible begins with God creating a good universe and world (Gen. 1:1–2:3) and ends with God bringing "a new heaven and a new earth" (Rev. 21:1). The Old Testament describes the creation and fall of God's good world and

---

1. C. S. Lewis, *Letters to Malcolm: Chiefly on Prayer* (New York: Harcourt, 1964), 17.
2. Dallas Willard, *The Spirit of the Disciplines: Understanding How God Changes Lives* (San Francisco: Harper San Francisco, 1988), xi, 18–19, 29–30; Doug Pagitt and Kathryn Prill, *Body Prayer: The Posture of Intimacy with God* (Colorado Springs: Waterbrook Press, 2005), 1–13. These works feature varying biblical reflection.

God's unfolding plan to restore this fallen world through one nomadic family that he makes into a glorious-but-imperfect kingdom. The Old Testament presents a rich picture of prayer not by way of instruction but rather through numerous personal experiences. Many of the records of these personal experiences also describe the physical posture of the ones praying.

Genesis 1–11 introduces God as a prayer-hearing God (cf. Ps. 65:2) without providing any instruction in the form, content, or practice of prayer. With the call of Abraham in Genesis 12, God begins to focus on one particular family through whom he will overturn the curse of sin and restore his people. God appeared to Abraham again when the latter was ninety-nine years old and reiterated this covenant and Abraham responded physically by falling "on his face," and God talked with him (Gen. 17:3). Abraham's posture indicates his deep respect for God as well as God's relational nature that is experienced through prayer.[3] Elsewhere, Abraham stands conversing with Yahweh, who treats him as a confidant (Gen. 18:22–33).

As Christopher Seitz has observed, one of the most striking features of prayer in the law of Moses is how little formal direction the law gives when contrasted with other forms of worship.[4] Moses, the lawgiver, prays often. Moses stands and prays barefoot before the burning bush, his face hidden for fear of seeing God (Exod. 3:5–6). In the midst of the plagues, Moses, God's chosen representative before Pharaoh, spreads out his hands to God, a posture of entreaty, and God stills the hail (Exod. 9:29, 33). The dramatic exodus from Egypt, marked by God's miraculous deliverance of his people through judgment, becomes a model for God's saving acts throughout the rest of Scripture.[5] As Moses stands atop Mount Sinai, praying to God, God stands with Moses and proclaims his covenant faithfulness and compassion. Moses appears awe-struck: "Moses made haste to bow low toward the earth and worship" (Exod. 34:5–8 NASB 1995).[6] Much later, when Israel rejected the report of the spies Moses had sent into the Promised Land, "Moses and Aaron fell on their faces in the presence of all the assembly of the congregation of the

---

3.   John H. Sailhamer, "Genesis," in *The Expositor's Bible Commentary*, vol. 2, ed. Frank E. Gaebelein and Richard P. Polcyn (Grand Rapids: Zondervan, 1990), 138. Elsewhere, Abraham again falls facedown and laughs at the prospect of God actually keeping his covenant with such an old man as he (Gen. 17:17). In Genesis 18, Abraham welcomes Yahweh and two companions, unaware of their true identity, by bowing down to the ground. He then hosts a lavish meal for his guests and has a remarkable conversation with the Lord in which Abraham learns that he will father a child within a year's time.

4.   Christopher R. Seitz, "Prayer in the Old Testament or Hebrew Bible," in *Into God's Presence: Prayer in the New Testament*, ed. Richard N. Longenecker (Grand Rapids: Eerdmans, 2001), 16.

5.   Graeme Goldsworthy, *Gospel and Kingdom* in *The Goldsworthy Trilogy* (Carlisle: Paternoster Press, 1981), 73.

6.   The Hebrew text of Exodus 34:8 emphasizes Moses's quick bowing in God's presence by altering the normal syntax of verb-subject-object to adverb-subject-verb.

sons of Israel" and there Moses interceded on behalf of the people (Num. 14:5, 11–19 NASB).

Following Joshua's conquest and the lawless period of the judges, Israel's longing to be like their neighbors brings about the period of the monarchy, first under Saul, and then under the unlikely warrior-poet David. David's kingship provides stability in which Israel flourishes, and God initiates a covenant with David to make his name great and to establish his kingdom through one of David's offspring (2 Sam. 7). Yet even this king after God's own heart sins by taking Bathsheba, the wife of Uriah, and she becomes pregnant, and God's judgment falls upon the couple's child (2 Sam. 11–12). During the child's illness, David "sought God on behalf of the child. And David fasted and went in and lay all night on the ground" (2 Sam. 12:16). David maintained his vigil for seven days until his son's death. For a heartbreaking week, David set aside the role of king for the role of father and interceded on behalf of his son. This story has important implications for the posture of prayer within the realm of biblical theology. First, even one whom God has chosen and blessed may not have his prayers answered according to his own desires. Second, even the most reverent and submissive postures do not guarantee that God will answer one's prayer.

David's son Solomon is the immediate fulfillment of Nathan's prophecy that one of David's descendants would build a dwelling place for God (2 Sam. 7).[7] First Kings 8:12–61 narrates a unique and important prayer of Solomon: important in that it contains the most specific description regarding the posture of prayer in the Old Testament and that it introduces a new era in God's dwelling with his people; unique in that "it is a prayer about the temple as the preeminent *place* of prayer."[8] Solomon stands before the altar with hands outspread toward heaven as he dedicates the temple (1 Kings 8:22–53). Solomon's prayer contains four parts: first, in 8:12–13, Solomon describes a transition in Israel's history: Yahweh, who dwells in "thick darkness" will now dwell in an "exalted house."[9] Verses 14–21 and 54–61 are both blessings to Yahweh and frame the petitions of 8:22–53. In 8:22–30, Solomon praises Yahweh's faithfulness and asks him to uphold his covenant, to hear his prayer, and to hear the prayers offered by generations of Israelites yet to come. Solomon specifically asks Yahweh to hear those prayers offered "toward this house/place" (8:29–31, 33, 35, 38, 42, 44, 48). Verses 31–53 are a sort of exposition on Solomon's request in which he describes different scenarios in which God's people would pray toward the temple. Samuel Balentine has noted that "Solomon's primary concern is that God will hear 'in heaven' the prayers and supplications

---

7. In response to Nathan's prophecy, 2 Samuel 7:18 notes that David "sat before the LORD" and prayed.
8. Samuel E. Balentine, *Prayer in the Hebrew Bible: The Drama of Divine-Human Dialogue* (Minneapolis: Fortress Press, 1993), 81.
9. The reference to thick darkness points to God's presence at Sinai (see Exod. 20:21; Deut. 4:11; 5:22).

directed toward the temple."[10] Thus the temple is a gateway to God.[11] Standing before the altar, Solomon moves prayer from the periphery to the center of Israel's worship.[12] Solomon establishes, for the first time in Israel's history, a posture and a place for prayer.

The books of Kings and Chronicles record prayers made by kings and prophets to a divided kingdom.[13] Elijah's confrontation with the priests of Baal illustrates the futility of ritual posture for those who seek false gods. When their vocalized prayers to Baal went unanswered, the priests "limped around the altar that they had made," mutilated themselves, and worked themselves into a raving frenzy, yet their prayers went unanswered (1 Kings 18:20–29). By contrast, Elijah needed only speak his prayer for a dramatic answer (1 Kings 18:36–40). Elijah's prayer occurs within the context of his call to Israel to return to covenant faithfulness.[14] Israel ultimately rejects this call, and both the Northern Kingdom and Southern Kingdom are defeated and exiled by their enemies and the temple, the "house of prayer" (Isa. 56:7), is destroyed.

Job stands at the front of the Writings section of the Old Testament and the book's narrator introduces Job as a mediator between God and his family (Job 1:4–5). Two prayers in the book provide insight into the posture of prayer. After learning of the disasters that have claimed his family and wealth, "Job arose and tore his robe and shaved his head and fell on the ground and worshiped" (Job 1:20). Here Job fuses common signs of mourning with a posture for prayer.[15] Later, Zophar, one of Job's friends, counsels Job to "spread out your hands to [God]," here a sign of entreaty and repentance (Job 11:13). The book concludes with a dramatic turn, as Job's three friends, all along sure that they were counseling a friend fallen into sin, are rebuked by God and must be restored by Job's mediating prayer (Job 42:7–9). Apart from advice on using careful speech when seeking God (Eccl. 5:1–3), the remaining wisdom books ignore the topic of prayer.

---

10. Balentine, *Prayer*, 84.
11. Graeme Goldsworthy, *Prayer and the Knowledge of God: What the Bible Teaches* (Downers Grove, IL: InterVarsity Press, 2003), 123.
12. So Daniel Block, *For the Glory of God: Recovering a Biblical Theology of Worship* (Grand Rapids: Baker Academic, 2016), 264. See also Jon D. Levenson, "From Temple to Synagogue: 1 Kings 8," in *Traditions in Transformation: Turning Points in Biblical Faith*, ed. Baruch Halpern (Winona Lake, IN: Eisenbrauns, 1981), 159. Note that in the 2 Chronicles 6 account, Solomon is not standing before the altar.
13. Although omitted for space reasons, the reader is encouraged to examine the prayers of Hezekiah (2 Kings 19:14–19; 20:2–3, and parallels).
14. In the New Testament, James remembers Elijah as an effective model of prayer (James 5:17).
15. David J. A. Clines, *Job 1–20*, Word Biblical Commentary, vol. 17 (Dallas: Word, 1989), 35. Clines notes that a technical term for verbal prayer is "only seldom connected with this term for worship," and that Job's posture is a common posture of prayer.

As described in Question 16 above, the Psalter is a collection presented in five books of various kinds of Jewish prayers and praises and was used in the public and private worship of Israel. The Psalms provide a "poetic commentary" on Israel's history and God's larger work of creation and redemption.[16] The following analysis of references to posture in the Psalms follows the five-fold division of books and will be necessarily brief.[17] Two psalms in Book One describe the postures of lifting hands and bowing (Pss. 28:2 and 5:7). Books Two through Four contain few descriptions of the posture of prayer. Psalm 63:4 associates lifting hands with blessing God and in Psalm 88:9, the sons of Korah spread out their hands as a physical sign of their prayer to Yahweh. In Psalm 95:6, the worshiper bows down and kneels before Yahweh as an act of homage to his creator. Book Five contains more descriptions of posture than the other four books. In Psalm 119:48, the psalmist lifts his hands to God's commandments as an expression of his delight in them. In the Songs of Ascent (Pss. 120–34), the psalmist lifts his eyes toward Yahweh as his source of help (121:1) and mercy (123:1). In Psalm 134:2, Yahweh's servants are called to lift up their hands toward Zion. David bows toward God's temple as a sign of thanksgiving (138:2). David lifts his hands as an evening sacrifice (Ps. 141:2) and stretches them out as a sign of his longing for God (143:6). This concentration of postures in Book Five may be intentional and focused on God's redeeming work. As Hamilton has noted, "Psalms 107–50 present the eschatological triumph of Yahweh through the conquering Davidic king, who decisively brings about the salvation that comes to Israel by means of judgment upon the enemies of Israel."[18]

The prophets called God's people to renew their covenant vows and to seek Yahweh. Given the volume of references to prayer in the prophetic literature, only selected instances will be noted here. Reiterating the notion that prayer is talking to God, the prophets consistently condemn pagan worship that diminishes genuine prayer, namely one-way conversation with idols (Deut. 4:6–8; Ps. 115:3–8; Isa. 44:12–20). Isaiah warned Israel that God had rejected their physical expressions of worship, including prayer with outspread hands, because of their failure to repent (Isa. 1:15). He also warned Israel that bowed heads and spread sackcloth paired with disobedient hearts dishonor God (Isa. 58:5). Jeremiah lamented that "Zion stretches out her hands; but there is none to comfort her" (Lam. 1:17). He instructed Jerusalem, "Lift your hands to him for the lives of your children" (Lam. 2:19) and asked the people to "lift up our hearts and hands to God in heaven" as physical signs of repentance (Lam. 3:41). Beholding God's

16. James. M. Hamilton, Jr. *God's Glory in Salvation through Judgment: A Biblical Theology* (Wheaton, IL: Crossway, 2010), 271, 276.
17. Hamilton provides a helpful discussion of recent trends in canonical scholarship that follow the theological themes of each of these five books. See Hamilton, *God's Glory in Salvation*, 276–90.
18. Hamilton, *God's Glory in Salvation*, 287–88.

glory, Ezekiel fell on his face in prayer (Ezek. 1:28–3:15; 3:23–27) as God set him apart for prophetic ministry. Daniel, whose prophetic ministry was performed in exile, regularly prayed three times a day, facing Jerusalem (Dan. 6:10). Daniel's practice is unique, but clearly fulfills Solomon's prayer that God's people, living in exile, might be restored by praying toward Jerusalem (1 Kings 8:46–53). Jonah prayed from inside the belly of a great fish (Jonah 2:1). Micah warns against bowing before Yahweh while forsaking justice, covenant loyalty, and humility (Mic. 6:6–8).

The book of Ezra chronicles the return from exile and the struggles of reestablishing religious life in Israel. One challenge Ezra faced was intermarriage between Israelites and pagan neighbors (Ezra 9–10). Upon learning that this practice was widespread, especially among Israel's leaders, Ezra performed ritual mourning (9:3–4) and "at the evening sacrifice I rose from my fasting . . . and fell upon my knees and spread out my hands to the LORD my God" (9:5). Ezra's posture is one of humility and need.[19] Ezra 10:1 further explains this scene, as according to the narrator, Ezra was "weeping and casting himself down before the house of God."

The Posture of Prayer in the New Testament

The New Testament describes Jesus of Nazareth as the one man through whom God will restore fallen men and women and ultimately the universe (Acts 4:12; Rom. 8:18–25; Rev. 21:1–2). Jesus and the first generations of his disciples inherited certain practices of prayer from Israel's past and from Roman and pagan cultures.[20] Jesus not only prayed, but taught his disciples to pray, and transforms all prayer, on earth and in heaven, including its posture.

As discussed in Questions 18–19, in his Sermon on the Mount, Jesus taught his disciples how to pray (Matt. 6:5–15). The passing mention of the Pharisees standing for prayer in 6:5 is not likely an indictment but a description of their practice. The Lord's Prayer of Matthew 6:9–13 and Luke 11:2–4 lacks a description of posture, yet the prayer is rich with theological imagery indicating the fulfillment of Old Testament patterns.[21] Mark's gospel records a passing reference to the practice of standing for prayer (Mark 11:25). At least one of Jesus's parables also provides insight into the posture of prayer.[22]

---

19. H. G. M. Williamson, *Ezra, Nehemiah*, Word Biblical Commentary, vol. 16 (Waco, TX: Word, 1985), 133.

20. See Asher Finkel, "Prayer in the Jewish Life of the First Century," in *Into God's Presence: Prayer in the New Testament*, ed. Richard N. Longenecker (Grand Rapids: Eerdmans, 2001), 43–65, especially 61–62.

21. See N. T. Wright, "The Lord's Prayer as a Paradigm of Christian Prayer," in *Into God's Presence: Prayer in the New Testament*, 132–54 for an excellent analysis of the eschatological nature of the prayer, especially as it portrays a new exodus.

22. The main point of Luke 18:9–14 is not which posture of prayer is preferable, but rather which person's heart is acceptable.

In a story parable in Luke 18:9–14, Jesus uses a Pharisee and a tax collector to illustrate the truth that self-exaltation leads to humiliation while humility leads to exaltation (Luke 18:14).[23] In the parable, both men stand in the temple praying. The Pharisee stands in self-righteousness while the tax collector stands "far off," refuses to lift his eyes to heaven, and beats his breast—postures that indicate a sense of unworthiness, timidity, and contrition.[24]

The Gospels also record the postures of other people in prayer, notably those who sought physical healing from Jesus. A leper kneeled, or fell on his face and begged Jesus to heal him (Luke 5:12–13; Mark 1:40). A Syrophoenician woman "fell down" at his feet and begged Jesus to heal her demon-possessed daughter (Mark 7:24–29). Another man knelt before him to ask for mercy for his epileptic son (Matt. 17:14–21). In one of the cruelest examples of irony in the New Testament, the Roman soldiers who prepared Jesus for his crucifixion mocked him by kneeling in homage before him (Matt. 27:29).

Acts depicts the church as a community of prayer (Acts 1:14; 4:23–31; 6:4; 20:36). The earliest church was primarily Jewish, and it is not surprising to find that Jewish customs influenced the early church's practice of prayer.[25] The disciples meet regularly to pray with one another (2:42), likely a practice carried over from the synagogue, and also pray at the temple, or at home, during certain set times (3:1; 10:3, 30; see Question 39). Acts describes several postures of prayer among early Christians. The most commonly mentioned posture is kneeling.[26] Stephen falls to his knees as he utters his final prayer on behalf of his executioners (7:60). Peter kneels to pray over the body of Tabitha (9:40). Paul kneels to pray with the Ephesian elders on Miletus (20:36) and with Christians at Tyre (21:5). The early church also practiced the laying on of hands in conjunction with prayer (6:6; 13:3; 28:8).[27] In Acts, the church prays at pivotal moments and these prayers further its mission, thereby connecting its prayer to the expanding reversal of the fall with the coming of Jesus's kingdom.[28]

---

23. Robert H. Stein, *An Introduction to the Parables of Jesus* (Philadelphia: The Westminster Press, 1981), 19–20. Stein identifies this parable as a "story parable." See also Craig L. Blomberg, *Interpreting the Parables* (Downers Grove, IL: InterVarsity Press, 1990), 256–58, on the interpretation of this parable.

24. Darrell L. Bock, *Luke 9:51–24:53*, Baker Exegetical Commentary on the New Testament (Grand Rapids: Baker, 1996), 1464.

25. M. J. Wilkins, "Prayer," in *Dictionary of the Later New Testament and Its Developments*, eds. Ralph P. Martin and Peter H. Davids (Downers Grove, IL: InterVarsity Press, 1997), 941–48.

26. In Acts, kneeling is expressed by a form of the verb *tithēmi* paired with the noun *gonu*. So Acts 7:60; 9:40; 20:36; and 21:5.

27. See Everett Ferguson, "Laying on of Hands in Acts 6:6 and 13:3," *Restoration Quarterly* 4 (1960): 250–52.

28. Peter T. O'Brien, "Prayer in Luke-Acts," *Tyndale Bulletin* 24 (1973): 123–24.

We consider Paul's prayers for churches in greater detail in Questions 22 and 23 of this book. Prayer was essential to Paul's ministry, yet his letters offer few clues into his physical practice of prayer. Two passages are important for this study: Ephesians 3:14 and 1 Timothy 2:8. In Ephesians 3:14, Paul introduces his prayer report with the phrase "for this reason, I bow my knees before the Father." Now, this reference may simply be Paul's rhetorical tool to indicate that he is praying, yet it need not exclude a posture of "homage or worship," and it is consistent with Paul's practice of kneeling in prayer as noted in Acts (Acts 20:36; 21:5).[29]

In 1 Timothy 2:8, Paul instructs Timothy on his wishes for a peaceable church service: "I desire then that in every place the men should pray, lifting holy hands without anger or quarreling." The primary point of this passage is that men ought not to pray in church when angry.[30] The imagery of "holy hands" is drawn from the Old Testament tradition.[31] Here the posture serves as a call to united prayer within a congregation. The prayers that Paul offers and receives serve a similar purpose as the prayers in Acts: the expansion of the good news of Jesus's coming kingdom.[32]

The Petrine epistles and Jude, though filled with prayers, lack details regarding its posture. Likewise, the Johannine epistles contain prayers and prayer requests, but do not address posture. While the epistle to the Hebrews explains both the earthly (5:7–9) and heavenly (7:25; 9:24) prayers of Jesus as well as the eschatological significance (9:26) of his redeeming work, the epistle offers no descriptions of the posture of prayer.[33]

The epistle of James contains three primary passages addressing prayer (1:5–8; 4:1–4; 5:13–18), and the final passage, directing the church to pray for physical healing, contains three imperatives regarding prayer within the church: First, a Christian who is ill must summon the elders of the church. Then, the elders are to respond by "praying over" him and "anointing him with oil in the name of the Lord." Douglas Moo notes that this passage is the only New Testament instance of this posture where prayer is concerned and

---

29. Andrew T. Lincoln, *Ephesians*, Word Biblical Commentary, vol. 42 (Dallas: Word, 1990), 202. Lincoln also suggests that the description may have carried more emotive force and emphasized the fervency with which the writer prayed.
30. So William D. Mounce, *Pastoral Epistles*, Word Biblical Commentary, vol. 46 (Nashville: Thomas Nelson Publishers, 2000), 105; George W. Knight III, *The Pastoral Epistles*, New International Greek Testament Commentary (Grand Rapids: Eerdmans, 1992), 129.
31. Mounce, *Pastoral Epistles*, 106. Mounce suggests that passages such as Exodus 30:19–21; Psalm 24:4; Isaiah 1:15; and 59:3 inform Paul's imagery. Additionally, Psalms 28:2; 63:4; 141:2; and 143:6 may be in view here.
32. Romans 15:30–32; Ephesians 6:18–20; Philippians 1:9–10; 2 Thessalonians 3:1–2; etc.
33. Hebrews does encourage believers to "draw near" to God (7:18–19, 25; 10:22; 11:6), which is likely a reference to prayer, yet this movement is metaphorical rather than gesticular.

this posture may indicate that the elders are laying hands on the sick person as they anoint that person with oil.[34]

In Revelation, John is given a vision in which he sees the throne room of heaven and hears the acclamations of the heavenly court for the thrice-holy God who is the creator of all things (cf. Isa. 6; Rev. 1, 4). Prayer is central to John's visions of earth and heaven in this book. Esther Ng has identified twenty-one recorded prayers in the Apocalypse and more prayers mentioned but not preserved.[35]

The twenty-four elders, at times joined by the four living creatures and the angelic host, fall down and worship in prayer (4:10; 5:8, 14; 7:11; 11:16; 19:4). The uncountable multitude of the redeemed stand before the throne (7:9) or by a sea of glass (15:2). The souls of martyred believers are found "underneath the altar," protected by God, from whence they pray for God to avenge their blood (6:9–10). Jesus's incarnation inaugurated his kingdom and his death secured redemption, and Christians martyred in his name extend the kingdom further.

Summary

While Scripture at time records the posture of God's people at prayer, neither the law of Moses nor the teachings of Jesus prescribe certain postures for prayer. The Bible describes a variety of prayer postures, most commonly standing, kneeling, or bowing one's face to the ground. Standing appears to have been the normal posture for prayer in Israel. Kneeling and bowing are nearly always presented as responses to God's presence. One does not assume certain postures in order to commune with God; rather, when one experiences communion with God through prayer, the common physical response indicates an awareness of God's divine majesty and our human frailty. These postures persist into the new covenant and even into the worship in heaven and are thus legitimate postures which Christians may adopt. Adopting a reverent posture, though, is no guarantee that one's prayer will be answered.

REFLECTION QUESTIONS

1. How does your Christian tradition emphasize or ignore the posture of prayer?

---

34. Douglas J. Moo, *The Letter of James*, Pillar New Testament Commentary (Grand Rapids: Eerdmans, 2000), 238.
35. Esther Yue L. Ng, "Prayer in Revelation," in *Teach Us to Pray: Prayer in the Bible and the World*, ed. D. A. Carson (Exeter, UK: Paternoster Press, 1990), 128.

2. In what ways might noting the place of our bodies in prayer help or hinder our praying?

3. What are several postures of prayer that express reverence or awe?

4. What are some biblical postures of prayer that you have ignored previously?

5. How might you encourage Christians who find it hard to pray with or without certain postures?

How Might We Fight Distraction in Prayer?

One common question that my students have asked over the years is how they can stay focused when they pray. In conversations, they often admit that their minds wander while praying and they suddenly become aware that they have no idea where their thoughts and words have gone! Distraction in prayer is a common complaint but it is hardly a modern one. In the Middle Ages, Thomas Aquinas asked whether attention was a necessary condition of prayer. He determined, helpfully, that it was not.[1] For a theologian as meticulous as Aquinas, the concession that distraction is part of the normal experience of prayer is reassuring, though I expect his sense of distraction may differ from my own. In this chapter, we want to consider the experience of distraction in prayer and look at some ways we might mitigate its impact.

Distraction Is Natural but Increasing

To be human means to be distracted. At a basic level, distraction is inevitable for created beings, because all of our faculties are limited. Attention is a finite thing. Only God is truly undistracted. As we will see shortly, Christians have reflected on distraction in prayer long before modern computing technology and the internet ever existed, but the perception that distraction is increasing over the past quarter century is common. Nicholas Carr has written about the internet-enhanced distractions of modern life, noting his own decline in memory and concentration.[2] Tony Reinke considers the particular ways smart phones have amplified distraction, likening distraction to an addiction, and suggesting that it "blind[s] souls from God," "close[s]

---

1. Thomas Aquinas, *Summa Theologiae* 2.83.13, https://aquinas.cc/la/en/~ST.II-II.Q83.A13.
2. Nicholas Carr, *The Shallows: What the Internet Is Doing to Our Brains* (New York: W. W. Norton, 2011).

off communion from God," and "mute[s] the urgency of God."[3] One hidden cost of instant and continual connectivity is its effect on our ability to focus. Distraction is inevitable, but it does seem to be increasing, at least by shared experience.

Distraction-free prayer can become an idol in the Christian life. Graeme Goldsworthy explains that reading stories of various "heroes" of the faith who prayed for several hours every day can easily make us feel inadequate.[4] Hearing such stories causes us to question whether our weakness in prayer, distracted as we often are, is normal or whether there is something wrong with us. While more mature Christians, be they "heroes" or not, have much to teach us about prayer, *their* practice is not the standard by which God measures our faithfulness. All Christians are to grow into "mature manhood," which Paul insists is "the measure of the stature of the fullness of Christ" (Eph. 4:13). The fact that I have included this chapter should indicate that distracted prayer is a concern for me as well, and that pursuing greater focus is a good thing, but I recognize that chasing distraction-free prayer can become an idol, a goal unto itself, a focus that is more intense than my focus on the experience on communion with God. Communion and fellowship are the goals of prayer.

Concentration is a skill that can be practiced and developed. Some people seem to have the ability to ignore nearly everything that is going on around them and get lost in their work, in their reading, or yes, even in their prayer.

Identify Sources of Distraction

To grow in our concentration, we begin by identifying the things that distract us. In the seventeenth century, pastor Nathanael Vincent addressed the topic of distracted prayer in a series of sermons on 1 Corinthians 7:35 (KJV), "And this I speak for your own profit; not that I may cast a snare upon you, but for that which is comely, and that ye may attend upon the Lord without distraction." Marriage is not sinful—quite the contrary—but our natural concern for our spouse divides our attention (1 Cor. 7:32–34). Distraction is a problem of the heart. Vain, wicked, or earthly thoughts may reveal that our hearts are not captivated by God as much as we would like to think they are. Sometimes distraction is a "hellish injection," suggested from without by the devil. At other times, that which distracts us is "unseasonable thought," things that are good, not wicked, but thoughts that come at the wrong time. Sometimes the setting and mode of prayer or worship distracts us. Sometimes we are distracted by our desire not to be distracted![5]

---

3. Tony Reinke, *12 Ways Your Phone Is Changing You* (Wheaton, IL: Crossway, 2017), 48.
4. Graeme Goldsworthy, *Prayer and the Knowledge of God: What the Bible Teaches* (Downers Grove, IL: InterVarsity Press, 2003), 10–11.
5. Nathanael Vincent, *The Cure of Distractions in Attending upon God* (London: Three Pigeons, 1695), 145–58.

Fighting Distraction in Prayer

How might we fight distraction in prayer? We can give attention to our surroundings, to our bodies, to our theology, and to our goals. One way we can mitigate distraction is to consider the spaces we pray in. Historically, the Roman Catholic and Orthodox traditions have placed greater emphasis on "sacred" spaces than most Protestant groups have.[6] Because the living and true God is not bound by geography or limited by architecture, and because we ourselves are the place where God dwells through his Holy Spirit, we might rightly pray anywhere, but sometimes we learn that the freedom to pray *any*where does not always mean that we pray *every*where with equal focus. Consider the "environmental" distractions surrounding your prayers: Is the space too hot, too cold, too loud, too comfortable, or too spartan? Do you find yourself thinking more about the kind of flooring or color of the paint in the space where you are praying than about the one to whom you are speaking? For many, finding a dedicated space in which to pray is an important part of fighting distraction, for it frees up their thoughts from answering the question, "Where will I pray today?" and lets them give their attention to God. Creating a simple space in your home, office, barn, garage, attic, basement, or bedroom may be a helpful step in fighting this sort of distraction.

Then, we pay attention to our bodies as we pray. Elsewhere I have mentioned C. S. Lewis's complaint that as he aged, his arthritis hindered his prayers. Lewis's point was that he prayed as a person, a unity of body and soul. Some who struggle to retain attention while praying may actually be struggling physiologically more than spiritually, or at least may be unaware of the impact that their physiology has on their prayer life. Hearing the value of praying early in the morning or reading about Christians who arose at 4 a.m. to begin prayer, we might seek to emulate their practice and find ourselves continually drowsy and distracted by the fact that we keep nodding off to sleep, when simply changing the time by twenty or thirty minutes might make a great difference. Similarly, trying to pray after we have consumed a carbohydrate-heavy meal, with all of our body's attention focused on digestion, might result in distraction. In a like manner, praying when we have consumed too much (or perhaps not enough!) caffeine may leave us jittery and anxious and unable to focus. Trying to pray when we have had too little sleep, or too much sleep, can leave us in a mental fog. Our natural frailty can be amplified by the effects of medicines we take, or should take; by pain from injuries or ailments; by the effects of aging bodies. While there may be little we can do about the distractions attendant within our bodies, we can become aware of them and make small adjustments to those things we can control, and such changes may temper distractions.

---

6. William R. McAlpine, "Sacred Space," in *Dictionary of Christian Spirituality*, ed. Glen G. Scorgie (Grand Rapids: Zondervan, 2011), 731–32.

Returning to Nathanael Vincent's advice, we ought to give attention to our theology in prayer so that we "have right apprehensions of God, whom we attend upon."[7] Following Bunyan's definition of prayer used throughout this book, we remember that God is one in essence and three in persons, and we recall the specific ministries of each person of the Trinity in our prayers. Vincent suggests we ought to remember that God is "an incomprehensible Spirit, of infinite Wisdom, Power, Truth, Holiness, Mercy and Goodness."[8] Our theology of spiritual conflict also plays a part in recognizing external, demonic distractions and seeking God's strength to stand against these schemes of the devil (Eph. 6:10). Finally, we also consider our goals in prayer. Here Scripture is so helpful, for the psalmist says, "Blessed are those who keep his testimonies, who seek him with their whole heart" (Ps. 119:2). Setting our goal to seek God "with our whole heart" is different from setting our goal as "today I will pray without distraction."

Summary

Distracted prayer is part of the human condition, a matter of body and heart. Practically, we can take several steps to limit our distractions: putting smart phones on "do not disturb" mode or out of reach while we pray, keeping pencil and paper nearby to write our prayer concerns down so that we do not get distracted by the lingering feeling that we are forgetting a need, keeping an open Bible nearby in order to read and pray Scripture, and giving attention to our space and bodies. These steps may all help us fight distraction in prayer.

REFLECTION QUESTIONS

1. What are the greatest sources of distraction you face in prayer?

2. How can "distraction-free" prayer become an idol?

3. What effect does our physical space have as a source of distraction?

4. How might giving attention to our bodies help fight distraction?

5. What is one step you will take to limit distraction in your prayer life today?

---

7.   Vincent, *Attending upon God*, 158.
8.   Vincent, *Attending upon God*, 159.

How Might Christians Pray Scripture?

We have considered how Scripture shapes prayer, from providing us with examples of people at prayer, to establishing our theology of prayer, and even to providing assurances of the hidden ministries of the Spirit and the Son in praying for us. In answering this chapter's question, we will explore an even more direct way that Scripture can help us pray: by shaping the very words we offer to God in prayer. While Christians from some backgrounds are accustomed to praying the words of Scripture as their own, for many others this practice is quite foreign. The practice is quite simple: as we read the Bible, we pause and begin to let the very words of what we read shape the way we pray.[1] This shaping might take the form of praying for things that we notice in the text, or, more commonly, beginning to take the words and phrases of Scripture as our words of prayer. This practice has a rich history in the church and has proven to be a life-giving means of strengthening and deepening prayer for many believers, myself included. We will begin by considering several biblical examples of this practice, and then trace briefly the way this practice has developed historically before concluding with particular advice on praying various parts of Scripture.

Scriptural Prayers

I recall a particular time of devotional Bible reading some years ago, while working through the Psalms, where I realized that I was hearing a familiar echo while reading Psalm 67. The psalm begins, "May God be gracious to us and bless us and make his face to shine upon us, *Selah*." I had read this psalm many times before and missed one obvious feature: the psalmist was quoting the Aaronic (priestly) blessing of Numbers 6:24–25. Now aware of this usage, I began to notice such interbiblical quotations elsewhere. Beyond the priestly blessing, Psalm 103:8 had a clear dependence upon God's self-disclosure in

---

1. See Donald S. Whitney, *Praying the Bible* (Wheaton, IL: Crossway, 2015), 26–27.

Exodus 34:6, as did Psalm 86:15 and Psalm 145:8. Jonah's prayer from the great fish (Jonah 2:2–9) was filled with allusions to various psalms. I was already familiar with Jesus quoting Psalm 22 while upon the cross but had somehow missed the Jerusalem church's use of the Old Testament in Acts 4:23–30. These passages, and many others, bear witness to the vital connection between the Word of God and our words in prayer. We may be tempted to see such usages through merely intellectual/academic lenses, and while they may prompt fruitful discussion, we must not overlook their practical significance: when expressing great praise or facing great suffering, believers turn to the very words of Scripture to give expression to their own thanksgivings and pleas for mercy.

A Brief History of Praying Scripture

Early Christian monastic communities practiced a pattern of reading and prayer that later came to be designated by the Latin phrase *lectio divina* (divine reading). This pattern emphasized a deepening engagement with the text of Scripture that moved from reading the words aloud (*lectio*), to reciting the words subvocally to oneself (*meditatio*), then to turning these recited words into prayer (*oratio*), and, finally, staying attentive and joyously in the presence of God (*contemplatio*).[2] The monastic *Rule of St. Benedict* documents this practice, although it clearly predates Benedict. By the Middle Ages a Carthusian monk named Guigo II codified this practice, and contemporaneous devotional authors recommended the practice as an almost meritorious work reserved exclusively for an elite class of the "religious." The practice remained well known at the time of the Protestant Reformation, for it was the daily practice by which Martin Luther learned the Scriptures, and he continued the practice, in part, years after he left the monastery, even as he offered insightful corrections to it, especially to the loosely defined aspect of "contemplation." Among early evangelicals, John Wesley proposed a formative reading of Scripture that looked in part like the fourfold approach of *lectio divina* but culminated in outward-focused teaching rather than inward-focused contemplation.[3] In the twentieth century, significant Roman Catholic and evangelical authors sought to revive this practice, with varying receptions.[4]

---

2. See Mariano Magrassi, *Praying the Bible: An Introduction to Lectio Divina*, trans. Edward Hagman (Collegeville, MN: Liturgical Press, 1998), 103–19.
3. See Lorinda Lewis Roberts, "John Wesley's Formative Reading of Scripture as an Applicable Model for Family Discipleship" (The Southern Baptist Theological Seminary, DMin Thesis, 2018).
4. Among twentieth-century Roman Catholic writers, see Thomas Merton, Thomas Keating, and M. Basil Pennington. Among evangelicals, two popular works are James C. Wilhoit and Evan B. Howard, *Discovering Lectio Divina: Bringing Scripture into Ordinary Life*

How might we assess this practice? It would be easy for Protestants to offer a summary dismissal of *lectio divina* because of its associations with works-righteousness and mystical undertones that seem to undercut the unique mediation of Jesus Christ. Equally tempting is to adopt this practice with little or no critique because of its antiquity, ecumenicity, or seeming novelty. Still others insist that Protestants have misunderstood aspects of this practice.[5] Martin Luther's approach, that of a critical practitioner, seems to provide us a helpful framework here.

As an Augustinian monk, Luther committed himself to adopting a rigorous, ongoing pattern of prayer and Bible study, a commitment he took very personally and fastidiously. Even after the posting of his 95 Theses in 1517, Luther continued the monastic life for several years, and even after abandoning the monastery, he continued some of the devotional practices that had marked him.[6] At the risk of drawing too general a conclusion from Luther's unique devotional life, his continued practice of praying the Scripture he read, even after a clear break with Roman Catholic doctrine concerning how we are made right before God (justified), seems significant. Focusing on the first three aspects—those of reading, meditating, and praying—has long been a part of Protestant spiritual practice. Developing a thoughtful and critical approach to the fourth aspect, contemplation, is necessary.

A Simple Way to Begin Praying Scripture

One of the simplest ways to begin praying Scripture is to identify and integrate specific one- or two-sentence petitions from Scripture into our own times of prayer. Pastor John Piper has recommended the acronym I.O.U.S. as a memorable way to connect prayer and Bible reading.[7] Piper draws heavily from the Psalms: "Incline my heart to your testimonies, and not to selfish gain!" (Ps. 119:36); "Open my eyes, that I may behold wondrous things out of your law" (Ps. 119:18); "unite my heart to fear your name" (Ps. 86:11); "Satisfy us in the morning with your steadfast love, that we may rejoice and be glad

(Downers Grove, IL: InterVarsity Press, 2012); and Eugene H. Peterson, *Eat This Book: A Conversation in the Art of Spiritual Reading* (Grand Rapids: Eerdmans, 2006).

5. One recent evangelical work on this topic is that of John H. Coe and Kyle Strobel, eds., *Embracing Contemplation: Reclaiming a Christian Spiritual Practice* (Downers Grove, IL: IVP Academic, 2019).

6. Timothy J. Wengert, "Preface," in *Luther's Spirituality*, eds. Philip D. W. Krey, Bernard McGinn, and Peter D. S. Krey, trans. Peter D. S. Krey and Philip D. W. Krey, The Classics of Western Spirituality (Mahwah, NJ: Paulist Press, 2007), xiii. "As Luther doubtless knew, the monastic encounter with biblical texts took place through a threefold *oratio, meditatio, et illuminatio seu contemplatio* (prayer, meditation, and illumination or contemplation). Luther, too, began with prayer *(oratio)*—not because he was pious, but because the biblical text overthrows all human reason and forces the reader to call upon the Holy Spirit for help."

7. John Piper, *When I Don't Desire God: How to Fight for Joy* (Wheaton, IL: Crossway, 2004), 150–52.

all our days" (Ps. 90:14). Piper's approach is a helpful introduction to the simplicity of praying Scripture and is commendable. In Psalm 119 alone, there are more than sixty petitions.

Letting Scripture Shape Our Prayers

One exercise that I have done with students in my graduate course in spiritual disciplines is to provide them with a printed text of a psalm and then ask them to spend twenty minutes in prayer. After this exercise I ask them to reflect as a class on the experience, and one question that always brings fruitful discussion is, "How many of you prayed for something you had not intended to pray about because of something you read in this psalm?" I cannot recall a time where students have failed to find something new to pray as a result of this practice. I have heard one church historian express this phenomenon by saying that without reading Scripture, our prayers tend to be self-focused. One caution in this regard is that we need to grow as readers of Scripture so we do not misinterpret Scripture or twist it. Yet the fear of getting some things wrong ought not keep us from letting the Bible shape the way we pray. What follows are several examples of how different passages of Scripture might direct our prayers of petition, thanksgiving, intercession, or adoration.

"Again, the kingdom of heaven is like merchant in search of fine pearls, who, on finding one pearl of great value, went and sold all that he had and bought it" (Matt. 13:45–46). In response to this parable, we might petition God as follows: "Father, help me to recognize how precious your reign as king over me and over this world is. Help me to treat it like treasure. Help me to remember that I cannot love the world or my possessions more than I love you. Help me to set aside all of my treasures in order to follow you."

"If then you have been raised with Christ, seek the things that are above, where Christ is, seated at the right hand of God. Set your minds on things that are above, not on things that are on earth. For you have died, and your life is hidden with Christ in God. When Christ who is your life appears, then you also will appear with him in glory" (Col. 3:1–4). We might intercede for a friend at church in light of this text like this: "Father, help my friend seek the things that are above and not be enamored with the things of this earth. Help her to recognize that she has died and that her life is hidden with Christ in God. Let her find comfort in being hidden in Christ; secure in your presence. Let her remember that Christ is her very life and that one day she will appear with him in glory."

"Though the fig tree should not blossom, nor fruit be on the vines, the produce of the olive fail and the fields yield no food, the flock be cut off from the fold and there be no herd in the stalls, yet I will rejoice in the LORD; I will take joy in the God of my salvation" (Hab. 3:17–18). We might confess in light of this passage this way: "Father, I want to take joy in you, the God of my salvation, but I am so overwhelmed by the pressures of raising my children and caring for my parents that I feel numb. I want to take joy in you, but I feel overwhelmed. I know I ought to have joy, and I confess my joylessness; Lord, help me rejoice again! Help me trust you, even though my world feels like it is spinning out of control. Restore my joy."

> And [Naomi] said, "See, your sister-in-law has gone back to her people and to her gods; return after your sister-in-law." But Ruth said, "Do not urge me to leave you or to return from following you. For where you go I will go, and where you lodge I will lodge. Your people shall be my people, and your God my God. Where you die I will die, and there will I be buried. May the LORD do so to me and more also if anything but death parts me from you." And when Naomi saw that she was determined to go with her, she said no more. (Ruth 1:15–18)

During the time of a famine in Israel, Naomi's husband moved his wife and sons to the land of Moab. After this move, Naomi's husband died. Ten years later, her sons, who had married Moabite women, also died. Naomi set her heart to return to her home in Bethlehem and implored her daughters-in-law to stay in Moab. The passage quoted above shows how Naomi's daughter-in-law Ruth responded in love. In light of this narrative of Naomi's loss and Ruth's faithfulness, we might offer thanksgiving for faithfulness we have received during our own times of suffering to this effect: "Father, thank you for showing your steadfast love thorough my friend, who has walked with me through my pain and cared for me like Ruth for Naomi. Thank you for forming him into this man of steadfast character and for the blessing he has been in reminding me of your faithfulness when I am tempted to sorrow. Thank you for making him tenacious in showing mercy, even when it costs him so much time. Help me to be this sort of friend one day, when you have brought me through this time of testing. Lord, encourage him that his kindness has been a blessing."

These examples illustrate how we might move from reading various kinds of biblical passages, to meditating upon them, to praying them in various ways that seek to preserve the meaning of the text and to apply them immediately to our lives. Of course, we might read the passages from which these texts are drawn, study the passages, and even do deep exegesis of their syntax or note their Christological significance and doctrinal distinctives. Yet we may also simply *pray* these texts, allowing them to interpret the world as God reveals it through his Word and ordering our lives in light of that truth.

Summary

Integrating our Bible reading and meditation into our prayers is one way to let Christ's word dwell richly in our lives, as individuals and as the church.

In our public prayers, we might read a short passage of Scripture and then pray in light of its message. Taking this approach allows God to help form us through his Word and to help us participate in the process of forming others through our prayers, as we both pray *for* them and pray *in the presence* of them. Jesus warns us against making an ostentatious show of our prayers in order to receive people's approval (Matt. 6), yet we must recognize that all public prayer is inherently didactic; it teaches those who hear it about God and about prayer. By letting Scripture shape our language and our requests, we may help keep our minds from straying, we rehearse the great truths that God has made known, we honor God by listening to him speak through his Word, we seek to conform our desires to his revealed will, we allow him to suggest the topics of our prayer and thus avoid self-focused praying, or at least minimize it—all these blessings we receive and so many others.

REFLECTION QUESTIONS

1. What are some benefits of letting the Bible shape our praying?

2. How has praying Scripture helped you vocalize difficult requests in the past?

3. What are some possible errors we might make in praying Scripture?

4. How might praying Scripture make us better students of the Bible?

5. How might praying Scripture be the culmination of our reading, meditation, and study?

Why Is It Important for Christians to Pray Together?

Nearly all the questions in this book have focused on prayer as an individual activity before God, but prayer is also a gift that God gives to churches and a congregational practice. Recalling John Bunyan's definition used above, prayer is "for the good of the church," and this chapter considers reasons why Christians must pray together. When I first posed this question in 2019, I would have answered it in the same way that I am doing now in 2021, yet the great disruption caused by the COVID-19 pandemic, especially among churches, has given this chapter new significance. Why is congregational prayer so important? How is praying with other Christians different from praying merely by ourselves? How do different kinds of prayer like confession, thanksgiving, and intercession take on new dimensions when practiced with other Christians rather than alone? How can we learn to pray together from Christians in prior generations?

Mature Christians Seek Prayer

As we grow deeper in our discipleship, we come to realize how important prayer really is and we ask other Christians to pray for us. Like Paul, we appeal to other believers to "strive together" with us in prayer (Rom. 15:30). One Baptist confession of faith speaks of this priority in the following way:

> As each church, and all the members of it, are bound to pray
> continually for the good and prosperity of all the churches
> of Christ, in all places, and upon all occasions to further it
> (every one within the bounds of their places and callings, in
> the exercise of their gifts and graces), so the churches (when
> planted by the providence of God so as they may enjoy op-
> portunity and advantage for it) ought to hold communion

among themselves for their peace, increase of love, and mutual edification.[1]

The Priority of Praying Together

The church is part of God's sovereign plan for the good of his people and the reconciliation of all things in Christ. Jesus promised to build his church and that "the gates of hell shall not prevail against it" (Matt. 16:18). In Christ, the church is "being built together into a dwelling place for God by the Spirit" (Eph. 2:22).

The early church understood the priority of praying with and for one another. In the book of Acts, we overhear the church at prayer. The church "devoted themselves" to prayer after Jesus's ascension (Acts 1:14) and prayed for God's direction in choosing an apostle to replace Judas (1:24–26). This devotion to prayer characterized scores of laity who were converted after Pentecost (2:42). A similar devotion to prayer marked the leaders of the church in Jerusalem (6:4). The church prayed for God's protection with powerful effect (4:21–31). The church prayed when setting apart men for ministries of service (6:6) and mission (13:3; 14:23). Peter commanded the would-be convert Simon the magician to repent of his selfish schemes and pray for God's forgiveness and Simon asked Peter to pray for him also (8:22–24). The church prayed earnestly for Peter when he was imprisoned (12:5), gathering for prayer in members' homes (12:12). Paul and Silas prayed together while imprisoned (16:25). Paul prayed with the elders of the Ephesian church who had come to meet him at Miletus (20:36).[2] This string of references to prayer is descriptive, but in describing the church, it is clear that prayer was a normal priority for these Christians and it ought to be so for our churches too. But making prayer a priority for churches means that praying with other believers ought to be a priority for us individually. We cannot lament a prayerless church if we are unwilling to pray with others ourselves. This word is for pastors or elders, deacons, lay leaders, and ordinary members. The early church responded to its challenges by gathering members together for prayer. When the church was unable to gather in large groups because of governmental persecution, they did not stop praying, but dispersed into smaller groups in people's homes to pray. Leaders prayed with other leaders and with members. Leaders prayed for other leaders and sent them out to minister. Members prayed for leaders enduring suffering for their commitment to Christ. These commitments to

---

1. *The Philadelphia Confession*, Article 14, *The Creeds of Christendom, with a History and Critical Notes: The Evangelical Protestant Creeds, with Translations*, vol. 3 (New York: Harper & Brothers, 1882), 740.
2. For a list that includes other individual prayers in Acts, see John Onwuchekwa, *Prayer: How Praying Together Shapes the Church* (Wheaton, IL: Crossway, 2018), 94–95.

corporate prayer are surely one reason for the early church's amazing growth and expansion, even in the face of Jewish and Roman opposition.

Confessing Sin and Praying for One Another

The New Testament also shows the early church confessing sin and praying for one another. James 5:16 is a pivotal text for congregational prayers of confession: "Therefore, confess your sins to one another and pray for one another, that you may be healed." We have examined this passage's context in an earlier chapter (see Question 25), but here we simply note that James envisions confession of sin as a congregational act. The verb "confess" (*exomologeisthe*) is plural and imperative, a pastoral command to a church and to our churches as is James's command to "pray" (*euchesthe*) for one another. Confession is an admission that we are wrong, that we have sinned, and James calls Christians to interpersonal confession within the church. Such confession is regrettably a missing hallmark of many Christian churches. Perhaps we ought not to be surprised that so many congregations seem so unhealthy when we ignore this command. Thankfully many churches do practice the sort of life-on-life discipleship that makes confession of our sin to other believers seem more normal, but some Protestants may be hesitant here because of associations with Roman Catholic practice. In the middle of the first millennium, Celtic Christians in England and Ireland played an important role in formalizing confession and shifting it toward a systematic practice of penance, a rubric-guided restitution for specific sins. By the early 1200s, confession before a priest was made obligatory, at least annually. Catholic critics noted abuses of these systems in the Middle Ages, and such abuses were a major catalyst for the Protestant Reformation of the sixteenth century. Yet even the German Reformer Martin Luther, whose own life as a monk was deeply marked by this sort of formal confession, urged churches to revive and retain biblical forms of confession and prayer.

Luther found the Lord's Prayer to teach congregational confession in the petition "Forgive us our debts" (Matt. 6:12) and he also appealed to James 5:16 for the practice. In light of the fact that Christians regularly sin against each other, confession should be a natural part of congregational life. Luther also saw a place for a more personal sort of confession between two believers:

> If something particular weighs upon us or troubles us, something with which we keep torturing ourselves and can find no rest, and we do not find our faith to be strong enough to cope with it, then this private form of confession gives us the opportunity of laying the matter before some brother.[3]

---

3. Martin Luther, *A Brief Exhortation to Confession*, in *Concordia: The Lutheran Confessions*, ed. Timothy Paul McCain, 2nd ed. (St. Louis: Concordia, 2005), 651.

Luther described this sort of confession as a gift related to Jesus's entrusting Christians with the ministry of priesthood, particularly of absolving one another of sins. Luther spoke about the ministry of the regular believer hearing another Christian's confession and reassuring them of the truth of the gospel, that Christ has indeed forgiven their sins, including *this* sin that is being confessed. The parallel imperatives in James 5:16 of "confess" and "pray" are for the purpose "that you may be healed" (*hopōs iathēte*). Here, "healing" is the restoration to wholeness that occurs after one's sin has been confessed and assurance of forgiveness given. Praying together is the way to bring about this wholeness and one reason why we must pray with other believers.

Concerts of Prayer for Revival

Beginning in the eighteenth century, a handful of pastors led their congregations to do something innovative: to come together to pray that God would awaken sinners and revive Christians. New England pastor-theologian Jonathan Edwards was one important promoter of these gatherings. Edwards had experienced a "surprising" movement of God in the mid-1730s, especially among younger members of his congregation. Beginning in 1739, he preached about the importance of prayer in connection with God pouring out the Holy Spirit upon his people, mentioning Zephaniah 3:9, which contains a prophecy about a future expansion of prayer among God's people.[4] Several years later, after a period of remarkable revival known as the Great Awakening, Edwards issued a more focused call for prayer in his work *An Humble Attempt*.[5]

Reading Zechariah 8:20–22 (KJV, emphasis added), Edwards found a biblical foretelling of a time of great concerted prayer on behalf of God's people:

> Thus saith the LORD of hosts; *It shall* yet *come to pass*, that there shall come people, and the inhabitants of many cities: And the inhabitants of one *city* shall go to another, saying, Let us go speedily to pray before the LORD, and to seek the LORD of hosts: I will go also. Yea, many people and strong nations shall come to seek the LORD of hosts in Jerusalem, and to pray before the LORD.

Edwards thought this passage ought to motivate Christians around the world to gather quickly for united prayer in order to seek the Lord and a fresh effusion

---

4. Jonathan Edwards, *A History of the Work of Redemption, The Works of Jonathan Edwards*, vol. 9, ed. John F. Wilson (New Haven, CT: Yale University Press, 1989), 142. See Thomas S. Kidd, "The Very Vital Breath of Christianity: Prayer and Revival in Provincial New England," in *Fides et Historia* 36 (2004): 19–33.
5. Jonathan Edwards, *An Humble Attempt, in The Works of Jonathan Edwards*, vol. 5, ed. Stephen J. Stein (New Haven, CT: Yale University Press, 1977).

of his Holy Spirit. He convened Christians in his own town of Northampton for such prayer, and through his wide correspondence with other ministers, encouraged similar gatherings in England, Scotland, and New England. In the late 1700s, Baptists like William Carey and Andrew Fuller revived these sorts of congregational "concerts of prayer" to support their vision of taking the gospel around the globe. Before the American Civil War, gatherings of lay members for prayer preceded and supported an important revival of religion that began in New York and spread around the English-speaking world in 1857–58.[6] In the twentieth century, congregational prayer played a significant role in a revival in Korea.[7] In the late twentieth century, evangelicals remembered and recommended gatherings of prayer like this.[8] As we mentioned in an earlier chapter, prayer is vitally connected with spiritual awakening among the lost and with revival among Christians. The brief historical summary above shows that evangelicals have committed themselves to this sort of prayer at various times over nearly three hundred years and have experienced the power of the Holy Spirit in these efforts. It is one way that we can and ought to pray with other Christians today.

Summary

So how can we grow in our practice of praying with other believers? First, we should remember that praying corporately need not be complicated. Pastor John Onwuchekwa's reflections on congregational prayer offer motivation and insight. Hearing other Christians express their struggles, concerns, and joys can help us learn to articulate our own hearts in prayer, even as it challenges us to pray about things we have overlooked.[9] Praying with other Christians might take place when the church is assembled for worship, or it might happen when smaller cells of the church meet outside the typical gathering time in people's homes, or even one on one as we confess and pray with other believers. We might pray in light of our common suffering, for believers in other parts of our country or world who are suffering hardship, or to ask God to bring renewed vitality to our congregations and for the conversions of the lost in our midst. Jesus envisioned us praying with others when he taught us to pray, "*Our* Father . . . give *us* this day *our* daily bread" (Matt. 6:9–11, emphasis added).

---

6. See Samuel I. Prime, *The Power of Prayer: The New York Revival of 1858* (Carlisle, PA: The Banner of Truth Trust, 1991).

7. See William N. Blair and Bruce F. Hunt, *The Korean Pentecost and the Sufferings Which Followed* (Carlisle, PA: Banner of Truth Trust, 2015).

8. See David Bryant, *With Concerts of Prayer: Christians Join for Spiritual Awakening and World Evangelization* (Ventura, CA: Regal, 1984).

9. John Onwuchekwa, *What if I Don't Desire to Pray?* Church Questions (Wheaton, IL: Crossway, 2020), 23–25.

REFLECTION QUESTIONS

1. How is praying with other Christians different from praying alone?

2. What does the book of Acts show about Christians praying together in the early church?

3. How might Christians practice confession and prayer together?

4. How might Christians pray for spiritual awakening and revival together?

5. What are your biggest fears about praying with others?

How Can I Set Aside a Day for Prayer?

Growing disciples of Jesus Christ will increasingly desire prayer. Throughout this book, we have considered ways to deepen our ongoing experience of daily prayer, but Christians have long recognized the need for special seasons of prayer. Looking to Jesus's example, we note that Jesus kept special times of extended prayer before calling his disciples (Luke 6:12–16), before revealing his forthcoming suffering to his friends (Luke 9:18–22), and before his arrest and execution (Matt. 26:36–46). When facing significant decisions or turning points in our lives, we might also set aside a day for extended prayer to seek the Lord's guidance in a special way. For some, spending a day in prayer is enlivening, but for many, the idea of spending a whole day in prayer seems daunting (how will I pass the time?) or perhaps foolish (isn't this just a wasted day?). In this chapter, we consider practical advice for how we might set apart special seasons for extraordinary prayer.[1]

Why Devote a Day for Prayer?

In light of earlier questions in this book, we remember that God does not hear us because of our many words (Matt. 6:5–8) and that we might practice restraint in our prayers (Eccl. 5), yet Jesus himself sometimes spent long hours (Matt. 14:23) or an entire night (Luke 6:12) praying; thus there seems to be nothing incompatible with praying simply but praying for longer durations. The fact that Jesus customarily prayed this way strengthens our case for occasional times of extended prayer. A day of prayer may seem "inefficient" to Western-minded workers, accustomed to associate time and productivity, yet efficacy, not efficiency, is the hallmark of genuine prayer.

Though we ought to cultivate ongoing, regular prayer as a pattern to maintain experiential nearness to God, some events or seasons in life bring our need

---

1. One book that provides a slightly different pattern for such a day is Gordon T. Smith, *Alone with the Lord: A Guide for a Personal Day of Prayer* (Vancouver: Regent College, 2003).

for prayer to the forefront of our minds and disrupt our normal patterns of life for a time. The loss of a job, a severe medical diagnosis, news of a friend's struggles, a child's death, the ending of a relationship, and many more situations that mark our lives might reveal our need for extraordinary prayer. Responding to these sorts of events with prayer is an appropriate way of reacting to events that are so important to our existence, yet extended prayer is also a proactive way to pursue godliness. Occasionally, we might set aside a day of extended prayer when there is no crisis or pressing need for the purpose of devoting ourselves to the Lord's presence and training ourselves to respond to future crises before they arise.

Start Small

For many, the desire for a day of prayer may outpace their discipline for such a day. Often, it is helpful for those who are not used to praying for long periods of time to set smaller goals, such as one to two hours, rather than attempting a full day. Remembering that prayer is a whole-person discipline that engages the mind and body as well as the spirit, praying for extended periods does require a measure of physical stamina. Some readers face significant physical limitations: loss of mobility, sense decline, post-traumatic stress, debilitating disease, lingering illness, side effects of medication, or hosts of other effects of a fallen world. Others of us are simply not used to focusing active mental energy for prolonged times. Still others would admit to laziness and procrastination as "besetting" sins. All believers are prone to the three-fold attack of the axis of flesh, world, and devil, which oppose our spiritual life at every step. Starting small, with goals that stretch your will and abilities, is a good way to begin expanding your natural abilities.

Plan for Prayer

Identify a day that you can set apart for this work. It may be today, but it may be better planned for a time when you can arrange your schedule to minimize other commitments. Commit to this day by adding it to a physical or electronic calendar. Mention it quietly to another believer to whom you are accountable, perhaps a small-group member, a Christian friend, your spouse, or a mentor. Ask that person to pray specifically for you on this day and to follow up with you later about your experience. Choose the best time of day for you, a time when you are most alert. For some, this time will be early morning, for others it may be mid-morning or even late at night.

Choose a place where you will spend this day. Depending on the time of year, this might be a local park, a retreat center, an empty worship center or classroom at church, a corner in your garage or basement, or some other location that best works for your purpose. Select a place where you will not become preoccupied with your surroundings or distracted by the happenings around you. You might consider spending part of your time walking to help fight grogginess or lethargy. If you choose a place outside, you might have a backup location indoors in the event of bad weather. Consider necessities like water, restrooms, and food (unless you are fasting). Determine what items you will need: a Bible, a notebook, a pen or pencil, a chair, a blanket, and so forth. Also consider leaving your mobile phone behind if possible, or at least keeping it out of easy reach and set to not disturb you during your time of prayer. Let someone else know where you will be and when you plan to return. When the day and time arrive, keep your commitment to the Lord by being at the place you have selected on time.

An Expandable Pattern

One exercise that I have used for several years involves spending four consecutive hours in Bible-directed prayer. Begin the time by dedicating it to the Lord. You might thank him for allowing you this opportunity to seek him. Ask for his help to behold wonderful things in his Word (Ps. 119:18). Ask him to help you be teachable. Read the Bible with an expectant spirit. For this time, you might focus on one book of the Bible that can be read in its entirety during your prayer time.[2] I have found the biblical wisdom books of Proverbs and Ecclesiastes, and the New Testament books of James, the gospel of Mark, and the epistles of 1 John, 1 Peter, and Hebrews particularly helpful for this approach. If the concept of praying the Bible is unfamiliar to you, you might review Question 35. Spend part of your time reading and part of your time praying in response to what you have read.

At the outset of your reading, ask that the Spirit would show you God's glory and that you might behold Jesus clearly in what you read. Ask that God would show you one particular virtue to be cultivated in your life. Further, ask that God might reveal one vice that needs to be uprooted from your life. As you read, be aware of these vices and virtues, perhaps writing them in a notebook, and pausing where Scripture addresses these matters to pray what you find in the text. You might keep a record of your prayers. Using this approach with a shorter book of the Bible like 1 John or Ephesians, I am often surprised at how quickly an hour passes, though one might read both books in less than thirty minutes. This method can be readily expanded if you have more time. This approach is generally a more proactive way of setting aside part of a day for prayer, but what about prayer that is responsive to the varied situations of life?

Concentrated Prayer for Needs

We might, from time to time, set aside a day of prayer for specific needs in our own lives or in the lives of others. Without sacrificing the value of praying

---

2. Thirty-three of the Bible's sixty-six books can be read in under thirty minutes. Even slower readers can typically read many other books in under two hours. Lists of Bible reading times are readily available online, such as at http://cdn.desiringgod.org/images/blog/DG_Blog_BibleReadingGraph_v.gif.

"at all times," setting aside a day for prayer can be very important when we are facing significant decisions or struggles for which we are acutely aware of the need for God's guidance. The act of dedicating a day for prayer can help shake us from the bonds of lethargy and distraction that sometimes mark our lives and help create a receptive disposition. It may also help us focus our prayers on the matters at hand. This refocusing can be helpful for our experiential sense of communion with God in prayer. We might set aside such a day for petition or for intercession, recognizing the need for God to work in the lives of others: our spouses, children, family members, friends, church members, political leaders, and so on. We might also set aside a day of prayer for thanksgiving, adoration, or confession, recognizing the value of these kinds of prayers. When we become focused on our own lives or the needs of others, we may incrementally forget to praise God or thank him. It may be that a day set aside simply to thank God for his care and provision or to praise him for his incomparable glory *is* the greatest need that we have.

Summary

Though Christians are called to pray "without ceasing" and to pray "at all times," setting apart special times of concentrated prayer allows us occasion to revisit our priorities and "reset" our agendas in light of God's kingdom. A faithful follower of Jesus might never set aside such a day during their lives, and by common testimony, many do not. However, marking out such a day, whether quarterly, annually, or with some other frequency may bear much fruit in our pursuit of fellowship with the Lord. As with many aspects of our physical health and well-being, we might be tempted to wait until we experience a crisis to give ourselves to intentional, focused action, yet in spiritual matters this approach is especially ill advised.

REFLECTION QUESTIONS

1. What are some circumstances where you might choose to set apart a day for prayer?

2. What is your greatest concern about setting apart a day for prayer?

3. What are some things to avoid in setting aside a day for prayer?

4. What is one practical step you can take to start small in this practice?

5. What are some ways other Christians can help you set aside a day for prayer?

PART 5

Prayer in Historical Context

What Can the Ancient Church Teach Us About Prayer?

Prayer is a practice that unites Christians to one another through the long, winding road of time and location. In this chapter and those that follow, we will consider ways in which Christians who have come before us can teach us about prayer. In answering this chapter's question, I want to look far back to the ancient church, to what has long been called the "patristic" era, from the Latin word *pater* (father). The period of the "fathers" of the church usually extends from about AD 100–500/600 and centers on Christians living in the Roman Empire or on its peripheries. This world seems far removed from our own in term of language, history, culture, and priorities, yet I hope to show you how prayer binds our worlds together in ways that may be encouraging. One challenge anyone faces in looking back in history is the distance between "then" and "now." This distance makes reflection on prayer in the ancient church challenging. Differences in language, culture, practice, philosophy, and so forth can create barriers to our hearing (well, reading) our forebears and understanding them. Despite these barriers, their voices are worth hearing.

Given the constraints of this chapter, we must avoid any kind of comprehensive analysis of prayer in the ancient church, for there are already fine works that do just that.[1] It is also challenging merely to summarize key concepts, for the way many of the ancient Christians mentioned in this chapter wrote defies simple itemization. Rather, my approach is to introduce and illustrate several important writings and examples of prayer in the ancient church in the hope that readers will benefit from such an introduction and that those interested in learning more will be able to follow the notes and sources to gain

---

1. Two important recent works are Christopher A. Hall, *Worshipping with the Church Fathers* (Downers Grove, IL: IVP Academic, 2009); and Robert Louis Wilken, *The Spirit of Early Christian Thought: Seeking the Face of God* (New Haven, CT: Yale University Press, 2003).

better acquaintance with these writers. Our sample includes men and women who lived and wrote in the 200s–400s across Africa, the Middle East, and Asia Minor: Origen, Macrina the Younger, and Augustine. Their voices are not the only ones who prayed in the ancient church, but they each have something helpful to teach us if we will listen to them pray.

Origen: Praying as We Ought

Origen was Egyptian, from the city of Alexandria, a city rich with Christian heritage, and was born around the year 185. He taught new believers the faith and led a rigorous, ascetic life. Origen was a Bible commentator, a theologian, and a philosopher. His philosophical speculations, shaped by Platonism, seem to have led him astray at various points of biblical theology, yet many of his original writings have been lost, making it difficult to assess his positions on some issues. Nevertheless, later Christians rejected much of his work. Origen ministered as a layman before being ordained to the priesthood, but was subsequently deposed. Moving from Alexandria to Caesarea, Origen established a school. In the year 250, he was imprisoned and tortured during an empire-wide persecution. He died around 254.

Origen wrote the treatise *On Prayer* around 233 after moving to Caesarea.[2] Throughout, Origen attempts to support his teaching from Scripture. In addition to exploring the Lord's Prayer and miscellaneous questions about place and posture, he frames his discussion around the concepts of "what" and "how" we ought to pray. The first category includes specific prayers drawn from Scripture while the second examines biblical descriptions of the attitude or frame of mind of the person who is praying. This synopsis focuses on the second category, praying "as we ought."

Praying "as we ought" involves thoughtful self-discipline. "First," writes Origen, "the person who composes his mind for prayer is inevitably profited in some way. Through his very disposition for prayer he adorns himself so as to present himself to God and to speak to Him in person as to someone who looks upon him and is present." Emphasizing the role of habit, Origen suggests that composing our minds for prayer has a place in sanctification: "If this [composing of the mind for prayer] happens frequently, those who have given themselves over to prayer with great constancy know by experience how many sins it prevents and how many virtuous actions it brings about." Origen suggests that Paul had instructed Timothy to undertake such preparation (1 Tim. 2:8) as had Jesus his disciples (Luke 11:4). Following the psalmist, Christians ought to pray by "lifting up their soul" to God (cf. Ps. 25:1) and

---

2. An accessible text is Origen, *Origen: An Exhortation to Martyrdom, Prayer, and Selected Works*, ed. Richard J. Payne, trans. Rowan A. Greer, The Classics of Western Spirituality (Mahwah, NJ: Paulist Press, 1979), 81–170.

abandoning malice toward others (Mark 11:25).[3] What can Origen teach us about prayer? The thoughtful act of preparing our hearts to pray can curb the appetites that invite sin and can help us walk in holiness.

Macrina: Praying in the Face of Death

When studying the ancient church, it is almost impossible to find surviving documents written by women. It is important for us to listen to women at prayer, but in the ancient church it is particularly challenging to hear their voices. One woman we need to hear praying is Macrina the younger. Macrina was born around the year 327 in Asia Minor and died on July 19, 379. She bore her grandmother's name, and her grandparents had survived imperial persecution, leaving a heritage of piety. Her parents were aristocratic landowners and committed believers. She was the first of ten children in her family, three of which siblings the Catholic Church recognizes as "saints."[4] Macrina learned the Psalms by heart as a young girl and used to recite them each day. Engaged to be married as an early teenager, her betrothed died suddenly, and she chose never to marry but instead to devote her life to God. She gathered with other women, some single, others widowed, and lived in a communal retreat for many years. In 378, her brother Basil died, and their brother Gregory came to visit her, arriving only hours before she too would pass. Gregory wrote the story of her life in a long letter, and near its end, he records Macrina's final prayer.[5]

> You have released us, O Lord, from the fear of death. You have made the end of life here on earth a beginning of true life for us. You let our bodies rest in sleep in due season and you awaken them again at the sound of the last trumpet. . . . You redeemed us from the curse and from sin, having become both on our behalf. You have crushed the heads of the serpent who had seized man in his jaws because of the abyss of our disobedience. You have opened up for us a path to the resurrection, having broken down the gates of hell and reduced to impotence the one who had power over deaths. . . . You who have on earth the power to forgive sins, forgive me, so that I might draw breath again and may be found before you

---

3. Origen, *On Prayer*, 97–100.
4. Remarkably, Macrina, her grandmother, and her brothers Basil and Gregory bear this distinction. Though the practice of designating certain believers as "saints" is foreign to the New Testament—which commonly uses the terms "saints" (holy ones) to describe all believers—and thus can be an off-putting practice for Protestants, this designation was not one which the family sought but was bestowed by later generations who recognized these individuals for their devotion to God.
5. A recent edition is Gregory of Nyssa, *The Life of Saint Macrina*, trans. Kevin Corrigan (Eugene, OR: Wipf and Stock, 2001).

in the stripping off of my body without stain or blemish in
the beauty of my soul, but may my soul be received blameless
and immaculate into your hands as an incense offering before
your face.[6]

Macrina's prayer is infused with Scripture's language and themes: the "last
trumpet," the crushed heads of the serpent, resurrection, Christ becoming a
curse to redeem his people from sin and its curse.[7] As Anna Silvas indicates,
Macrina's use of "you" as direct address to God, followed by a recounting of
his saving acts, is a form of adoration.[8] The prayer is brief but marked with
deep reverence for God. Macrina shows us how to pray in order to prepare
ourselves to stand face to face with God at death.

Augustine: Praying *coram Deo*

The Latin phrase *coram Deo* means "before God" or "in God's presence."
Through prayer, believers come into God's presence, and few ancient writers
capture this movement like Augustine (354–430). Raised by a Christian
mother, converted from secular pursuits at age 30, and indescribably important for the development of Christian theology and ethics, Augustine became
bishop of the Roman city of Hippo in North Africa in the late 300s and remained there until his death in his late seventies. Near the midpoint of his life,
Augustine wrote his *Confessions*, an autobiographical reflection on the ways
God had shepherded him to spiritual life in Christ. *Confessions* is part of the
canon of Western literature and new translations from the original Latin continue to appear every few years.[9] For our purposes, what makes *Confessions* so
important is that the work is really one (very) long prayer.

From the *Confessions'* opening line, "You are great, Lord, and highly to
be praised," to its final sentence, "Only you can be asked, only you can be
begged, only on your door can we knock. Yes indeed, that is how it is received,
how it is found, how the door is opened," Augustine leads readers with him
as he reflects on God's grace and providence in his life. It might be helpful to
think about *Confessions* as a long-form example of Paul's exhortation to "pray
without ceasing" (1 Thess. 5:17), for this is what Augustine does, in literary

---

6. Gregory, *Life of Saint Macrina*, 41–42.
7. The full prayer is only two pages of text and contains more than twenty biblical allusions or
   citations.
8. Anna M. Silvas, *Macrina the Younger, Philosopher of God*, in *Medieval Women: Texts and
   Contexts*, vol. 22 (Turnhout, Belgium: Brepols Publishing, 2008), 133.
9. All of the quotations we will examine come from *Saint Augustine Confessions*, trans.
   Henry Chadwick, Oxford World's Classics (Oxford: Oxford University Press, 1991).
   Augustine wrote *Confessions* in thirteen "books," which are actually long chapters. In citing
   Confessions, the standard approach is to give the book.chapter.paragraph, rather than a
   page number, since so many translations exist. We follow this approach here.

form, for about three hundred pages. The first thing Augustine shows us about prayer in *Confessions* is, then, that all of life can be lived intentionally as a prayer to God and that prayer involves continually interpreting our lives in light of God's presence and activity. Past events, former misunderstandings, our sins, sudden deaths, lifelong friendships, a mother's prayers, unexpected insights from Scripture, God's redeeming grace: all of these things make up the stuff of our prayers.

    Confessions is also a prayer filled with prayers. That is, although Augustine composed the entire work as a prayer, the work contains numerous individual prayers that allow us to listen to Augustine the bishop as he talks to God.[10] These specific prayers offer a second way that Augustine can teach us about prayer. We examine three here.

> Who are you, my God? What, I ask, but God who is Lord? For "who is the Lord but the Lord," or "who is God but our God?" (Ps. 17:32). Most high, utterly good, utterly powerful, most omnipotent, most merciful and most just, deeply hidden yet most intimately present, perfection of both beauty and strength, stable and incomprehensible, immutable and yet changing all things, never new, never old, making everything new and "leading" the proud "to be old without their knowledge" ... always active, always in repose, gathering to yourself but not in need, supporting and filing and protecting, creating and nurturing and bringing to maturity, searching even though to you nothing is lacking: you love without burning, you are jealous in a way that is free of anxiety, you "repent" (Gen. 6:6) without the pain of regret, you are wrathful and remain tranquil. You will a change without any change in your design. You recover what you find, yet have never lost. Never in any need, you rejoice in your gains (Luke 15:7). . . . You pay off our debts, though owing nothing to anyone; you cancel debts and incur no loss. But in these words what have I said, my God, my life, my holy sweetness? What has anyone achieved in words when he speaks about you? Yet woe to those who are silent about you because, though loquacious with verbosity, they have nothing to say. (*Confessions*, 1.4.4)

In this first prayer, we hear Augustine's voice of adoration through a string of God's attributes: "Most high, utterly good, utterly powerful, most omnipotent," and so on. We also hear thanksgiving: "You pay off our debts, though

---

10. John Rotelle identifies multiple dozens of prayers in his *Saint Augustine: Prayers from the Confessions,* trans. Maria Boulding, ed. John E. Rotelle (New York: New City Press, 2003).

owing nothing to anyone; you cancel debts and incur no loss." We also hear the sweet irony of such prayer when Augustine asks rhetorically, "What has anyone achieved in words when he speaks about you?" and immediately rejects the possibility of anyone remaining silent about God regardless of how much other talking they do.

> My love for you, Lord, is not an uncertain feeling but a matter of conscious certainty. With your word you pierced my heart, and I loved you. But heaven and earth and everything in them on all sides tell me to love you. Nor do they cease to tell everyone that "they are without excuse" (Rom. 1:20). But at a profounder level you will have mercy on whom you will have mercy and will show pity on him whom you will have pity (Rom. 9:15). Otherwise heaven and earth would be uttering your praises to the deaf. (*Confessions*, 10.6.8)

In *Confessions* 10, Augustine has shifted from talking about his past experiences to the present time in which he was writing the book, grounding his love for God not in emotion but in the "conscious certainty" that God is calling all, through creation and Scripture, to worship, while showing particular mercy to some according to his goodwill. A third prayer will stand without further comment.

> Late have I loved you, beauty so old and so new: late have I loved you. And see, you were within and I was in the external world and sought you there, and in my unlovely state I plunged into those lovely created things which you made. You were with me, and I was not with you. The lovely things kept me far from you, so if they did not have their existence in you, they had no existence at all. You called and cried out loud and shattered my deafness. You were radiant and resplendent, you put to flight my blindness. You were fragrant, and I drew in my breath and now pant after you. I tasted you, and I feel that hunger and thirst for you. You touched me, and I am set on fire to attain the peace which is yours. (*Confessions*, 10.27.38)

Summary

What can the ancient church teach us about prayer? By listening to Origen, we learn to prepare our hearts for prayer and in doing so to pursue holiness before we have even sought it propositionally. In listening to Macrina, we hear how a life of reflection on Scripture can prepare us to pray at the end of our life as we ready ourselves to meet God. In listening to Augustine, we learn to make all of life a prayer and to reflect on our whole life as a testimony of God's mercy and appropriate to remember in prayer.

REFLECTION QUESTIONS

1. How does Origen encourage believers to pray "as we ought?"

2. In what ways might Macrina's prayer comfort Christians facing death?

3. How does Augustine express adoration and thanksgiving to God?

4. Why is it important for us to listen to Christians from the past at prayer?

5. What is one way these ancient Christians have challenged you in prayer?

What Can the Medieval Church Teach Us About Prayer?

For Protestants, mentioning the "medieval church" often evokes several reactions. Like many in the nineteenth century, some Protestants will be moved with romanticized images of an era marked by chivalry, virtue, and beauty. For others, the term "medieval" calls to mind violent religious wars, biblical illiteracy, theological error, and ecclesial captivity. Yet others, maybe many, have only vague impressions of this period and wonder why we ought to bother with such a far-away time and distant lands.

There are good reasons why Christians ought to remember the medieval period. For one thing, it comprises a considerably long period of time—roughly one thousand years (from around AD 500–1500). That seems like an awful lot of history to ignore! Then, many of Christianity's most significant theologians and teachers lived during this era: Anselm of Canterbury, Bernard of Clairvaux, Thomas Aquinas, Bonaventure, and others. These teachers shaped the trajectory of our theology and ought to be remembered. In the West, the Roman Catholic Church grew in influence during this period as did major institutions like the papacy, the monastery, and the university. This fact will make some readers uncomfortable and perhaps raise barriers worth addressing.

During this period, Christians prayed much as they had done for centuries before and have done since. Prayer is one recognizable link that we have with the church of this period. The way medieval Christians practiced prayer began to change, though. Some Christians started addressing prayers to notable Christians who had died—"saints" whom they presumed might help them gain attention in heaven—or to Mary, Jesus's mother, who took on an increasingly prominent place in the devotion of Christians of the age.[1] Some Christians

---

1. See Jaroslav Pelikan, *Mary through the Centuries: Her Place in the History of Culture* (New Haven, CT: Yale University Press, 1996).

prayed while undertaking pilgrimages to lands they thought holy. Some prayed in the presence of physical relics they thought special. Some prayed in attempts to gain God's favor for their devotion. Some prayed stylized scripts with a hope of spiritual release. During this time, some aspects of prayer became detached from biblical moorings, yet many Christians prayed with a sincere desire to draw close to God and in ways consonant with Scripture. One such development worthy of careful consideration was the growth of regular or "set" hours of prayer. This practice encouraged Christians to pause for intentional prayer at set or fixed times each day and, with thoughtful appropriation, it can help us better practice disciplined prayer.

What Are the Origins of Set-Hour Prayer?

As the days of the ancient church were drawing to a close around the mid-400s (what historians call "late antiquity"), some Christians in modern-day Syria, Egypt, and even in Europe were practicing set-hour prayer. Precisely who first suggested this approach has been lost to us, but key figures such as John Cassian (d. ca. 430) and Benedict of Nursia (d. ca. 550) documented and stylized this practice for later generations.

Born in central Europe (modern Romania) around 360, John Cassian lived as a monk in Bethlehem, the town of Jesus's birth, in the mid-380s. Later Cassian travelled throughout Egypt, studying and documenting the varieties of monastic experience he encountered. Ordained in the early fifth century, he founded two monasteries near present-day Marseilles, France, and wrote several books, including two on the monastic life: *The Institutes* and *The Conferences*. These books describe Egyptian and eastern monasticism as Cassian found it during his travels in the 380s–390s. Cassian observed that daily patterns of fixed-hour prayer were part of "the most time-tried customs of the most ancient fathers."[2]

The most enduring ancient work to establish a pattern of daily set-hour prayer is the *Rule of St. Benedict* (RB), a handbook developed originally for the monastic community at Monte Cassino in Italy. The *Rule* was part guide and part constitution: its documents prescribed various ways monks were to live and the monks agreed to abide by the stipulations of these documents. Though Benedict's *Rule* was one of many such handbooks in late antiquity, it became the most influential. In the centuries after its appearance, monasteries across Europe adopted the RB, making it an almost universal pattern in the medieval period. Benedict's rule still shapes the daily pattern of spirituality for globally dispersed monastic communities today. In RB 16, Benedict appeals to the longest chapter in the Bible, Psalm 119, to support the practice of rising at night for prayer and for maintaining a pattern of seven daily "hours"

---

2.   John Cassian, *The Institutes*, trans. Boniface Ramsey, Ancient Christian Writers, no. 58 (Mahwah, NJ: The Newman Press, 2000), 37.

of prayer.[3] Benedict read Psalm 119:164, "Seven times a day I praise you for your righteous rules," as establishing seven mandatory times of prayer that monks were to observe. He found Psalm 119:62, "At midnight I rise to praise you, because of your righteous rules," to teach that the faithful should awake in the middle of the night in order to praise God. Together, these directions called monks to practice eight intentional times of prayer daily, as summarized in the table below.[4]

Latin Name	Time of Day[5]
Matins	2 a.m.
Lauds	5 a.m.
Prime	6 a.m.
Terce	9 a.m.
Sext	12 p.m.
None	3 p.m.
Vespers	6 p.m.
Compline	7 p.m.

During these times, monks would recite certain verses from select psalms as an opening prayer and then chant/sing specific psalms together before listening to several chapters of Scripture or works of early-church writers.[6] Monks would then return to the psalms before closing with a memorized prayer. Though the number and structure varied based on the time of day, monks would typically pray/sing at least three psalms per designated hour and recite portions of New Testament passages from memory. At this pace, monks would engage all of the psalms each week in prayer.

---

3. Readers will note that Benedict's actual references are to Psalm 118, following the Latin enumeration of the Psalms from Jerome's Vulgate.
4. See *The Rule of St. Benedict in English*, ed. Timothy Fry (Collegeville, MN: The Liturgical Press, 1982), 44 (RB 16.1–5). Abbreviated as RB with the common chapter and verse references.
5. The various times of day are a modern approximation.
6. Benedict was careful to distinguish the Bible as having "authority" though, RB 9.8. In the Latin text, the Old and New Testaments are called *auctoritatis*, which Fry translates "inspired" (RB 39), but which might be better rendered "authoritative."

This pattern in Benedict's *Rule* spread widely and shaped the daily and weekly rhythm of countless men and women who sought lives of devotion to God. As mentioned above (Question 31), the late Middle Ages saw a growing number of devout rulers and lay people begin to adopt a version of this practice through the publication of many "books of hours," which were richly illustrated handbooks to lead readers through formalized prayers at specific times each day. Set-hour prayer was not only a Catholic or monastic practice though.

Martin Luther (1483–1546), preeminent voice for the Protestant Reformation, immersed himself daily in set-hour prayer for a decade in an Augustinian monastery and continued this practice until 1520, several years after his break with the Roman Catholic Church.[7] The Genevan Reformer John Calvin (1509–1564) encouraged Christians to recognize their own weaknesses at prayer and to set apart five specific times for prayer during their daily routines. Calvin suggested Christians pray "when we arise in the morning, before we begin daily work, when we sit down to a meal, when by God's blessing we have eaten, when we are getting ready to retire."[8] The English Reformer Thomas Cranmer (1489–1556) incorporated morning and evening prayers into his daily liturgy for the Church of England in the *Book of Common Prayer*. The quasi-monastic Protestant community in the English village of Little Gidding observed these canonical hours.[9] The prolific Baptist pastor-theologian John Gill (1697–1771) suggested that Psalm 55:17 showed a thrice-daily pattern of prayer at "*evening, and morning, and at noon*" and insisted that the practice was worth following when approached with the proper theological framework.[10] Contemporary Presbyterian pastor Timothy Keller suggests various prayers for morning, midday, and evening.[11] These examples are representative of some Protestants who have found set hours of prayer helpful, yet other godly Protestant readers have remained skeptical of this practice because of its associations with Catholicism.

Is Set-Hour Prayer Biblical?

What should we make of this pattern of praying at specific times throughout the day? Particularly, how well does this pattern of prayer fit with a biblical

---

7. See Herman Selderhuis, *Martin Luther: A Spiritual Biography* (Wheaton, IL: Crossway, 2017), 56.

8. John Calvin, *Institutes of the Christian Religion*, ed. John T. McNeill, trans. Ford Lewis Battles, vol. 1, Library of Christian Classics (Louisville, KY: Westminster John Knox Press, 2011), 917–18.

9. Richard F. Lovelace, *The American Pietism of Cotton Mather: Origins of American Evangelicalism* (Eugene, OR: Wipf and Stock, 1979), 124.

10. John Gill, *A Complete Body of Doctrinal and Practical Divinity: Or a System of Evangelical Truths, Deduced from the Sacred Scriptures*, new ed., vol. 2 (London: Tegg & Company, 1839), 692.

11. Timothy Keller, *Prayer: Experiencing Awe and Intimacy with God* (New York: Dutton, 2014), 263.

spirituality? First, we ought to recognize that the desire to pray more consistently is a mark of spiritual maturity and that we learn to pray by praying. Practices that foster more prayer rather than less would seem helpful. Second, we ought to commend Benedict's stated intention of remaining faithful to Scripture. Still, there are good reasons to question the biblical rationale for a sevenfold daily pattern of prayer. Although some Protestant interpreters suggest otherwise, there is no evidence that Jewish readers of Psalm 119:164 saw what Benedict would later see: a command to pray at seven specific times each day.[12]

The Old Testament contains no legal directives regulating prayer the way it does other forms of worship. From around the time of the Babylonian exile (597–538 BC), daily prayer became increasingly important in Jewish life, especially in connection with the synagogue. During the time of the second temple (ca. 500 BC), Jewish sages codified a thrice-daily practice of praying: morning, afternoon, and evening.[13] The clearest biblical example of an individual maintaining a set time of prayer is the threefold pattern of daily prayer that Daniel practiced (cf. Dan. 6:10),[14] and one significant postbiblical Jewish source connects the normative threefold practice of prayer with Daniel's example, though other traditions date the practice from Israel's patriarchs Abraham (morning), Isaac (afternoon), and Jacob (evening).[15] In Acts, the apostles seem to participate in prayer in the afternoon and evening. By the end of the first century AD, some Christian leaders were recommending praying the Lord's Prayer three times daily.[16] In sum, it seems clear that by the early fourth century some Christians had developed a pattern of praying at seven specific times each day, although this pattern does not enjoy as clear biblical evidence as many have claimed. Setting aside specific times for prayer does indeed have biblical warrant, and a threefold pattern was very typical in the centuries prior to Christ's incarnation and in the earliest days of the church.

---

12. See Greg Peters, *The Story of Monasticism: Retrieving an Ancient Tradition for Contemporary Spirituality* (Grand Rapids: Baker Academic, 2015), 18; and Robert Benson, *In Constant Prayer* (Nashville: Thomas Nelson, 2008), 29. Both authors assert Psalm 119's influence on Jews and the earliest Christians, but provide no evidence to support their claims. Mention of the psalm seems absent from rabbinic literature, which constructs patterns of daily prayer from other passages.

13. Sometimes the order is afternoon, evening, and morning. See the Babylonian Talmud *Berakoth* 4. On the growth of prayer, see Bernard Martin, *Prayer in Judaism* (New York: Basic Books, 1968), 5.

14. See the helpful discussion in John Joseph Collins and Adela Yarbro Collins, *Daniel: A Commentary on the Book of Daniel*, Hermeneia (Minneapolis: Fortress Press, 1993), 268–69.

15. Babylonian Talmud *Berakoth* 31a for Daniel's influence. *Berakoth* 26b regarding the Patriarchs.

16. Francis X. Glimm, "The Didache or Teaching of the Twelve Apostles," in *The Apostolic Fathers*, trans. Francis X. Glimm, Joseph M.-F. Marique, and Gerald G. Walsh, vol. 1, The Fathers of the Church (Washington, DC: The Catholic University of America Press, 1947), 178.

A Simple Set-Hour Prayer

Recognizing that Scripture gives us freedom to pray at all times and does not set apart certain hours as more appropriate for prayer frees Christians to pray "at all times" (cf. 1 Thess. 5:17), but praying "always" can still include set times. What are some ways to begin praying at set times? First, we might consider setting apart time twice each day, morning and evening, specifically for prayer. These times might not be long at first, perhaps five to ten minutes as a starting point. As you practice this pattern, you might add in a time at midday or in early afternoon. The prevalence of personal fitness monitors and smart phones might help us set simple reminders throughout the day to stop our work and pray. Tim Keller proposes a threefold "daily office" that integrates Bible reading and prayer in the morning, midday, and evening.[17]

Summary

Christians have the freedom to practice set-hour prayer or to avoid such a practice. The New Testament pattern of praying "without ceasing" is not at odds with praying at certain times; rather, it encompasses such times. The discipline of praying at set times took on greater significance in monasticism during the Middle Ages, but it had its roots in Jewish and early Christian practices. The clearest expression of a threefold daily prayer is Daniel, and his example may prove instructive to us in this regard. Establishing set times of prayer may lead to a form of legalism, thinking that God hears our prayers and accepts us because of our consistent devotion, but it need not lead to this conclusion so long as we balance the truth that prayer is a blessing of the gospel, not a condition of God's acceptance in the gospel. Establishing regular times of prayer can help us to keep God at the forefront of our day by regularly coming into his presence and remembering his goodness toward us in Christ, even as we seek his provision for ourselves or others.

REFLECTION QUESTIONS

1. What can Daniel's example of praying three times daily teach us about intentional, set prayer?

2. How does Christian freedom from the law relate to praying at specific times?

3. What are the traditional hours of prayer as practiced in monasteries?

4. What are practical reasons we might adopt set-hour prayers?

5. What are your concerns about praying at set times during the day?

---

17. Keller, *Prayer*, 263–64.

What Can the Puritans Teach Us About Prayer?

Though the term "Puritan" is no more favorable today as it was in earlier centuries, these pastors and godly laypeople from England, the Netherlands, and America's past have much to teach us about prayer if we will listen. In several chapters of this book, I have integrated reflections from various Puritan authors like John Owen, Joseph Symonds, and Thomas Goodwin; and of course, the whole book is framed around John Bunyan's definition of prayer. In this chapter, we will first consider who the Puritans were, and then mention several authors who can help us in our own practice of prayer today.

Who Were the Puritans?

Puritanism was a movement of spiritual renewal, spawned by the Protestant Reformation, late in the sixteenth century in England. Puritanism arose out of a concern regarding the extent of reform within the Church of England and encompassed a variety of Protestant sects in Europe and the New England colonies, united by a vision of a biblically ordered, pure church. It called Christians to a serious and devout lifestyle grounded in Scripture and patterned after the model of Jesus. The very name "Puritan," however, was a derisive term meant to mock those who seemed always unsatisfied with the state of the church, and those who used it viewed the great majority of church members as insincere. The label stuck. To describe Puritanism as a primarily spiritual movement is not to discount its social, political, and economic significances, yet the Puritan movement was at its core one that emphasized "daily communion with Christ, energized by the Spirit and guided by a biblically ordered set of beliefs and values."[1]

---

1. Kelly M. Kapic and Randall C. Gleason, *The Devoted Life: An Invitation to the Puritan Classics* (Downers Grove, IL: InterVarsity Press, 2004), 24.

From roughly 1570–1680, Puritanism shaped the spirituality of England and the Netherlands, while its influence lingered into the eighteenth century in New England. Historian Jerald Brauer notes the difficulties of defining this phenomenon. On the one hand, Puritanism was a diverse movement that encompassed a wide range of denominations and views about how one could be saved.[2] Baptists, Congregationalists, Presbyterians, and other "independent" groups existed alongside ministers who remained in the Anglican Church. On the other hand, the Puritans had certain common qualities and goals.[3] Broadly, Puritans sought to foster a biblically guided, personal communion with God and emphasized the depths of human sin and the heights of divine grace which was made real in the believer's life through the work of the Holy Spirit and pursued through various means.[4] Many Puritan leaders were trained as theologians, primarily Oxford or Cambridge men in England and Harvard men in New England, yet theirs was by and large a *pastoral* theology.[5]

In the Netherlands, the *Nadere Reformatie* ("Further Reformation") developed in parallel with English-speaking Puritanism. Technically, this Dutch movement was distinct from Puritanism, but because it shared similar emphases on personal piety and experiential faith drawn from Scripture and lived out in every sphere of life, because it existed at the same time and in close proximity to Puritanism, and because many of its writers addressed similar concerns as their anglophone peers, it seems appropriate to include their insights here.

Nearly all Puritan authors were churchmen who were involved in the tasks of ministry and in the lives of families under their spiritual care. The number of general Puritan writings available to interested readers is massive, and Puritan works focusing on prayer are numerous.[6] One helpful introduction to this literature is *Taking Hold of God*.[7] In this chapter, we will look briefly

---

2. Jerald C. Brauer, "The Nature of English Puritanism: Reflections on the Nature of English Puritanism," *Church History* 23 (1954): 100. See also Kapic and Gleason, *The Devoted Life*, 23–24.

3. Brauer saw four common marks: (1) a "deep dissatisfaction" with the extent of Anglican reforms and with Roman Catholic theology, (2) based on a "deep religious experience" which (3) gave rise to a zeal for reform structured primarily on (4) a framework of covenant theology. Brauer, "The Nature of English Puritanism," 100.

4. Kapic and Gleason, *The Devoted Life*, 24–31, note several of these emphases. Among the chief means used by the Puritans were Scripture, prayer, communion, and fellowship.

5. The Puritan movement was wide enough to accommodate men of the highest academic credentials, like John Owen, as well as men with no formal theological training, like John Bunyan.

6. Interested readers might also consider the influential work of Isaac Watts, *A Guide to Prayer* (Carlisle, PA: Banner of Truth Trust, 1991). Watts's *Guide* is a comprehensive look at nine aspects of prayer.

7. Joel R. Beeke and Brian G. Najapfour, *Taking Hold of God: Reformed and Puritan Perspectives on Prayer* (Grand Rapids: Reformation Heritage Books, 2011).

at four Puritan writers on prayer to illustrate how valuable these Christians can be in helping modern readers deepen our own prayer lives. The authors represent a cross section of Puritan traditions. First, we will consider Henry Scudder's *The Christian's Daily Walk*. Then we turn to Welsh Presbyterian Matthew Henry's *Method for Prayer*. From the *Nadere Reformatie*, we look at Willem Teellinck's *The Path of True Godliness*. We end with Boston pastor Cotton Mather's private devotion to prayer captured in his *Diary*.

Henry Scudder: *The Christian's Daily Walk*

Puritan authors wrote various kinds of books: theological treatises, controversial pieces, collections of sermons, and devotional manuals among them. This last type, devotional manuals, offered detailed directions on topics such as trusting God during illness, preparing oneself to take the Lord's Supper, engaging in self-reflection and confession, arranging one's day to focus on God, and a variety of similar themes.[8] Prayer was one frequent topic in these devotional guides, and Henry Scudder's (d.1659) *The Christian's Daily Walk* offered readers guidance on prayer.[9]

Puritans typically commended the practice of bookending one's day with prayer: using morning prayer to stir the mind toward God and evening prayer to review the day and confess sins. Scudder is representative of this approach:

> In the instant of awakening let your heart be lifted up to God
> with a thankful acknowledgment of his mercy to you. For it is
> he that "giveth his beloved sleep" (Psal. 127:2); who "keepeth
> you both in soul and body while you sleep" (Prov. 6:22); who
> "reneweth his mercies every morning." (Lam. 3:22, 23)[10]

Scudder directs readers to consider various biblical texts and how to pray before getting out of bed, as they are dressing themselves, as they look at themselves in the mirror, as they begin their work, and so forth. The emphasis of morning prayer, according to Scudder, ought to be renewing our faith in Jesus Christ and our peace with God by confessing sins that we have committed since the last time we prayed.[11] In the evenings, Scudder suggests a pattern of prayer which the faithful ought to follow after family Bible reading (the last

---

8. For a deeper look at Puritan devotional handbooks, see my article "The Doctrine of the Trinity in Puritan Devotional Writings," in *The Spirit of Holiness: Reflections on Biblical Spirituality* (Bellingham, WA: Lexham Press, 2020), 1–14.
9. Henry Scudder, *The Christian's Daily Walk in Holy Security and Peace* (Philadelphia: Presbyterian Board of Publication, n.d.). Numerous editions of this work appeared in print in the seventeenth through nineteenth centuries. Scudder served as rector and pastor of an Anglican church at Collinbourne-Ducis in Wiltshire, England.
10. Scudder, *The Christian's Daily Walk*, 29.
11. Scudder, *The Christian's Daily Walk*, 32–36.

social event of the evening). The aim of evening prayer is to review one's conduct during the day, offering prayers of repentance for sinfulness and thanksgiving for God's faithfulness before committing oneself to God's care for the night, as one changes clothes, lies in bed, and falls asleep.[12]

Chapters 2–6 of *The Christian's Daily Walk* provide nearly seventy pages of meticulous detail regarding how Christians might order their normal day for the purpose of living a godly life, and prayer is a large part of this pattern. Though Scudder's advice may seem excessive, and readers will need to use wisdom to determine how best to appropriate his very full schedule, his purpose was to help believers live with intentional devotion in all aspects of their day through prayer.

Matthew Henry: *A Method for Prayer*

Most readers who know the name Matthew Henry (1662–1714) will recognize him as a Bible commentator, but he also enjoyed a fruitful ministry in Chester, near Wales, from 1687–1712 before answering the call to a church in the north London suburb of Hackney. Henry died in an accident in 1714. Henry completed his *Method for Prayer* shortly before relocating to London. It contains several chapters of biblically saturated reflection on each aspect of our prayers (the address, confession, petition, thanksgiving, intercession, and conclusion) and is almost always accompanied by three sermons on prayer that Henry preached in August, 1712.[13]

Henry's *Method* is simple but full. In each chapter, he provides a brief introduction to a different aspect of prayer and then develops brief points to explain that chapter's focus, illustrating every point with Scripture. Henry's desire to allow Scripture to consciously shape his prayer is commendable, for it emphasizes how sufficient a guide to prayer Scripture truly is. On average, Henry provides about three hundred biblical citations per chapter to support his views on prayer. It is not the mere presence of this many citations that is impressive, but the pastoral wisdom with which they are deployed. Space permits only one sample of Henry's approach, minus the illustrating support.

In Chapter 3, Henry considered supplication. He emphasizes the need for Christians to pray for the continued grace of God in our lives, including for our instruction, truth, memory, conscience, and our natures. With regard to our natures, we need continual sanctification, thus we should pray for faith; for the fear of God; "that the love of God and Christ may be rooted in us, and, in order thereunto, that the love of the world may be rooted out of us"; for tender consciences; for increased "charity and brotherly love" toward others;

---

12. Scudder, *The Christian's Daily Walk*, 94–96.
13. Various editions of Henry's book are in print and available electronically as well. Matthew Henry, *A Method for Prayer: Freedom in the Face of God* (Ross-shire, Scotland: Christian Focus, 1994).

for the grace of self-denial; for humility and meekness; for "the grace of contentment and patience, and a holy indifference to all the things of sense and time"; for the grace of hope; and "for grace to preserve us from sin, and all appearances of it and approaches towards it."[14] Henry is not suggesting that every prayer must include all of these elements, but rather showing the scope of biblical teaching on the various ways that Christians depend on God's grace for continuing spiritual growth. This summary represents just one of twelve different kinds of supplication Henry considers in this single chapter.

Willem Teellinck: *The Path of True Godliness*

A popular pastor in Middelburg, Netherlands for sixteen years, Willem Teellinck (1579–1629) preached and wrote of experiential Christianity grounded in the life of church participation and private devotion and sustained by the practices of regular Bible reading, participation in the Lord's Supper, works of mercy, Sabbath keeping, and prayer. *The Path of True Godliness* (1621) is a guidebook to intentional spiritual growth written in nine sections or "books."[15] Book Six emphasizes the place of prayer in a Christian's vigilant self-watch.

Puritans emphasized vigilance, a continual self-awareness of one's internal and external temperament and circumstances. This practice was often designated "watching," a reference to Jesus's admonition to the disciples in Matthew 26:41 that they "watch and pray" to avoid temptation. Prayer was part of this watching. Teellinck advised Christians to keep alert and watch what was coming and to "be much in prayer":

> When he is on sentry duty, the Christian's heart should constantly be lifted up to God in prayer. By these prayers—arrows shot directly from earth to heaven—he should make his requests known to God, his heavenly Father, so that he will not be dismayed about anything.[16]

Christians ought to pray "in every situation" daily, during our emotional highs and lows, during our work, during good and bad times. Particularly, Christians ought to seek the Holy Spirit's presence daily: "We must continually pray that [God] will lead us into all truth by his Spirit." We also seek the spiritual blessings needed for our daily tasks as well as the wisdom to use these blessings rightly. In sum, "We should watch and pray so that we will be edified and, by the right use of the means, reach our true purpose in life and

---

14. Henry, *Method for Prayer*, 60–67.
15. Willem Teellinck, *The Path of True Godliness*, trans. Annemie Godbehere, ed. Joel R. Beeke (Grand Rapids: Reformation Heritage Books, 2003).
16. Teellinck, *Path of Godliness*, 196.

further godliness."[17] Teellinck's guidance on prayer is helpful because he calls on Christians to maintain a spiritual "situational awareness": an alertness to God's work, our needs, and the enemy's presence. Rather than walking passively through each day, praying only when a crisis arises (though Teellinck would have us pray then!), Christians should approach each day and each situation actively seeking God's help moment by moment.

Cotton Mather: *Diary*

Cotton Mather (1663–1728) came from a family of pastors with deeply Puritan roots and ministered at the Old North Congregational Church in Boston from 1685 until his death. Mather's name is most often associated with the Salem witch trials, yet he was a prolific author, able theologian, concerned pastor, and charitable benefactor within his parish. Mather remained deeply committed to prayer from his childhood until his death, as the following survey highlights. Rather than examine one of Mather's works on prayer, though many exist, it seems better to present a short synthesis of his approaches to prayer to illustrate its priority in his life and ministry.[18]

From age fourteen on, Cotton Mather set aside entire days for the purpose of prayer and fasting, a practice he learned from reading Henry Scudder's *The Christian's Daily Walk*.[19] By one analysis, Mather kept around 450 such days of private fasting and prayer over about forty years of ministry.[20] Some entries in his diary let us see what this experience was like:

> But this day, I set apart for prayer, with fasting, before the Lord. I humbled and loathed myself before God, for my former iniquities, and my present infirmities. I confessed my unworthiness of all mercies . . . and the Lord assured me that he would be with me.[21]

> This morning, my heart was melted, in secret prayer before the Lord, when I used these words: "Lord, I am in thy hands, a poor, broken, sorry despicable vessel. But it is with Thee to make me a vessel of Honour. Oh! Do so! This, even this, is

---

17. Teelinck, *Path of Godliness*, 196.
18. Readers who want to dig more deeply into Mather's writings on prayer should begin with Richard F. Lovelace, *The American Pietism of Cotton Mather: Origins of American Evangelicalism* (Eugene, OR: Wipf and Stock, 1979).
19. Samuel Mather, *The Life of the Very Reverend and Learned Cotton Mather* (Boston: 1729).
20. Ralph and Louise Boas, *Cotton Mather: Keeper of the Puritan Conscience* (New York: Harper and Brothers, 1928), 258.
21. Cotton Mather, "April, 1691," *Diary of Cotton Mather, 1681–1708*, Massachusetts Historical Society Collections, Seventh Series, vol. 7 (Boston: Massachusetts Historical Society, 1911), xxvii.

the greatest of my desires. I am worthy to be nothing forever, But Oh! Let thy name have glory by me. Thou art worthy to be exalted forever and ever. Oh! Do these things in me, and for me, and by me, that upon my account it may be said, 'O the power, the wisdom, the grace and the truth of the great Jehovah!' Lord, thou art my aim, and my all, and my exceeding great reward."[22]

I sett apart this Day for the Exercises of a Fast in my Study; and for *extraordinary Prayer*, tho' I had not many Occasions but the ordinary and perpetual Ones. . . . I enjoyed something of the Divine presence with me, this day.[23]

I kept a day of thanksgiving in my study. And I enjoy'd some intimate communion with heaven; when acknowledging and glorifying of God the Father, and the Son, and Spirit, in his infinite perfections; and when mentioning his particular favours to myself, on each article whereof, I mentioned a particular aggravation of my own sinfulness, to render me more unworthy of it.[24]

These samples are representative of Mather's *Diary*. Recognizing that Mather intended for his children to destroy this document rather than to publish it, we suspect that it is an accurate record of Mather's sentiments rather than a document edited for personal advancement. Mather's writings are so many that it is difficult to even compile a list of publications on the topic of prayer, let alone summarize them. One sermon published after a public day of prayer in Boston will suffice for a different perspective on prayer's purpose. According to Mather,

One end of prayer is, that we may reverently realize the attributes of that God, who is greatly to be had in reverence by those that come about him. 'Tis a veneration of God, as well as a petition to God. Our God whose throne is in the highest heavens, would be enthroned in the high thoughts of our souls; now 'tis by prayer that we are put upon the forming of such God-adoring thoughts.[25]

---

22. Mather, "June, 1681," in *Diary*, 21–22.
23. Mather, "December, 1701," in *Diary*, 408.
24. Mather, "August, 1702," in *Diary*, 439.
25. Cotton Mather, *The Day and the Work of the Day* (Boston: B. Harris, 1693), 25.

To this "end" Mather added that of making the doctrines of Christianity truths that we can practice, expressing our dependence upon God, nourishing "an humble communion with the God who humbles himself to take notice of us," preserving a "good order of soul, and to "unload our hearts under our griefs."[26]

Summary

No generation of people are perfect exemplars of Christ on earth. The earliest disciples of Jesus were flawed followers, and every subsequent generation of disciples are liable to their own faults. Yet the Puritans certainly had an uncommon ability to reflect in great detail upon the experiential aspects of the Christian life as perhaps no generation before them had done, at least not in written records. This is not to say that the Puritans were the first "spiritual theologians," for there were others before them, but merely to recognize that in this diverse group of generally English-speaking Christians, there exists a richness and depth to the Protestant spiritual life that has long been the privilege of specialists to discover. The accessibility of Puritan writings through library databases, modern reprints, and online libraries can help current and future generations of Christians discover these writers and their works for themselves.

REFLECTION QUESTIONS

1. Who were the Puritans?

2. How did Henry Scudder suggest Christians integrate prayer into their day?

3. Are there specific "graces" that Matthew Henry suggests we ought to pray for that are new to you?

4. Following Willem Teellinck, how might Christians use prayer to cultivate a spiritual "situational awareness"?

5. In what ways does Cotton Mather's commitment to prayer challenge you?

---

26. Mather, *The Day*, 22–32.

Epilogue

How Can I Start Praying Today?

It seems only right to end this book with a practical summary of the previous forty questions about prayer. Perhaps you have thumbed (or scrolled) your way to the end first, or maybe you have just completed the whole work. I want to leave you with a brief encouragement to begin praying now. In my own life, I know that I should pray but do not always pray. I know that I should pray with and for my family, my church, my friends, my coworkers, my leaders, my neighbors, and even complete strangers, but I often *know* more than *pray*. That situation is not right. Maybe you are in the same situation, and you have picked up this book because you are interested in a few topics, a friend suggested it, or a professor assigned it. If you are a Christian, you know you should be praying. How can you and I start today?

Understand and Avoid Legalism

Legalism is the general idea that God accepts us because of our performance. That definition is quite basic, but it is a problem that has faced the church since its earliest days. Perhaps the earliest of Paul's letters was to the churches of Galatia, where he confronted a form of legalism that called Christians to trust Jesus *and* keep the Jewish law. Paul rejects this idea, and so should we. We face legalism of a different sort, and sometimes it involves prayer.

It can be easy to confuse legalism and discipline. Discipline says, "I love God, therefore I must pray." Legalism says, "I want God to love me, therefore I must pray." Legalism says, "I must pray *in this* way," but discipline says, simply, "I must pray." Throughout this book, I have tried to gather helpful reflections and specific practices of prayer that might give you and me a variety of ways to approach the throne of grace: praying Scripture, praying in solitude, establishing set hours for prayer, and so forth. The goal is that we commune with

God through prayer, not that our prayers take a certain form. To focus on the form as the goal of prayer is to miss the point of prayer. If these recommendations form a barrier, cast them aside, and simply pray. Remember, God does not accept you because you pray. You pray because he has accepted you in Christ.

Practice the Discipline of Prayers

Frame your days with prayer. When you awaken, thank God for the day he has set before you; seek his blessing upon your work; ask him to help you depend on his strength for the day; consider who he is, what he has done, and praise him. As you end your day, confess sins, ask for forgiveness, seek grace, and knock with expectation. At midday, set apart a few minutes to reflect on the morning's activities and pray. Consider the responsibilities of the afternoon, and seek the Spirit's help.

Throughout the day, pray. Ask God's help to see situations clearly, to provide wise leadership to your employees, to your children, to those you are around. Lift up the concerns of those whom you have encountered. Ask God for opportunities to speak the gospel of Jesus and the wisdom and courage to speak as you ought. Pray Scripture. As you read and study the Bible, ask the Spirit for more light to understand and see the wonderful things in God's Word. As you learn these things, thank God for your learning. Ask him to help you teach someone else.

Dear reader, take the greatest concerns of your heart, your anxieties, your burdens, and cast them upon Jesus, knowing that he cares for you.

Select Bibliography

Block, Daniel. *For the Glory of God: Recovering a Biblical Theology of Worship*. Grand Rapids: Baker Academic, 2016.

Bloesch, Donald G. *The Struggle of Prayer*. Colorado Springs: Helmers and Howard, 1988.

Bonhoeffer, Dietrich. *Psalms: The Prayer Book of the Bible*. Translated by James H. Burtness. Minneapolis: Augsburg, 1970.

Bunyan, John. *I Will Pray with the Spirit, and I Will Pray with the Understanding Also, or, A Discourse Touching Prayer, from 1 Cor. 14.15*. 2nd Edition. London: 1663.

Carson, D. A. *Praying with Paul: A Call to Spiritual Reformation*. 2nd Edition. Grand Rapids: Baker Academic, 2015.

_____, ed. *Teach Us to Pray: Prayer in the Bible and the World*. Exeter, UK: Paternoster Press, 1990.

Goldsworthy, Graeme. *Prayer and the Knowledge of God: What the Whole Bible Teaches*. Downers Grove, IL: InterVarsity Press, 2003.

Goodwin, Thomas. *The Heart of Christ in Heaven, to Sinners on Earth*. In The Works of Thomas Goodwin. Vol. 4. Edinburgh: James Nichol, 1862.

Henry, Matthew. *A Method for Prayer: Freedom in the Face of God*. Edited by J. Ligon Duncan III. Fearn, Scotland: Christian Heritage, 1994.

Holladay, William L. *The Psalms through Three Thousand Years: Prayerbook of a Cloud of Witnesses*. Minneapolis: Fortress Press, 1993.

Keller, Timothy. *Prayer: Experiencing Awe and Intimacy with God*. New York: Dutton, 2014.

Longenecker, Richard N., ed. *Into God's Presence: Prayer in the New Testament.* Grand Rapids: Eerdmans, 2001.

Lovelace, Richard F. *Dynamics of Spiritual Life: An Evangelical Theology of Renewal.* Downers Grove, IL: InterVarsity Press, 1979.

_____. *Renewal as a Way of Life: A Guidebook for Spiritual Growth.* Eugene, OR: Wipf and Stock, 1985.

Luther, Martin. *A Simple Way to Pray.* In *Little Prayer Book, 1522 and A Simple Way to Pray, 1535: The Annotated Luther Study Edition.* Edited by Mary Jane Haemig and Eric Lund. Minneapolis: Fortress Press, 2017.

Millar, Gary J. *Calling on the Name of the Lord: A Biblical Theology of Prayer.* New Studies in Biblical Theology. Vol. 38. Edited by D. A. Carson. Downers Grove, IL: InterVarsity Press, 2016.

Miller, Paul J. *A Praying Life: Connecting with God in a Distracted World.* Colorado Springs: Navpress, 2009.

Owen, John. *A Discourse of the Work of the Holy Spirit in Prayer.* In The Works of John Owen. Vol. 4. Edited by William H. Goold. Carlisle, PA: The Banner of Truth Trust, 1967.

Packer, J. I. and Carolyn Nystrom. *Praying: Finding Our Way through Duty to Delight.* Downers Grove, IL: InterVarsity Press, 2006.

Sire, James W. *Learning to Pray through the Psalms.* Downers Grove, IL: InterVarsity Press, 2005.

Ware, Bruce A. "Prayer and the Sovereignty of God." In *For the Fame of God's Name: Essays in Honor of John Piper.* Edited by Sam Storms and Justin Taylor. Wheaton, IL: Crossway, 2010.

Whitney, Donald S. *Praying the Bible.* Wheaton, IL: Crossway, 2015.

Scripture Index

40 QUESTIONS SERIES

40 QUESTIONS SERIES